HAUNTED BY HOME

HAUNTED BY HOME

THE LIFE AND LETTERS
OF LYNN RIGGS

by

Phyllis Cole Braunlich

UNIVERSITY OF OKLAHOMA PRESS : NORMAN AND LONDON

Library of Congress Cataloging-in-Publication Data

Braunlich, Phyllis.
    Haunted by home : the life and letters of Lynn Riggs / by Phyllis
Cole Braunlich.—1st ed.
        p. cm.
    Bibliography: p.
    Includes index.
    ISBN 0-8061-2142-4 (alk. paper)
        1. Riggs, Lynn, 1899–1954. 2. Dramatists, American—20th
century—Biography. 3. Oklahoma in literature. 4. West (U.S.)
in literature. I. Riggs, Lynn, 1899–1954. II. Title.
PS3535.I645Z59 1988
812'.52—dc19
[B]
                                                              88-4874
                                                                   CIP

To my dear husband, Frank,
whose encouragement made this work possible.

CONTENTS

ILLUSTRATIONS

PREFACE

ROLLIE LYNN RIGGS (1899–1954) was unquestionably one of America's most distinguished playwrights and poets. Yet he is relatively unknown today, although the record-setting musical *Oklahoma!* (first produced in 1943) still plays around the world and is based faithfully on his *Green Grow the Lilacs*, a Broadway hit in 1931. Little attention has been paid to Richard Rodgers and Oscar Hammerstein's acknowledged debt to Lynn Riggs.

Riggs wrote twenty-one full-length plays, thirteen of them published and eight others produced though unpublished. He also published one-act plays, television plays, and short stories as well as dozens of poems. His plays usually told of the colorful and troubled people of his Oklahoma childhood, struggling against their primitive beginnings.

Throughout his life he published poems in magazines, which resulted in two published volumes of his poetry. He took a leading role in the development of the "little theater" movement of the thirties. Perhaps this biography will help regain for him a well-deserved place in American literature and theatre history.

While Riggs's plays use the authentic colloquial speech of early Oklahoma, his poems are in his own voice and highly literate in form and structure. They express his unique sense of beauty and his personal anguish. Quotations from his later poems—views of his inner landscape—are used to introduce each chapter of this biography.

Riggs's personal story is as compelling as his plays: the story of escaping a dark childhood, discovering his homosexual orientation, finding new freedom in the world of the arts, struggling for theatrical and literary success. Ironically, he found many prominent friends and received honors but often missed the popular and critical acclaim that he needed. He had sworn to honesty in his plays, but they therefore lacked commercial appeal, since he often dealt with the worst in human frailties. Producers and audiences often preferred light comedies. His plays, which he saw as universal, were branded as regional, since they were usually set in early-twentieth-century Oklahoma. He found his part-Cherokee ancestry mysterious and spent much of his life developing the only play that he wrote about it, *The Cherokee Night;* however, he had no use for Hollywood-style "movie Indians" in his works. No cowboys-versus-Indians themes are to be found in his plays.

Related to his writings was his love for singing folk songs, accompanying his mellow tenor voice on his guitar—to the delight of his friends and, occasionally, larger audiences. Because of Appalachian and railroad people in his childhood, he had a large repertoire, and he preserved many of the old songs in an anthology, *Cowboy Songs, Folk Songs, and Ballads from "Green Grow the Lilacs."*

Riggs knew the famous people of Broadway, Hollywood, and the college drama departments and little-theatre circles of his time. Among his close friends were movie stars Bette Davis, Joan Crawford, and Jean Muir. Finding him a sensitive and genial companion, they helped protect his homosexuality from publicity. He always feared condemnation from the folks back home, who had never been sympathetic.

Many friends called him "a prince of a fellow," but his lovers faded out of his life while he still needed them. One died suddenly at age forty-two. Others left. Only Ida Rauh

Eastman was his loyal, motherly friend to the end. He died of
cancer at age fifty-four in New York City's Memorial Hospital
in 1954.

His sister gave his papers to his hometown, Claremore,
Oklahoma, including a trunkful of photographs, as well as
manuscripts and memorabilia. These are now in the Lynn
Riggs Memorial at Rogers State College Library in Claremore.
During six years of research I discovered hundreds of his
letters in archives around the United States. The greatest
number were written to three friends: Barrett H. Clark, his literary agent and a theatre historian; poet Witter Bynner; and
Walter S. Campbell (Stanley Vestal), writer and professor in
the University of Oklahoma. Also helpful were Dr. Arrell
Morgan Gibson's taped interviews with Riggs's close friends
Betty Kirk Boyer and Willard Johnson, in the University of
Oklahoma Western History Collections. I examined hundreds
of clippings about his career, public interviews, magazine
articles, and playbills in Riggs's four oversize scrapbooks,
which were graciously made available to me by his niece,
Bernice Cundiff Hodges.

I also interviewed many of Riggs's contemporaries. I am
grateful to the many friends of Riggs who so generously gave
their time to me in interviews and shared with me their documents about Riggs. Most of them are named in these pages. I
have pursued Lynn's ghost as closely as I could for ten years,
yet I am sure there are more people and letters to see, more to
be learned. I would like to hear from those I may have missed.

I would especially like to thank Jean Tanner, retired librar-
ian of Rogers State College and a never-failing source of information and encouragement during the early years. Also
happy in my memory is the generous help, by mail, phone,
and personal interview, of the late Dr. Paul Green of Chapel
Hill, North Carolina. He and his wife, Elizabeth, welcomed
me to their gracious home one spring day, and there among
antiques and magnolias, Dr. Green gave me many important

facts, sources, and contacts that led me further into Lynn's life. I'm sorry this great man, whose mind in his eighties was still powerful and active, did not live to read this book.

Unpublished dissertations by Eloise Wilson and Charles Aughtry also were very helpful. In this work I have not touched on the special language of Riggs's plays, which is the subject of a 1948 dissertation written at the University of Tulsa by Ilse L. Nesbitt, "Study of Dialect in Oklahoma in the Plays of Lynn Riggs."

Lynn Riggs is still the only playwright to tell the world of the joys and conflicts of early Oklahoma life as Indian Territory shed adolescence to become a state in 1907. He attempted only to tell individual stories out of his experience, not to write historical dramas; yet his writings contain truths of time, place, and people that can be found nowhere else. Nonetheless, if his musical, emotionally charged poetry were his only literary legacy, it should earn for him a solid place in American letters. His courage and conviction, his firm but tender love of the word, are an example for writers everywhere who believe in their material, and who know that what they have to say must be said, in spite of all.

Tulsa, Oklahoma   PHYLLIS COLE BRAUNLICH

HAUNTED BY HOME

CHAPTER 1

THE GOLDEN WORLD OF SANTA FE

(1923–1925)

> *Guitar on yellow wall is good.*
> *The room receives you, takes you in,*
> *and the stove is tongued with pinion wood*
> *less for the spirit than the skin.*
>
> *The ginger lamp is honey light.*
> *Two tables start their disarray*
> *right at the edge of waxen night—*
> *man cannot work who cannot play* . . .
> —from "The Shaped Room," by Lynn Riggs[1]

ONE GOLDEN AUTUMN DAY in 1923, Rollie Lynn Riggs stepped off the Santa Fe train at Lamy, New Mexico, and into a new life. A young man in rumpled professorial tweeds, he surveyed the unfamiliar landscape through thick horn-rimmed glasses. In contrast to the green, rolling hills of Oklahoma, he saw buff-colored mountains dotted with low pinion trees, cresting like waves around the wide valley. Beyond the station was a cluster of modest adobe homes, a white-steepled church on the slope above them. In the dusty road in front of a weathered saloon he saw Old John Longjohn waiting beside his horse and buckboard wagon. "Going to Santa Fe?" Riggs asked. A grunt was Longjohn's terse reply.

Longjohn's leathery face showed no expression as Riggs loaded up his guitar case and a battered footlocker containing

3

Riggs in Santa Fe, 1924. He wrote on this photograph for Joseph Benton that he looks "the decadent poet" in his Navajo shirt and concha belt. *Western History Collections, University of Oklahoma Library*

all his possessions from college days—his sparse wardrobe, his published poems, the college magazines that he had edited, photographs—all past history. He climbed up on the seat next to the driver, and they began the eighteen-mile trip up to 7,000-foot Santa Fe.

At age twenty-four, Riggs thought he might have come to Santa Fe to die. Instead, Santa Fe was about to teach him how to live and to set him on the path toward becoming a great playwright of the American Southwest.

The blue mountains across the valley were dusted with snow under a bright November sky as they climbed along the old Santa Fe Trail. Once in that town, the road wound past light brown adobe houses nestled against the foothills. A few staid brick houses with shady verandas bordered the central plaza with its white octagonal bandstand and its monument shaft honoring New Mexico's war dead. In the shady portal of the Palace of the Governors, Indians sat cross-legged, their silver and turquoise jewelry and blankets spread out before them to sell.

The wagon road curved along the Acequia Madre ("mother ditch") and up the winding Camino del Monte Sol ("road of the Sun Mountain"). Fragrant pinion-wood smoke from chimneys spiced the wine-fresh air. Tiny yards leading to carved wooden doorways were bare of grass but shaded by golden-leaved cottonwood trees.

As the horse strained up the final rise of the mountain road, Riggs saw the two-story main lodge and the new east building of Sunmount Sanatorium. Both were pink adobe with many windows, shaded by cottonwoods and aspens and surrounded by a hay-colored lawn. Along the drive the sloping hillside was crowded with square tent-roofed cottages, among which children played and adults sat in the sun.[2]

For twenty years tuberculosis patients had been coming there to take Drs. Frank and Harry Mera's famous fresh-air cure: pure mountain water, wholesome food, plenty of rest, and especially, Santa Fe's high altitude and sparkling air. As flame-colored trees glowed across the Sangre de Cristo range behind Sun Mountain, the bright New Mexican sun descended across the valley through a sapphire sky.

Inside the lodge was like a ranch resort: white-washed walls, heavy carved ceiling beams, tapestries and wrought-iron candelabra on the walls, bright Indian rugs on polished wood floors. People sat, talking, on Spanish-style furniture, played cards at corner tables, or clacked the balls around the billiard table.

In Riggs's room up the stairs were a wardrobe, a small Indian rug, and a wicker chair before a writing desk. French doors opened onto the sleeping porch, where a narrow white iron bed was surrounded by window walls on three sides. Here he was to stay until he felt better or his money ran out, whichever came first.

He was grateful for a place where no demands would be made on him, where there would be no criticism of him, no brave front he must put up in public. He had left the University of Oklahoma in the midst of his senior year, the place of his greatest happiness, his many successes and honors, and had left there everything he cared about. None of it was recoverable: the teaching assistantship, the life of a promising student-poet, the fraternity, the almost-won bachelor's degree, and the beauty queen with raven hair and violet eyes who had slipped out of his arms and eloped with someone else. His ailments had been diagnosed as consumption, severe depression, or a nervous breakdown.

The poet Witter Bynner, who had been a visiting lecturer at the university the previous winter; his doctor, whose name was Mayfield; and Riggs's close friend and teacher Walter S. Campbell; all had urged Riggs to go to Santa Fe to recover his health and spirits. Bynner had settled into Santa Fe's growing community of writers and artists the previous year. It was in a letter to Bynner on October 14, 1923, that Riggs, making a valiant effort to get through the fall semester, had written, "nothing at all interests me, nothing gives me pleasure, nothing seems worth doing—in fact, I find it almost impossible to do anything. Can't seem to concentrate."[3] He added that he would love to come to Santa Fe, but he was a "vassal of the state," having a teaching agreement with the university. He was not able to see that assignment through, however.

Bynner, a mentor to many young poets, noted in the margin of the letter that Riggs was "on the edge of melancholia" when he arrived, adding, "I worked hard to straighten his spirit." By December 3, Riggs was able to write Bynner (in New York) from Sunmount in a much happier mood: ". . . Feeling much better, thanks to you. Only it will take several decades to overcome wrong habits of thought, won't it? I'm beginning Decade 1. . . . I finished a thing called "Sanatarium" [sic]. . . . and am two scenes deep in a one-act play; hope to finish "Santa Fe" right away. . . . Hal, you saved my life, you know—to Humanity the burden."

How was this astonishing turnaround accomplished in only a few weeks? The cure was in the unique qualities that characterized Sunmount and Santa Fe. Even more than the academic world that Riggs loved, Santa Fe accepted the artistic, sensitive person and excused individual idiosyncrasies. In addition, life at Sunmount was more like a health resort than pity and pills. Riggs and other self-admitted patients may not actually have had tuberculosis; such cases made rapid and complete recoveries at Sunmount.

According to a Santa Fe New Mexican article honoring Sunmount's founders, Dr. Frank Mera believed that the patient's mental outlook had a great deal to do with his recovery, and so he produced a homelike atmosphere, plenty of congenial companionship, and stimulating entertainment.[4] The common rooms were decorated with pine and chamiza for Thanksgiving and Christmas; music groups and speakers were frequent. Most of the patients were ambulatory and enjoyed Sun Mountain's famous climate, year-round sunshine, and mild, dry, invigorating winters.

The *New Mexican* article added, "Sunmount became a social
and cultural center in the life of Santa Fe due largely to the
many intellectual and artistic people who came there for their
health." Among those were painter Arthur Musgrave, poet
and educator Ivor Winters, and his wife-to-be, novelist Janet
Lewis. Roark Bradford, whose wife was at Sunmount, came
and read from his books; Alice Corbin, coeditor of *Poetry*
magazine, lived there with her husband, painter William Pen-
hallow Henderson, and their family in one of the tent cottages. Due to her influence, famous poets such as Carl Sandburg and Vachel Lindsay recited their poems in the great
parlor.

More than the culture, more than the exhilarating air, was
rare to Oklahoman Lynn Riggs: Santa Fe's free acceptance
buoyed his spirit, stifled from a youth spent in a home filled
with rejection and criticism. Santa Fe in its long history of in-
vasions had learned tolerance; first were the Indians, then
came the Spanish explorers, then Hispanic and American
pioneers and businessmen, then archaeologists, vacationers,
and health-seekers. Taking them all in stride, local businessmen mingled freely with the writers and artists and held celebrity dinner parties which helped the humble adobe poets
stay alive.

As Riggs's spirits revived, he explored the local culture. On
November 25, 1923, he wrote his former University of Oklahoma professor Walter Campbell that he had a day-labor job
carrying mud for plaster on a friend's adobe house. But he
put it off for a day or two, commenting: "There is the altitude
too, you know. Everything adverse is blamed on the altitude
by newcomers."[5]

He had gone to dinner at Witter Bynner's house, then to
visit two Indian pueblos, San Felipe and Santo Domingo.
Bynner and his other guests, Alice Corbin Henderson and
two others, were members of the New Mexican Indian Associates, working to protect Indian rights. Riggs joked, "The

pueblo life must be wonderful—the real communal life. And to think of how they are being contaminated by the damned whites and the stinking Mexicans! (You see I already speak the lingo of the Pueblo enthusiasts.)." He introduced Campbell to the people of Sunmount:

> "Sunmount," where I am staying, is full of tubercular patients from everywhere: there is a Miss Conkey next to me who lives in New York and reads a lot, and is a friend of all the wild young radicals who come out of Chicago and Denver—Ivor Winters, Janet Lewis, John Meem, etc.; there is a Mlle. Breviere, who has a sun-bath every morning—her legs are a rich chocolate with overtones of smoldering red like an overheated stove; there is a Katherine Stinson, a famous flyer, who was in the A.E.F. in France and is now down with T.B.—she's a Texas girl; . . . there is a young Harvard graduate who likes Havelock Ellis, and damns the "young generation"—as I do.

He explained his loss of enthusiasm for F. Scott Fitzgerald and Joseph Hergesheimer, but new interest in Willa Cather and Robert Frost. He concluded his letter wistfully: "Tell everybody I'm alive."

From the time of his arrival, Riggs published poems in *The Laughing Horse*, a magazine started as a "horse laugh" against the establishment by Willard ("Spud") Johnson and two students at the University of California in 1921. Authorities there objected to its publications, which included a denunciation of university professors by Upton Sinclair and a review by D. H. Lawrence of an allegedly obscene novel by Ben Hecht, *Fantasias Mallare*. Two students were prosecuted, but the resulting notoriety brought the magazine many subscribers.[6]

Transferring to the University of Colorado, Johnson had met Witter Bynner, a visiting lecturer on poetry there, and had come to Santa Fe in 1922 as Bynner's secretary and companion. He continued to publish *Laughing Horse* until 1939, with numerous distinguished contributors from Santa Fe's colony of writers.[7] Riggs's contributions included his best-

known poem, "Morning Walk—Santa Fe," and other Southwest poems, many of which were later included in his 1930
poetry volume, *The Iron Dish.*

Flourishing in Santa Fe, Riggs continued to write and publish poems in national magazines and began to take a serious
look at playwriting. He wrote Campbell on January 19, 1924,
"I weigh 9 or 10 lb. more than I ever did and am feeling first-
rate." He described an attempt to see an Indian ceremonial
dance during Christmas week at San Felipe Pueblo, likening
his group of inexperienced friends to silly characters from the
play *Cuckoo* that he had written at the University of Oklahoma:

> It was muddy, cold—we got stuck on a hill because of a box-
> like Ford with all the family (from Lisa to Grandpap) aboard,
> which crawled down the hill like a snail. We got stuck in the
> mud, dismounted for lunch, and finally arrived at the village.
> Dancing was over, but there were rumours that it would start
> sometime in the afternoon. We waited.
>
> A drum began, far-off, and we decided it came from the
> kiva. We waited. The drum was intermittent. Once we drove
> up near the kiva and the sound stopped. We drove away and it
> began. Finally one of the party went to investigate. Behind the
> kiva two little overalled tots were playing the drum; when they
> got tired they stopped beating it!

The party returned by way of Santo Domingo, which was
the "New York of the Pueblos," Riggs said, because "the
people even lock their doors when they leave." Friends had
seen the dances there and, in particular, a performance by a
tall Indian with a suitcase, umbrella, and linen duster. "He
scattered candy to the children and cried in Spanish: 'How do
you do? You *nice* Indians! I'm from New York and I think
you're *so* interesting!' And people are fond of believing they
have no sense of humor!"

Always putting up his most cheerful front in his letters to
Campbell, Riggs wrote of an "invasion" of painters, sculp-
tors, and writers from Denver, who provided a Christmas
puppet show at Sunmount. He gossiped that Alice Corbin

Henderson was a "week-old grandmother." Her daughter Alice had married John Evans, son of Mabel Dodge Evans Sterne Luhan, heroine of Van Vechten's 1922 novel, *Peter Whiffle*. "It is rumored," he added, "that she is about to divorce Luhan, the Taos Indian, and marry a Chinaman in California." The much-married Mabel, a bright thread running through the fabric of Santa Fe–Taos society, entertained many celebrities and sparked many rumors with her flamboyant style. Like others, Riggs was sometimes in her favor, sometimes not.

Little was hidden in this colorful, historic town of eight thousand people, three thousand of whom were Anglos. It was along the winding Camino del Monte Sol that many artists chose to make their homes and studios. There, for example, Mary Hunter Austin, who was a health-seeker as well as an artist and writer, built "La Casa Querida" ("the beloved house"). Riggs and other friends often sat on its broad terrace facing the Sangre de Cristo Mountains on the north. Her long library–living room, with its Indian rugs, pierced-tin light fixtures, carved tables, and pottery, reflected her strong interest in native arts. Austin was a large woman who wore her dark hair on top of her head and fastened with a Spanish comb. She built her house in 1924 and lived there for ten years along with her niece Mary Hunter.[8]

Austin wrote in her autobiography, *Earth Horizon*, that the perpetual flow of Santa Fe's interesting visitors included Marie Garland, Sinclair Lewis, John Galsworthy, and Grant Overton. She added, "Lynn Riggs came; he used to spend evenings with young Mary, sitting out on the *placita*, playing the *guitarra*, and singing Oklahoma folk songs."[9] Although she was an Anglo, Austin worked to preserve native culture and supported the Spanish and Indian Trading Post, where Riggs worked for a time after leaving Sunmount.

Issues of the *New Mexican* tell the story of two gifts that nature brought to the young state of New Mexico during Riggs's first year there: the end of a three-year drought and the discovery of large quantities of oil on the Navajo Reserve. These riches strengthened the state and revitalized the economy.

Many of the Anglos were by this time old families in Santa Fe. Social leaders such as banker Levi Hughes and his wife, Christine, mingled with the wealthy Witter Bynner and other not-so-wealthy poets and artists, giving them occasional odd jobs. Some, for example, cleaned the swimming pool on the estate of Will and Sally White and their daughters, Amelia and Elizabeth. This sewing-machine magnate "hunted to hounds" in the Santa Fe hills. Riggs attended some of the large parties for two hundred or more people at the Whites' rambling adobe house with its large patio garden.[10]

The unchallenged majordomo of Santa Fe, six-foot, two-inch, Witter ("Hal") Bynner, liked to tell stories and make puns, drank and smoked with abandon, played piano, and was inclined to conduct monologues in conversation. Close to forty when Riggs arrived, Bynner was balding, but strong and brown, with a whooping laugh and a quick walk. He frequently traveled in the Orient, translated Chinese poetry into English, and liked to wear Chinese robes when he was not wearing a velvet Navajo blouse gathered with a belt of silver and turquoise medallions. The poet Wallace Stevens described him thus: "The manner of a girl, the divination, flattery, and sympathy of a woman, the morbidness and reverie of a poet, the fire and enthusiasm and ingenuousness of a young man."[11]

Bynner's classical poetry seemed old-fashioned in an innovative literary period, but his flamboyant hospitality moved and shook Santa Fe society. He and Mary Austin were notoriously antiwar, a stance which had cost Bynner many friends while teaching at Berkeley during World War I. Austin sometimes spoke of the young poet Alan Seeger (much admired by Riggs), whom she had known in New York before he died on the battlefield in France. Bynner shocked even Santa Fe society by publicly acknowledging his homosexuality in 1931,

when he published a long autobiographical poem describing
his male lover, Paul.[12]
  Widely published in magazines, Bynner often used his influence to interest editors in the work of young poets. Warmed
by Bynner's geniality, Lynn Riggs used him as a role model in
many ways; but although he shared most of Bynner's views,
Riggs preferred privacy. Newly freed by the recognition of his
own homosexual orientation, he nevertheless was constantly
wary of Oklahoma's judgments, and never quite so full of self-
esteem as Bynner was. Like Bynner, after success came, Riggs
seized every opportunity to promote the careers of young
writers and artists.

  Except for a regressive visit home to Claremore in February,
1924, Riggs found the courage to accept the unconventional
self he had discovered in Santa Fe, but it was too easy to slip
back into depression and doubt. He clung to Bynner's lifeline
in a cryptic letter from Claremore on February 6:

  I am here at last—in a snow-drift, literally and metaphorically.
  . . . I have met great kindness at the wrong end of life that is
  all. . . . The forces of earth rise to crush the weak things, the
  tortoises without a protective shell. This later complication
  (which you know about, dear Hal) would have been little difficulty had there not been earlier, unsolved ones. You would
  understand if you were here in this squalor and dirt and misery and harshness from which I have never been absent. What
  little work I have done in poetry has been not realization but a
  feeble attempt to escape from a birthright. So the sonnet I sent
  you in New York about "I have sung of beauty where I have
  seen no beauty" remains my truest utterance. . . .
  I remember you as a clear flame—with the strength I thought
  I possessed and the wisdom I hoped to acquire. And I shall try
  not to write in this strain again.

  Two younger half-brothers were growing up in the home
of William Grant and Juliette Riggs, Lynn's father and stepmother, but the discord in that home, and the rejection that
always overwhelmed Lynn there, kept him from returning

more than a few times during his adult years. Never a sup-
porter of Lynn, Bill Riggs was absorbed in his own problems,
which led to divorce five years later. One of Lynn's later
poems, "I Knowing . . . ," recalls the feeling of returning to
an unhappy home with silent regret, a place that "is not the
same," even though the paintings on the wall and the faded
quilt his sister made were the same:

> Yet no one is aware
> but me, of how awaited,
> non-reiterated
> words can cloud the air . . .
>
> And still the gray is growing.
> And still miasmic blight
> rifles the room of light
> . . . and I knowing.[13]

His life in Santa Fe expanded like a bright sail in the wind.
He and Spud Johnson, Bynner, Alice Corbin, and Haniel
Long formed a poetry group, meeting weekly in their homes
to read and appraise each other's current work. Johnson said:

We called ourselves the "Rabble" which was supposed to be
from Rabelaisan. That was a slight exaggeration, of course, but
still shows how informal it was, so we could say whatever we
liked and write whatever we liked and felt a very sympathetic
understanding among the group. Sometimes we played a
game going around the circle, writing a Shakespearian sonnet,
rhyming a, b, a, b, c, d, c, d and so on. Then each attempted to
write a sonnet using those words. It was very amusing how
sometimes they were quite good poems, and how different
they were . . . Lynn and I were both just out of college, working part time, penniless poets . . . We were asked out to dinner quite a lot.[14]

Johnson was working at a restaurant downtown that was in
a former farmhouse on the river. Riggs lived in a chicken
house and took care of the chickens for his rent.
After he left Sunmount in the spring, tending chickens on
the McComb ranch amused Riggs and provided healthful

physical labor. The experience inspired his successful comedy *Russet Mantle,* written in 1934. The hero of that play is a poet who applies for work tending chickens; one scene is set in the section of the adobe chicken house where he lives much as Riggs did.

Riggs often visited the Hughes home, and with young Mary Christine and her brother Jimmy went to picnics and parties, or gathered with friends at a popular sidewalk café. He wrote Dr. Campbell on June 16, 1924:

> Time is so limited at the ranch that we have to strain at an hour to swallow a moment. I am trying to write this before breakfast, the only leisure moments I have, and it means getting up earlier. But I'm getting so damned healthy, it's disgusting. I have done some new work, principally the SONNETS FROM A SANTA FE PRIVY, and a fairly decent thing called "A LADY." Here it is. Hal wants me to do a whole series on Santa Fe characters.

He exchanged works with Campbell, and they discussed each other's poetry with their writing groups. He encouraged Campbell to visit that summer, mentioning among recent visitors Dr. George Pierce Baker, of the famed Harvard Drama Workshop, and Carl Sandburg. Others coming for the summer included western author Harvey Fergusson. The D. H. Lawrences and their friend Lady Dorothy Brett had arrived in March to visit Mabel Dodge Luhan.

Most influential, however, among Riggs's Santa Fe friends was the actress and sculptor Ida Rauh Eastman. At age forty-four, she became a surrogate for the understanding and supportive mother he had never had. Divorced from the socialist Max Eastman in New York in 1922, she had moved to Santa Fe shortly before Riggs, bringing her young son Dan. The beautiful and opinionated actress had led the innovative Provincetown Players and directed Eugene O'Neill's first one-act play, "Where the Cross is Made." She had organized the Players with George Cram Cook and his wife, Susan Glaspell, the radical writer Jack Reed, and O'Neill. In 1905, at age twenty-seven, she had received a law degree from New York University, but after 1920 she enjoyed mostly sculpture and painting, dabbling in poetry writing and in local theatre.

A free spirit and an avid follower of Margaret Sanger, Ida Rauh was arrested in 1916, at age thirty-six, and charged with "obscenity" for passing out birth-control pamphlets. A suspended sentence left her undaunted. Her former husband, Eastman, once described her as "gifted and graceful, thoughtful and witty, ambitious of freedom, very good to look at."[15] This woman did more than anyone to put Lynn Riggs back on the track of his career, and she was his friend both in need and in good times the rest of his life.

It was she who challenged him to put his dramatic talents to use, producing his second one-act play, *Knives from Syria;* and she organized and directed the Santa Fe Players in its production. The Syrian pedler, who went about the countryside to sell to country women exotic wares such as lace, perfume, and egg beaters, was a common figure known to Riggs in his Oklahoma youth. He returns in Riggs's best-known play, *Green Grow the Lilacs.*

In *Knives from Syria* the heroine, Rhodie Buster, is eager to accompany the pedler and see something of the world beyond her own limited place, rather than marry the convenient hired man. Here is one of Riggs's recurrent themes, the yearning of middle- or lower-class rural young people to find wider horizons and more freedom than their restricted lives offer. He wrote Betty Kirk, a journalist friend from Norman, Oklahoma, on January 6, 1925, that Ida was advising him on this first serious drama, and also that his poem "Santo Domingo Corn Dance" was to be published in *The Nation.*[16]

The community gathered for the presentation of *Knives* in the Spanish mission–style Saint Francis Auditorium built in 1918. Carved wooden beams supported the room's high ceiling, and the stage protruded into the room, without a front curtain. Arched religious tapestries, like stained-glass windows, hung high on the white walls. Patrons sat on heavy wooden pews.

The place lent a quaint dignity to Riggs's brief play, which was published in 1927 in Samuel French, Inc.'s *One-Act Plays for Stage and Study, Third Series.* Alan Downer compared it to Mark Twain's tales or to Synge's *The Shadow of the Glen.*[17] *Knives* continued to be popular with amateur drama groups as late as 1956, when it had been given a total of 134 performances in thirty-six states.[18]

The summer of his first year in Santa Fe found Riggs living on the Acequia Madre, working for the Spanish and Indian Trading Company, and typing a new play by his friend Roy Chanslor, one of the founders of *The Laughing Horse.* The squat adobe house, with its rounded corners, small windows, oval fireplace, and carved doorways, gave Riggs a feeling of coziness that he loved.

He wrote Betty Kirk on July 24 from El Hogan Ranch, discussing his expanding philosophy about writing, saying he felt then that Scott Fitzgerald was decadent and a bad influence on younger writers, whereas Shakespeare's gusto was the epitome of good writing. He added, "And remembering the enormous gusto and delight of the Elizabethans, I am no longer ashamed of healthy delight, emotional, even to tears. . . . Art never thrives in a sophisticated hothouse."

He faced honestly his own emotions and affirmed that his art would genuinely reflect life (a position that later brought him much conflict with New York producers). He said of his return to vigor: "I confess to being utterly done up, spiritually, when I left Norman. Well, I've been vaccinated, as it were, and am quite safely over it."

The letter's gossipy chatter reflects the pleasant rhythms of his literary life. Alice Corbin had passed along the confidential information that Carl Sandburg was working on a life of Lincoln. Corbin was publishing her new book of lyrics in the fall. Haniel Long had published a book of poems and was working on short stories and a novel. Hal Bynner was working on a Chinese translation. "It's a great bunch," Riggs said.

His experiences with Mabel Dodge Luhan, however, had

already turned negative. He wrote: "She does take hold of people (she has unlimited means, and a good family), plays with them until she is tired of them, and throws them away. She gives them cars, houses to live in on her Taos estate, makes of fine people dependents and of ordinary ones flabby apes. She's a meddler. She thinks she's God."

Times for introspection always led Riggs to an outpouring of poems, often followed by a flurry of publishing. His Santa Fe poems appeared in *New Republic, Smart Set,* and *American Mercury. Laughing Horse* published "Sanatarium," about a woman with hair the color of corn shucks in a tuberculosis sanatarium, in its ninth issue, December, 1923. Number 10 (May, 1924) carried "The Choice," and number 11 (September, 1924), "Boot Heels." Number 12 (August, 1925) carried two Santa Fe sonnets entitled "Spring" and "Summer," which included the following lines:

> *Go not, spring, with your delicate*
> *petals of the pear tree, and your lazy rain*
> *purring in the dust of the road—till*
> *your ultimate leaf is born,*
> *your last Christ risen again.*

Working steadily after the success of *Knives from Syria,* Riggs in 1925 completed *The Primitives,* a New Mexican play that he subtitled *A Satirical Comedy in Three Acts,* which he later destroyed. He then wrote *Sump'n Like Wings,* set in the Oklahoma town of "Claremont" just after statehood. In it Willie, aged sixteen, seeks something more than her monotonous life. Twice disappointed in love, she concludes: "I got to live my own life. I got to do fer myself." The reckless and loving Willie chose not to be promiscuous like the kitchen helper, Elvie Rapp, saying, "It's the way people are made that's to blame" for what they become. She is made to desire a freer life and resolves to rise above her poverty and lack of education rather than accept her circumstances.

Feeling ready for Broadway, Riggs in 1925 took the first step

CHAPTER 2

GROWING UP: OKLAHOMA TERRITORY
CHILDHOOD (1899–1920)

But this is something I shall never name,
seeing it darkly and darkly bearing it:
to know the summer withered and its flame
minutely warm in seeds for the following season;
to hear the quick blood dropping bit by bit
on a scoured stone, and never know the reason.
    —from "Listen, Mind"[1]

LYNN RIGGS'S MOTHER, born in northeast Indian Territory, was
one-eighth Cherokee Indian. His father, born in Missouri,
came from a family of railroad and hotel workers of Appalachian stock.

His grandfather, Joseph S. Riggs, was born March 2, 1832,
the son of James Riggs and Polly Stewart, in Scott County,
Virginia. In 1855, Joseph married Sarah Estep. Soon they left
the green mountain country and followed the railroad to La-
Clede County, Missouri, where he worked on the construction crew. Among their children were James W., born February, 1857; Mary, born April 27, 1861; and William Grant, born
January 14, 1869. Sarah died on October 1, 1874.[2]

On November 3, 1878, Joseph Riggs, forty-six, married
Martha Bolenger Ferguson, forty-two, a widow; and the
united families moved in a covered wagon to Indian Territory.
There Riggs built a house three miles southwest of Claremore
on the Collinsville Road.

21

Pension records describe Joseph Riggs's appearance as very
much like that of his grandson Lynn. He stood five feet, nine
inches tall, with a fair complexion, light hair, and blue eyes.
An able horseman, he served during the Civil War as a private
with Company F, Second Regiment of the Kansas Cavalry,
from 1863 through 1865. He was captured by the Confeder-
ates in 1864 and taken to Tyler, Texas, as a prisoner of war,
where he contracted disabling and chronic diarrhea. He lived
near Claremore the rest of his life. After his death in 1902, his
widow, Martha, received a small pension, and she lived on
with her daughters.

On October 28, 1890, Joseph Riggs's son William Grant,
aged twenty-one, married Rose Ella Buster Gillis, a widow,
whose frail two-year-old daughter, Hattie Gillis, died a few
months later. A small, quiet woman with delicate features,
Rose Ella ("Rosie") was one-eighth Cherokee through her
mother, Mrs. John ("Mattie") Buster.

Rosie Buster had been born October 5, 1868, in Cooweescoowee District in the Claremore area of Indian Territory,
into the Go-Sa-Du-I-Sga clan of the Cherokee Nation. According to Indian census records, she bore W. G. ("Bill") Riggs
five children, three of whom lived past infancy: Mattie A. M.
(Mary Martha) in 1896; William Edgar, 1898; and Rollie Lynn,
August 31, 1899. Ethel F., born in 1891, died a year later;
Joseph B. H., 1892, died in 1895.

Rosie's short, sad life was ended by typhoid fever in November, 1901, depriving the children, especially the youngest, of the mother's love they sorely needed. She and her
daughter Hattie, who died in infancy, are buried in the Buster
family Indian cemetery, a small plot on the old Buster farm
north of Claremore. As a child Lynn played in this meadow
near Claremore Mound, where narrow stones mark the dozen
or so graves of his Indian ancestors, sheltered by a grove of
oak trees.

During Lynn's first year his mother enrolled herself and her children in the Cherokee tribe and received an allotment of 160 acres of land under the Dawes Allotment Act of 1887, which was designed to change ownership of land in Indian Territory from tribal to individual. The act had been extended to the Cherokees and other Five Civilized Tribes in 1893.[3]

Since every acre of land in the eastern half of Oklahoma was allotted to tribal citizens, Joseph Riggs, a noncitizen, could no longer own the land on which he had settled. It stayed in the family, however, becoming part of Rose Ella's allotment, and was divided among the children when Lynn was three years old, with Bill Riggs as guardian. The grandparents, Joseph and Martha, lived on the farm that Lynn inherited, adjacent to his brother Edgar's land, which was used for pasture. Across the road were Mattie's land and Rose Ella and Bill Riggs's farm.

Swonnie Hensley, a fifteen-year-old cousin, came to stay with the W. G. Riggs family and care for the children when Lynn was born in 1899, and she stayed after his mother died until his father remarried. On June 22, 1902, six months after Rosie's death, Bill Riggs married Juliette Scrimsher Chambers, twenty-eight, who was one-fourth Cherokee. Born near Claremore on November 28, 1873, Juliette had attended Cherokee Nation schools and had graduated from the Cherokee Female Seminary at Tahlequah and Fort Worth Business College.[4] Joseph Riggs died on July 14, 1902, soon after his son's second marriage.

Lynn apparently never knew his mother's parents, but the Cherokee heritage he prized came through her line. Her people probably came to Indian Territory during the great migrations from the Southeast on the Trail of Tears. A proud nation, the Cherokees prided themselves on their learning, and they had built a well-developed governmental and educational system in Indian Territory. But after their tribal lands had been distributed to individuals, their control began to slip away from them in the territory that was supposed to be theirs forever. At the time of Lynn's birth statehood was fast approaching. It was made official in 1907—a significant event in his writings.

According to a cousin, Lillie Brice Warner, Rose Ella left a fine farm with many outbuildings and an orchard on it, to which Bill Riggs brought his second wife. Bill's sister, Mary Riggs Thompson, after she was divorced in 1905, lived on Lynn's farm with her eight children and her brother Jimmy. During the lean days when he was putting himself through college, Lynn mortgaged the land and the mineral rights on it several times—a burden of debt he did not escape for many years. Eventually, he sold the land, which had served him well although he never lived on it as his own.[5]

Lynn's stepmother, Juliette, was dark, strong-featured, strong-willed, and ambitious. Although she apparently did not abuse her stepchildren physically, her relationship with them ranged from indifference to total emotional rejection. A relative said she "didn't want anything to do with them." Many sources confirm that she was a difficult woman. Her marriage to William Grant Riggs broke up after the children were grown, in 1929. Juliette became the model for the wicked stepmothers in Lynn's plays, especially *The Lonesome West*, *Some Sweet Day*, and *The Cream in the Well*.

Juliette's youngest stepchild often received the brunt of her irritation and was punished by confinement in the "dog house," one of the outbuildings on the farm. His sister, Mattie, just four years older, sometimes slipped food under the door to him and tried to comfort him. Physically more frail than his older brother, Lynn was never able to please his father, who rarely stood up for him against his stepmother. Lynn's plays and poems often convey a nightmarish imprisonment, a betrayal by women, and the vulnerability of innocents. Several of his plays feature a cold, harsh woman and a stern father. Rebellious youth, rejecting the ways of the older generation, was a natural and important theme for him.

When Lynn was six, the family moved to a new two-story

Wedding picture, 1902, of Riggs's stepmother, Juliette Chambers, and father, William Grant Riggs, with the baby, Rollie Lynn, his sister Mattie *(standing)*, and his brother Edgar. *Lynn Riggs Memorial, Rogers State College, Claremore, Oklahoma; the source of all photographs except those for which another source is indicated.*

Riggs's Aunt Mary Thompson Brice, *center*, with her first husband, Raymond Thompson, and, *from left to right*, her daughters, Jessie, Doll, Goldie, Laura, and Lillie, who were important companions during Riggs's childhood. Mary Brice was the model for Aunt Eller in Riggs's play *Green Grow the Lilacs* and Rodgers and Hammerstein's musical version, *Oklahoma!*

house on Eleventh Street in Claremore. Bill Riggs, a rancher and a stockholder in the bank, eventually became president of the Farmer's Bank and Trust Company. Two sons were born to him and Juliette: Lee Grant, in 1908, and Joseph Vann, in 1914. Two daughters died in infancy.

After meals in the Riggs house the kitchen and common rooms were closed to the children. They were sent to the upstairs bedrooms immediately after supper. Although the well-to-do Riggses had no social relations with Bill's sister Mary and her large family of twelve children (eight of whom survived to adulthood), they often sent their children to stay with Aunt Mary. Bill would bring them over whenever Juliette would get excessively angry with them, then bring them home again when she would calm down.

Therefore, Lynn grew up very close to his cousins and received from Aunt Mary some of the mothering he lacked at home, where care and respect were given only grudgingly. Yet he carried psychological scars throughout his life which adversely affected many of his relationships, especially with women.

Eloise Wilson said, "Lynn so loved and admired his Aunt Mary that he made her America's 'Aunt Eller' in *Green Grow the Lilacs*. . . . Aunt Mary's churn, her palm leaf fan, her sassafras tea, her observance of birthdays, even her own marital difficulties appear in Lynn's various Oklahoma plays."[6] Riggs wrote in 1947, "Aunt Eller is based on my wonderful Aunt Mary (Mrs. John Brice) and some of the things I vaguely knew about my mother—who died when I was two. (Her name, too, was Ella, "Eller" as people called her.)"[7]

James Riggs, a bachelor in his forties, brightened the lives of the Thompson and Riggs children. When Aunt Mary went into town to work to support her six daughters and two sons, she left them in his care. The children of Bill Riggs were often there, too, with gentle, musical, unique Uncle Jimmy (who appears in Lynn's play *A Lantern to See By*).

The family did not have much, but Uncle Jimmy managed

to have popcorn on hand, stick candy, which he bought in five-pound bags, and apples by the bushel. In the evenings each child who had behaved well during the day was rewarded with a stick of candy. Occasional explorations to pick up pecan nuts or gather blackberries provided special treats. While the children enjoyed snacks, Uncle Jimmy hammered out tunes on his old dulcimer and taught them to sing the old songs that Lynn learned to love.

The best times of childhood for Lynn were spent with his kindly uncle and his cheerful, high-spirited girl cousins. As young women they were models for several of his heroines. According to Lillie Brice Warner, Bill Riggs, too, had once sung cowboy songs on the range—"My Old Beaver Cap" and other favorites that Lynn anthologized—but after Rose Ella died, he sang no more.[8]

Lynn's play *The Boy with Tyford Fever* uses incidents remembered from age eleven, when he had suffered from the common and dreaded disease of typhoid, of which his mother had died. One day when Lynn was acting cranky, Juliette ordered him to go to the "dog house," but his father noticed his flushed face, felt his forehead, and found he had a high fever. On this one occasion his father interceded for him. When Juliette refused to nurse the sick child, Bill Riggs sent for Aunt Mary. It was she who took turns with Bill, sitting up twenty-four hours a day for several days until the fever left Lynn.

Bill helped his older brother James (Uncle Jimmy) finance the building in 1909 of the St. James Hotel across from the Claremore Missouri Pacific Railroad station and train yards. Jimmy added for his sister Mary a boarding house and dining room at the side rear of the hotel, where she cooked for boarders and hotel guests. Often in the evenings at the hotel, Uncle Jimmy and the family would sit on the porch and sing together. The railroad section hands, who stayed in a bunkhouse at the yards, came over to sing with them, teaching them more folk songs from all parts of the country.

A childhood friend recalled a carnival, a big event coming to the small town. As she and Lynn set out to spend ten cents on a movie, they were lured aside to see "Bosco the Snake-Eater." When the ordeal was over, both children sat on a curb and vomited.

She said Lynn learned his love of horses early, often riding a five-gaited sorrel mare belonging to Billy Rogers, uncle of Claremore's most famous native son, the comedian Will Rogers. The children sometimes rode or walked out to Big Lake, site of one of Riggs's early plays. In late fall they sometimes engaged in persimmon fights, choosing up sides and pelting each other with the wild fruit, then calling a truce to sit in the shade and eat picnic lunches.[9]

Lynn also became stagestruck early. In 1931 he recalled in a letter that he had made his debut at the age of eleven in *The Miller's Daughter*, and he said that he had just rediscovered a copy of the play among his papers. He had played "that great nobleman, Lord Harrington, alias Basil Lawrence."[10]

By the time Lynn reached Eastern University Preparatory School in Claremore in 1912, at age thirteen, he had found ways to ingratiate himself and receive recognition from his peers through music and drama. He starred at the Friday night literary "speakings" at the school, and he often played on his guitar and sang some of his growing repertoire of folk songs and play-party dance songs. He dreamed of becoming an actor.

He said later that he liked to read "trash," such as Diamond Dick and Horatio Alger stories. During the summers he worked on his father's farm, but he hated farm work. He compromised by running the plow around the field once, then stopping under a tree to read a book, setting an alarm clock for ten minutes, then circling with the plow once again.[11]

Since his father also traded in cattle, shipping small herds to Baxter Springs, St. Louis, and Chicago, Lynn became an experienced horseman and knew the cowboy life. He also earned money driving a grocery delivery wagon and sang

James W. Riggs with his niece Mattie A. M. Riggs and his nephew Rollie Lynn Riggs.

songs in the local movie house. His voice teacher, Miss Minnie Owens, accompanied him on the piano.

A life-threatening experience, apparently a sunstroke, sent Lynn's Uncle Jimmy indoors in 1910, shortly after he completed the St. James Hotel. He took up residence in his room there and, wary of the sun, did not leave the place for twenty-four years. His sister Mary persuaded him to come out on May 5, 1934, for her seventy-third birthday party. On that occasion he took his first automobile ride to her home, as reported in the *Claremore Progress* on May 6. One of his nieces drove him around the area, showing him all the new sights, which included Lake Claremore, the Hotel Will Rogers, and Oklahoma Military Academy (formerly the Eastern University Preparatory School). He saw the Will Rogers Airport, named for a boy that he had trotted on his knee and chased to "tan his hide," the son of his close friend Clem Rogers. Although, during the ride to Mary's, James Riggs insisted that the car go down alleys to avoid traffic, he enjoyed the trip so much that he decided to see "anything and everything" at age seventy-seven.

Graduating from preparatory school in 1917, Lynn Riggs left the eccentric people of his childhood behind and signed as a cowpuncher on a cattle train bound for Chicago. There he worked in the claims department of the Adams Express Company for a few months. He went on to New York, where he tried several kinds of work: he was an extra in cowboy movies being produced in Astoria and the Bronx, sold books at Macy's department store, and read proof for the *Wall Street Journal*. He went to all the plays he could afford.

Although he enjoyed this first taste of freedom from the disapproving atmosphere of home, poor health forced Riggs to return to Claremore in 1919. Recovering, he went to work that summer as a reporter for the *Oil and Gas Journal* in Tulsa. In his reading that year, he "discovered" poetry and began to write it—"reams of bad poetry," he said later.[12]

PHOTO BY CARSON
CLAREMORE, OKLA.

Riggs relatives and hotel guests in front of the family's St. James Hotel in Claremore, of which Lynn's uncle, Jimmy Riggs, was the proprietor. His aunt, Mary Brice, ran the boardinghouse and dining room in the rear on the left.

But Riggs had seen something of the exciting young world of filmmaking, and he soon hopped a freight train to Hollywood, where he worked again as a film extra. He was a natural as a cowboy, but he told of one film where he and others, dressed in tuxedos, watched young Rudolf Valentino repeatedly fall off a balcony for the cameras. Riggs was to have a lifelong relationship with this industry and the drama, fake and real, that centered around its people. In those early days he counted among his many friends actors Pauline Frederick, Jack Pickford, Wallace Reed, and Hobart Bosworth.

He tried writing a film script, "The Treasure Chest," which was an autobiographical romantic comedy about going to Chicago on a cattle train. It was rejected by Goldwyn Pictures in a letter of January 10, 1920, addressed to "Robert L. Riggs, 715 S. Hope St., Los Angeles." [13] Apparently he destroyed this script.

Riggs earned his living between screen jobs by reading proof for the *Los Angeles Times*, even though he found this work a strain on his myopic eyes. It was on this job that he got the lucky break which enabled him to enroll at the University of Oklahoma and pursue the writing and music career that he really wanted.

Working late one spring night in 1920, Riggs was in the building when a bomb went off, set by disgruntled former employees of the *Times*, and several people were killed. He wrote and sold an eyewitness report to the McClure Syndicate. With the resulting three hundred dollars, he returned to Oklahoma and enrolled in Norman as a fine arts major interested in music and drama. [14]

Although Riggs rarely returned to the scenes of his unhappy childhood, he treasured the good things about it, especially the songs. He remembered the many colorful characters at home and used the real stuff of life there in his stories. Often criticized for presenting the darker side of life, he recognized the truths of human nature and tried to portray it honestly. His play *Big Lake*, for example, features a schoolboy

Rollie Lynn Riggs on graduation from Eastern University Preparatory School in Claremore, 1917.

and girl who become lost and involved with evil adults. A poetic kind of play, it contrasts the innocence of youth with the suspicion and oppression laid on them by adults. A common theme of Riggs's works continued to be the corruption of innocents by the harsh realities of adult life around them.

His heritage had given him two important things: knowledge of the diverse Oklahoma culture and people and some inherited land. When he was twenty-one, he petitioned to become legal owner of his land instead of his guardian, his father. Then he mortaged the land to help pay his way through college—an expense which his father refused to pay, although he was certainly financially able to do so.[15] Although an impoverished student, Riggs managed to scrape by and enjoy the rich intellectual, creative, and social life that college had to offer him. Never before and never again would his life be so full and rewarding, so happy and complete, as it was at the University of Oklahoma.

CHAPTER 3

BREAKING OUT: OKLAHOMA
UNIVERSITY (1920–1923)

Here lies a bag of bones—here lies my love.
Here I lie too, who never meant to die
at last unloved, and face ignominy—
for such it is for such as I, by love.
Immutably the standard flown above
splits in the wind, announcing one poor guy,
unrewarded by the wizardry
that love is . . .

—"Epitaph"[1]

LYNN RIGGS entered the University of Oklahoma in the fall of 1920 with a meager wardrobe, a few dollars, and a determination to absorb literature, music, and drama. Almost destitute during his student years, he maintained his dignity, pursued extramural activities with enthusiasm, and worked and studied long hours. In spite of hardships, these were radiant years, and he almost made it all the way to the gold at the end of the rainbow. But when his personal life collapsed in his senior year, his health, energy, and courage broke down, too. Had he been living at last the life he was meant to live? Or was he again, as he said, "just outside the rush of light"?[2]

To stay in school, he mortgaged his Indian allotment lands at Claremore. He also washed dishes for his room and board at the new Pi Kappa Alpha fraternity house, was initiated into the fraternity, and lived there in the basement. Later he moved

37

to the home of fraternity brother Joseph Benton, where he was like a son to Mrs. Benton, who had lost two younger sons. He and Joseph, a singer who became an operatic performer, remained lifelong friends. Benton said that Lynn was like a brother to him.[3]

Riggs was older than most of the students because of the three years that had elapsed between his high school graduation and college. He made all As and Bs in college except for one C in physical education. In January, 1921, he changed his major from fine arts (music) to English, minoring in French and English philosophy. He formed another lifelong friendship with Darwin Kirk and his family. Kirk's younger sister Betty idolized her brother's literary classmate. Later, as a journalist, she often wrote about Riggs, and she eventually contributed her Riggs correspondence file to the university's Bizzell Memorial Library.

Riggs joined the Men's Glee Club as a second tenor and the Pi Alpha Tau honorary drama fraternity, in addition to editing the campus literary magazine. He wrote a short farce called *Cuckoo*, a folk comedy that included ballads. The farce was produced in May, 1922, and produced again in July when he was on tour. On a brief visit home to Claremore in August, he wrote Betty Kirk a lively letter about attending dances and parties. He loved ballroom dancing and once said he "never missed a dance or a football game" in college.[4]

His college years, in retrospect, do seem to have been a perfect time. Riggs was involved in the music, writing, and drama that he loved, surrounded by friends and encouraged by teachers. He joined Battle Ax, the honorary freshman society, and he graded English papers for thirty-five dollars per month. In 1922 he became a member of Blue Pencil, the honorary literary fraternity. He was associate editor of the yearbook, *The Sooner*. His income was boosted with an appointment to teach a class in freshman composition for sixty-five dollars a month during his second and third years. He and other students also published independently a humor magazine called *Whirlwind*. Founded in May, 1921, it sold for twenty-five cents at the university and in local high schools. In 1922 the busy student also saw the first of his poems published in *Smart Set*: "Song" and "I Was a King." The August *Smart Set* had "Puritans" and "Summer." He wrote two poems to visiting poets, "To Vachel Lindsay" and "To Witter Bynner," and on December 6 he wrote Bynner to thank him for critiquing some of his poems. His first checks for his writing were from *Smart Set*: fifteen dollars from H. L. Mencken for poetry and a second check from George Jean Nathan for a short story.[5]

Warmed by Bynner's friendship and nonjudgmental views, Riggs wrote him this poem:

> *The orchard here is near and homelike—*
> *Thus Carl Sandburg said: and you*
> *Have, orchard-wise, put out authentic blooms*
> *From dawn to dew.*
>
> *And we who part must do so casually*
> *Lest we betray*
> *Too much of what it means renouncing home*
> *To go away.*[6]

The summer of 1922 offered Riggs a rich experience travelling with the Sooner Quartet from the University of Oklahoma through the Midwest on the Chautauqua entertainment circuit. Riggs sang second tenor with Joe Benton, first tenor; Elmer Fraker, bass; Laile Neal, baritone; Skeet Carrier, dancer; Jack Froose, pianist and speaker; and Charles Green and Leo Morrison, chalk talkers. They traveled from Elmira and Niagara Falls, New York, to Indianola, Iowa, in less than luxury, sometimes dressing in the back of their car. In Red Cloud, Nebraska, Riggs met Willa Cather. A woman fortune-teller on the circuit, known as Mother Lake, also impressed him greatly and was to become the subject of a short story that he wrote near the end of his life, called "Someone to Remember."

Riggs's fascination with words flourished at the university.

Oklahoma University's Sooner Singers in Indianola, Iowa, on a Chautauqua tour, July 5, 1922. *From left to right,* Jack Froose, piano accompanist; Joe Benton, first tenor; Lynn Riggs, second tenor; Laile Neal, baritone; and Elmer Fraker, bass. The Chautauqua tent is in the background. *Western History Collections, University of Oklahoma Library*

Incongruously, he used quotations from Shakespeare in his farce *Cuckoo,* where a ranting suitor waves an imaginary sword while exclaiming, "Out, out damned spot! By heaven, I'll make a ghost of him that lets me. I say away!" The play also featured music, including a Shakespearian song, "I am Titania," as well as its hillbilly heroine, wearing big plow shoes, who plays the organ and sings.

Benton said: "Once I came upon him reading the Psalms. I teased him about the Bible and he looked up, his eyes luminous, 'Why this is the most beautiful literature I've ever read,' he said." Benton added, "Lynn was no Christian in a dogmatic sense. Writing bubbled up in him like a volcano. . . . Music was as natural to him as breathing."[7]

Leo Morrison wrote in 1957 to Frances Baker of Quapaw, Oklahoma, that he remembered Riggs as an intellectual and artistic person, "a rather quiet fellow with a keen and subtle sense of humor, often making off-hand remarks that would cause everyone to chuckle." He continued,

> There were eight boys on the Chautauqua tour and all the rest of us, except Joe, were out having a big time after our program in each town, while Lynn and Joe spent their time with the older and more cultured people of the town. As soon as we got to a town, Lynn would head for the book store and spent all his spare time browsing and always carried a book or two of poetry with him which he read while traveling.[8]

Riggs wrote Witter Bynner on January 24, 1923, discussing poetry and considering how he, a "vassal of the state," might get free of obligations so that he could come to Santa Fe. Bynner corresponded with several students from the university after visiting there. He had written Harriet Monroe at *Poetry* magazine on Riggs's behalf. After *Poetry* bought his poem "Rhythm of Rain," Riggs wrote, "I've an idea it's your fault that I'm there—you wrote, I remember, to H.M. and she promised to watch out for me." Monroe dedicated a whole issue of *Poetry* to Riggs in the summer of 1923.

In the spring of 1923, Riggs was poetry editor for the *University of Oklahoma Magazine* and continued in the Men's Glee Club and the Blue Pencil literary fraternity. It was in Blue Pencil that he came to know Eileene Yost, a Delta Gamma sorority member from Norman, an artist, and a yearbook beauty queen.

Faculty members Andy and Elizabeth Anderson, Walter Campbell, and his wife, Isabel, befriended the student literary group, holding informal meetings in their homes where students would read and discuss each other's work. Campbell published under the pseudonym of Stanley Vestal. Osage writer John Joseph Mathews was in this group, as was Betty Kirk. During Betty's senior year of high school, Riggs and Phil Gully brought her books to read by writers they admired, among them Carl Van Vechten, F. Scott Fitzgerald, Joseph Hergesheimer, Edna St. Vincent Millay, Eleanor Wylie, Robinson Jeffers, Dorothy Parker, and James Branch Cabell.

Riggs told Betty Kirk that his father came west from old Appalachian stock and "had very little interest in him because he was not like his rugged cowboy brothers." She said, in 1968, "Although physically frail, Lynn was not weak. He was emotionally and intellectually powerful. He would have had to be to overcome so many handicaps. . . . He had a quiet but unshatterable courage." [9]

By the fall of 1923, Riggs had fallen in love with Eileene Yost, the dark-haired Irish beauty with violet eyes, whose mother worked in the college extension division. Riggs called her a "Hergesheimer woman," having charm and glitter like characters of his favorite author. But Eileene wanted to marry, and Riggs had no money and no evident prospects. At midterm along came Hod Byer, a dashing geology student, son of a beer baron from Wisconsin, who swept Eileene off her feet. Byer drove a Stutz speedster and had a well-padded wallet to add to his attractions. Their elopement one winter weekend shattered Lynn. Betty Kirk later said, "He was so totally stricken that he collapsed and had to resign his position. . . . The loss of Eileene was a definite turning point in Lynn's emotional life. I'm fairly sure he never again fell wholly in love with any other woman." [10]

Riggs went into a deep depression. Although he tried to continue his schedule in the fall semester, he showed symptoms of tuberculosis, such as chills and fever. Dr. Mayfield, the Campbells, and the Bentons advised him to follow the call to Santa Fe.

The gaiety and triumphs, the hilarious performances of *Cuckoo*, the broadening Chautauqua tour, the publications of his poetry, the teaching of English and editing of university publications, membership in fraternities and honorary societies—all these were turned to ashes. As a child Lynn had felt deserted by his mother's death, emotionally rejected by his stepmother, and ignored by his father. Now the final rejection by Eileene, who symbolized all the best things that had ever happened to him, was too much. His self-esteem hit bottom.

He lost the will to write, temporarily, and lost the glowing view of what the future could hold for him. When he dared to look ahead at a writing career, he feared the continuous struggle that such a life forecast. He did not yet envision how he would become the spokesman for the inarticulate people of his home country, how he would campaign all his life for their story to be told. Poetry was his way of self-expression, of catharsis; drama would become his way of portraying what he saw of southwestern life for the rest of the world to understand. Suffering from tuberculosis, depression, or a nervous breakdown—possibly, all three—Riggs fled to Santa Fe.

CHAPTER 4

THE BIG TIME: BROADWAY, YADDO, AND PARIS (1925–1928)

You'd think, erased in line and contour, he
the watcher washed, would flow as waters run
down among fibrous root and cellular
organic waste and worm to be as one
with wider reaches of identity:
vapor and ocean, rock, and farthest star.

—from "You'd Think" [1]

FOR THE FALL SEMESTER of 1925, Lynn Riggs left Santa Fe to take a position teaching English in evening classes at the Lewis Institute of Chicago. [2] While working there and living in Oak Park, he wrote *Big Lake*, his first play to be produced in New York.

Subtitled *A Tragedy in Two Parts,* this play is about two adolescents, Betty and Lloyd, who wander away from a school picnic and seek shelter in a dugout with an evil couple. Butch, a bootlegger, has just murdered an informer and schemes to pin the murder on Lloyd. He looks upon Betty with lust. After they escape from the situation and return to their friends, the ugly accusations of their classmates and teacher repel them. They flee out onto the lake, where death pursues them. This play was produced on April 8, 1927, by the new, experimental American Laboratory Theatre founded by director Richard Boleslavsky and actress Maria Ouspenskaya, both

former members of the Moscow Art Theatre. It was staged by
George Auerbach.

Barrett Clark said in his introduction to the play, which was
published by Samuel French, Inc., in 1925, that *Big Lake* cap-
tures the adolescent's joy in the beauties of nature and the
horror of lurking evil. In the program, he had commented,

> There is a winged lightness in the words he [Riggs] puts into
> the mouths of his young people, a sort of lyricism which is ab-
> sent from nearly all the plays of our generation. But Mr. Riggs'
> lyricism is not primarily a verbal matter, and his words are not
> just a part of some dramatic pattern; his plays are lyric dramas
> because they have been conceived and felt lyrically. . . . I am
> sure that in Lynn Riggs our American theatre has found a poet
> who can bring to it an authentic note of ecstasy and passion,
> expressed in terms of drama. He is one of the few native drama-
> tists who can take the material of our everyday life and mould
> it into forms of stirring beauty.[3]

Although praised by Burns Mantle of the *Daily News* and
Walter Winchell, the play was called by some New York critics
an amateurish first attempt. It remained popular with off-
Broadway theatre groups, however, and was still offered in
the Samuel French, Inc., catalogue of 1988, along with other
Riggs plays: *Green Grow the Lilacs, Hang On to Love, Roadside,*
and *Russet Mantle.* Charles Aughtry likened Riggs's plays
about the dreariness and frustrations of rural life to Eugene
O'Neill's *Beyond the Horizon* (1920) and *Desire Under the Elms*
(1924), Owen Davis's *Icebound* (1923), and Dan Totheroh's
Wild Birds (1925).[4]

When Riggs left Chicago for New York in February, 1926,
he hoped *Sump'n Like Wings* would soon see production. But
producer Otto Kahn took an option for five hundred dollars
only to drop it later, and the play was never produced in New
York. Riggs had come east on the invitation of Kenneth Mac-
Gowan, Ida Rauh's Provincetown Theatre friend, and he continued work that spring on his next play, *A Lantern to See By.*

Riggs wrote Betty Kirk in July about *Big Lake:* "The lovely leading lady in the tragedy I wrote last winter is named Betty. I hope you don't mind. I've stolen your name and put it on a very blond, pale, delicate flower of the backwoods who is a little too fragile for the world of the dark woods, and finally drowns herself in the lake."[5]

Riggs wrote Hal Bynner from Roy Chanslor's place at 244 Thompson Street, New York, on July 26, 1926:

> Will you please come back here and bring along some gaiety. Everybody, dead already, is decomposed by the heat. And I'm leaving, before I leave off having a good time, myself. I'm going to help Hatcher Hughes farm in Cornwall, Conn. Do you know him? He seems very grave, but a Pulitzer prize winner can afford to be. We are to farm in the afternoon, write in the morning. I may start the new play . . . again.[6]

He passed along some compliments for Bynner from Oklahoma writer May Frank, for his "noble poems," and said Bynner's secretary, Paul Horgan, is "a pleasant young chap" (Horgan later became a novelist, poet, and historian). The dramatist Hatcher Hughes had won the Pulitzer prize in 1923 for *Hell-Bent for Heaven*. He taught English at Columbia University between 1922 and 1924.

It was a mark of his continuing, though fragile, prosperity that Riggs was released from mortgages on his property near Claremore on April 2, 1926, and January 27, 1927.[7] He continued to keep in close touch with his friends in Santa Fe, where Bynner in 1926 published *Cake: An Indulgence Play*, part of his continuing feud with Mabel Dodge Luhan.

On July 27, 1926, Riggs wrote Bynner that he had finished his new play, or was

> . . . delivered, as it were, of a monstrosity in 3 acts, tragic by title, dramatic by spurts, and comic by general accord. No, the fact is, aside from phrase-making, it's the best thing I've done. It's called *A Lantern T'See By*, and now is in the hands of Arthur Hopkins, Kenneth MacGowan, Robert Milton, and the Theatre Guild. As soon as possible, I want to send a copy to Santa Fe.

Soon, for the sake of clarity, he changed the "T'" in the title to
"to."

He had spent a week at George Cronyn's place at Brewster,
New York, where he had typed Roy Chanslor's new play,
which Riggs said was about a little episode in the lives of
people Bynner knew. Moving on to a discussion of arguments
with friends, Riggs adds: "There's nothing in this world I'd
fight for, and least of all an idea. I'll even go to war next time,
most likely, because, although I disapprove, I might learn
something from discipline." This unusual expression from a
pacifist is followed by, "This isn't quite it. But it's a hot day.
And I sit here in my room, almost nude, in a state of coma."

Three of his poems, "Epitaph," "Slight Monument," and
"The High Words," were to appear in *The Bookman*. His poem
"Spring Morning—Santa Fe" had been selected for an anthology. He comments that the play season was "lean, lean"
except for *The Great God Brown*. He discusses actors being
considered for *A Lantern* and adds that he and Roy Chanslor
are proposing to dramatize DuBose Heyward's *Porgy*. He adds:
"Barring permission to do *Porgy*, my next play will be a bleak
tragedy, called *The Lonesome West*. . . . Patterson McNutt is
reading *The Primitives*, thanks for a word Peggy Wood told
him about me. . . . I've got to go. Roy is entertaining his aunt,
the old lady from Dubuque. I promised to help." Riggs later
destroyed *The Primitives*. It is likely, however, that some of the
plot and characters turned up again in later plays, since such
recycling was his custom.

Sump'n Like Wings and *A Lantern to See By*, labeled "two
Oklahoma plays," were published by Samuel French, Inc.,
in 1928 and dedicated to Ida Rauh. *Sump'n Like Wings* takes
place in the Oklahoma town of "Claremont" just after Oklahoma became a state in 1907. Willie Baker, a girl of sixteen, is
frustrated in her attempts to find love and happiness and de-
cides that she must struggle for self-reliance. *Lantern's* hero,
Jodie Harmon, nineteen, is the sensitive son of a cruel and ty-

rannical farmer. After his overworked mother dies, Harmon's father hires Annie Marble to do the domestic work, but Annie's desire is to escape the farm by becoming a prostitute. When Jodie, who loves Annie purely, discovers his father's illicit relationship with her, he kills his father, then learns of Annie's consent to the relationship. Caught in poverty and ignorance, these people have a "dim light to see by." Goaded by his father's trickery, Jodie says he is glad that he killed him: "My mind ud got dim . . . it's brighter now."

According to records kept in his scrapbook, Riggs destroyed another play written in 1926, called *The High Mountain.* The title reappears, however, on one of the episodic scenes in *The Cherokee Night*, completed in 1936.

On April 30, 1927, in a New York apartment at 13 Cornelia Street, Riggs wrote the Guggenheim Foundation asking for a fellowship application. June 2 he wrote to Barrett Clark, who had said in *An Hour of American Drama* that Eugene O'Neill, Lynn Riggs, and Paul Green equaled any European dramatists:[8]

> After your word on *Big Lake* I'll have to get down to work and deserve it. That's the way I feel. I'm a little abashed even at appearing in the same paragraph with the lords of the American drama. But I'm shameless too I'm afraid—it gives me a nice warm glow of delight. Thank you for this—and for your continuous encouragement and help.[9]

In the summer of 1927, Riggs was among distinguished and promising talented people on the Saratoga Springs estate of Spencer Trask, opened in 1926 as Yaddo, a place of artistic retreat. Creative artists in such fields as painting, literature, music, and sculpture were recommended by established critics and art patrons for a stay at Yaddo, where "isolation and insulation" from the world was offered during a six-month season. In 1899, after the sudden deaths of their children, the Trasks had willed their estate to the arts. They developed studios for the residents in various rooms of the house and grounds: the wooden Outlook Studio, at the edge of Pine Grove; the Hillside Studio, made from the never-used Piggery; the Meadow Studio east of it, with a view of the nearby Green Mountains; the Stone Tower Studio, with its vaulted roof, huge stone fireplace, and wide window overlooking the lake. On the grounds were four lakes fed from clear springs, an arboretum, a rose garden, and a rock garden. These were graced with statuary that included a sundial inscribed with a Van Dyke poem; a poignant line reads, "Time is too long for those who grieve . . ." Inside the mansion Tiffany windows, Persian rugs, an elaborate oak staircase, and classical bronze statues created an atmosphere of leisurely elegance.[10]

Riggs arrived June 29, 1927, and was joined the next day by his friend and former professor, Walter S. Campbell of Oklahoma University, and his wife, Isabel. Campbell wrote vivid descriptions of the Yaddo experience in his journal:

> We were delighted with our rooms (just vacated by the dramatic critic Dickinson) which overlook the Green Mts. The bedroom is big with eight large windows in a bow looking east. Adjoining it is a 6 by 10 marble bathroom and beyond it the Garden Studio, a cosy little room, cheery . . . We dined at the long table and enjoyed meeting the other guests. . . . After dinner we were shown through the gardens, laid out by the Founders to suit themselves before they lost their four children and left it all to us—and artists. It made me sad to see the grounds intended for their children (they lost 2 within an hour to diphtheria). . . . The gardens are old fashioned, but have a certain charm, and a sort of damp resignation about them, a little air as of having gone to seed that is in key with the memories of the place. We passed up towards the collonade [sic], and the cut-ups (Lynn and Lange) rolled down the grassy slopes, posing a little. I was saddened all the evening—damp and cool—by the thought of the grief of the Founders, and the solemn croak of the old frog kept up the mood all night. I slept badly.

After breakfast he and Isabel worked. Lunch was brought to their rooms, but an attempted nap was spoiled by hammering upstairs by a young sculptor, named Gutman. "We thought it was carpenters, or people pushing carpet sweepers about, or putting down rugs, or moving furniture, or juggling boxes," Campbell wrote. "But I am glad to know that Mrs. Ames will stop it. It makes work impossible for us." At Yaddo noise was restricted following breakfast until 4:00 P.M.[11]

After dinner, with what Campbell described as an odd assortment of guests, writer George O'Neil played the piano. This meeting began a lifelong close relationship between him and Riggs. Campbell said Riggs's grass-rolling friend Lange was "a blonde and somewhat soft young man," commenting:

It is gorgeous to have the freedom and uninterrupted peace of this great old place. Some of the young men—conventionally, after the manner of patients having the disease of youth— sneer at the old-fashioned things here. But they stay on. I wonder if they have as yet a suspicion that our poses of today will seem as ridiculous in turn as those of the nineties.

Riggs stayed at Yaddo until mid-October. He wrote Barrett Clark at Samuel French, Inc., on July 2, 1927:

What a swell place this is. A certain decayed grandeur can be discounted. I've a tower studio, the beginning of a play, good company (Irwin Edman, George O'Neil and others), the race track nearby beginning to hum with exercising feet. All is lovely. My new play began itself yesterday—much to my surprise. It's *Borned in Texas*, a romance of the roads.
    I'm not in it very deep yet, but the mood grows. It's rough and comic, and of the folk who travel the roads in ramshackle wagons through Oklahoma, stopping at night by a stream, stealing roasting ears and young chickens. What a racy, good-for-nothing lot! There is Hanney Rader, a juicy gay one, Pap Rader, a cheerful sly devil. Red Ike and Black Ike, cousins, and that roaring scalawag, Reckless, who got drunk once and yelled publicly:

> *"I'm wild and reckless,*
> *Borned in Texas,*
> *Suckled by a bear.*
> *Steel backbone,*

Tail screwed on,
Twelve feet long.
Dare any sonofa bitch to step on it!"

The native cops suppressed him; and a jovial judge threw him
in the hoosegow for twelve days—"one day for ever foot of tail
you got." There are tall tales of "William Penn from acrost the
Verdigree," and one about buffaloes. There are songs, "Way
Out in Idyho" and a scandalous one about—"They chew to-
baccer thin in Kansas." And I mustn't forget "the banana that
weighed 150 pounds."

This play became *Reckless,* which was published by French
in 1928 in *One-Act Plays for Stage and Study, Fourth Series,* and
later it became a full-length play, *Roadside,* also known as
Borned in Texas.

Riggs discusses in the same letter to Clark his new play, *A
Lantern to See By,* which was to be handled by French as the
exclusive agent for all Riggs's plays. *Big Lake* was going to
press, and Helen Westley was reading *Sump'n Like Wings* with
a view to reviving the Theatre Guild's interest in it. Riggs
asked Clark for a fifty-dollar advance on his work—a frequent plea from him in those days.[12]

On July 17, Riggs wrote Betty Kirk, who had just written
about him in *My Oklahoma,* that he wondered if people there
would be "irate Oklahomans when my plays are published—
in all their fever and horror and brashness and lewdness and
all the things that accumulate and throw their shadows over
the inner gentility and fragility which is at their core."

Through a summer of suffocating heat, Riggs worked at
Yaddo and corresponded with Clark about attempts to get his
plays into production. July 17 he wrote that Thomas H. Dickinson was looking at *Sump'n* and *Big Lake* that weekend, and
that Mrs. Ames, the Yaddo director, had asked Riggs to read
Big Lake to the guests: "Last night I did, and if they didn't fall
out of their seats at least they strengthened me in the knowledge that I can present a play so that it lives. And that may be,
if worst comes to worst, something to be grateful for."

He followed this to Clark on July 21 with a summary of his playwriting thus far:

I actually wrote my first play—a wild, 1-act farce based on an experience of friends of mine doing geology work in the Arbuckle Mountains—while a student at the University of Oklahoma, in 1922. It was pretty dreadful, but it played uproariously. It was called *Cuckoo*—and it was. It was given two performances at the university.

Then in January, 1925, while in Santa Fe, I made my first honest attempt to do something with Oklahoma life in a 1-act play, *Knives from Syria*, which under the direction of Ida Rauh (once of the Provincetown Players, and largely responsible for my doing it at all) was given four performances by the Santa Fe Players. I played the farm hand myself.

Next I did a satirical comedy of Santa Fe life, called *The Primitives*. This was not very satisfactory. Strangely, the best people in it were the Mexicans, whom I didn't know I knew at all.

Sump'n Like Wings, my first serious long play, grew out of a talk with Miss Rauh about people I had known in Oklahoma. This play, I believe, is called experimental.

Big Lake was written in Chicago the same year, 1925. It is my only attempt to write a play in one mood, fusing certain realistic and non-realistic elements.

In 1926, I came to New York, and wrote *A Lantern to See By* in a tiny room noisy with elevated rumbles and the screaming of Italian children in Washington Square.

That summer, at a farm in Connecticut, I wrote a very bad piece called *The High Mountain*. This I destroyed.

At the moment, in Saratoga Springs, I am deep in Oklahoma again doing a bleak study of frustration called *The Lonesome West*.

Roadside's perennially popular Bunyanesque hero, Texas, claims he was born fully grown, wearing a ten-gallon hat and boots. A rowdy braggart who outsmarts the representatives of law and order, Texas realizes that he needs a woman with enough spunk to match his own. He recognizes her in Hannie, a restless but sympathetic woman, who travels in a covered wagon with her ne'er-do-well "Pap" and likes to keep moving on. Texas sees that he is getting older and needs some permanence in his life, and sees by extension that the same thing is happening to his state. The frontier is "closin' with barb' wire," and life will never again be so free and reckless as it has been.

At Yaddo and later, Riggs continued work on an anthology of the many old folk songs for which he knew both words and music, many of which he recorded on paper for the first time. He also worked on *The Lonesome West*, writing to Clark on July 21, after only three weeks at Yaddo, that he was developing a "masterpiece": "It's a play such as America has never seen—an epic of frustration that follows pioneering in the Middle West. Well, let me boast! I'll probably go mad—but I'll finish it."

He adds an afterthought: "I'm just raving today. And thinking, 'Poor old Chekhov! How you must envy me!'"

The Lonesome West was an autobiographical play set on the eighty-acre farm of the Bingham family near Blackmore, Oklahoma, about 1910. In setting the scene, Riggs describes buildings like those of his childhood. The children—Marthy, twenty-five, Ed, who is married, and Sherman, eighteen— correspond to Riggs's older sister Mattie, his brother Edgar, and himself. The father, Bill Bingham, resembles Bill Riggs; and Lynn's stepmother's maiden name was Chambers, like Kate Chambers, the stone-hearted stepmother in the play. Henry Roth wrote in 1930:

> In *A Lantern to See By*, the farmhouse, the center of Oklahoma country life, was merely background; in Lynn Riggs' . . . *The Lonesome West*, the farmhouse becomes dynamic. Here it is resolved into its elements—living-room, partly-underground potato house, porch, roof, etc.—each of which becomes a plane for the dominant feelings of a certain character—his aspirations, elemental or unaccountable impulses, transitions, and ecstatic release or vision. . . . For instance, Ed, an earthy creature and lover of the soil, belongs to the sphere of the partly-underground potato house, while Sherman, mad, visionary, and poetic, is the only one to attain the roof of the house.[13]

In the play, Kate Chambers dominates Bill and makes the lives of her three step-children miserable. She persuades her husband to move to town in the end, leaving the children to run the farm. Although one critic of the 1936 Hedgerow Repertory Theatre production considered Kate a hackneyed character, this wicked stepmother was for Riggs a very real part of his past. He must have found some catharsis in picturing Sherman old enough to consider strangling her—although Sherman forgoes the opportunity.

Riggs wrote Clark in August that he had completed the first act of the play, the longest and hardest, and was determined to finish the rest before leaving Yaddo. Another guest, Irwin Edman, had quoted a poem of Riggs' in the leading article on "Books" in the Herald Tribune, saying that it "sums up with acid beauty the spirit of this lost age." Riggs suggested that review copies of his newly published Big Lake go to the Tribune, The Nation, Poetry, and to reviewers in Oklahoma City and Norman.

Riggs completed the play and sent it on September 26, 1927, with a note to Clark defending his dominant use of setting:

> Here it is at last. No murders, no deaths (well, hardly any), nothing but transmitted fevers—in some abundance. If the set looks vaguely like The Field God, I can't help it. It's actual—almost as it stands, and was planned last summer before I knew anything about Paul [Green]'s play. I've thought it best not to point out the "levels of action." This, as you will see, is the set that is to "out-construct constructivism." I'm tired, tired as hell. I'll be here, I believe, until the 10th. But I'd like a word on The Lonesome West. Please!

Riggs and Clark discussed at length possible changes in the play, considering a title change to Children of the Pioneers or In This Country. Riggs said in a letter of October 18 that the play expressed his original idea, that it was about more than one person or one couple, that it was strange, and that it is,

like symphonic music, completely visible and meaningful only
at last. I know my disagreeing this way about it won't alienate
you at all. All the same, I've been reluctant as hell to say I'm
afraid I can only swear by the play as it is, not as it might be if I
worked on it from now until 1930. Let me know you support
me even in what may easily be poor judgment. I honestly feel,
Barrett, that this play determines my right to be in the theatre
at all.

In spite of Riggs's personal investment, this play was seldom
produced and never published.

By November 14, 1927, Riggs had returned to the Hotel Al-
bert in New York City and had almost completed the first act
of yet another play, *Rancour*. Saying he was "pleased with it,
and excited as hell," and that it was a good theatrical study,
he asked Clark to use his influence to get him another cash
advance from French: "I'm at the middle of the month again,
and so wrapped up in the play that I can't hunt a job, and I
wonder if another advance would just about put me in wrong
all around. You'll say honestly, won't you?"

That busy autumn Riggs was gathering his poems of the
years from 1925 to 1929 for publication as *The Iron Dish* in
1930, continuing to circulate copies of *Lonesome West* and
Sump'n Like Wings to producers, arranging for an Oklahoma
lecture tour, pursuing a Guggenheim fellowship, and writing
Rancour. *Big Lake* was favorably reviewed in the *University of
Oklahoma Magazine*, and Clark praised Riggs's work in an article in the *English Journal*.

On October 13, Riggs applied to the John Simon Guggenheim Foundation for a fellowship in "creative writing in
drama and study of the European theatre." His only listed
"disability" was myopic eyes. He cited knowledge of French
and Spanish languages, and said that, though he was profi-
cient in neither language, he was studying French again. His
distinguished references included Clark, Witter Bynner, and
Paul Green, plus some newer acquaintances from the Yaddo
period: Mrs. John Carroll Ames, Yaddo director; Thomas H.

Dickinson, drama critic; and Dr. Irwin Edman, poet and philosopher, of Columbia University.

For accomplishments he cited five plays, three of them published, and summarized his plans for study thus:

> Believing that a knowledge of the European theatre would be helpful to a dramatist, I want to see what the theatres of Paris, Berlin, Vienna, Rome and, possibly, Moscow are doing; and believing that a year abroad would be a station from which the American life I know might be more penetratingly viewed, I want to settle down somewhere in France for several months and write a new play of American life.[14]

On December 13 he added to his application reviews of *Big Lake* from the *New York Times*, *New York Graphic*, and the *Daily Oklahoman*, plus Clark's article, "Plays," from the *English Journal*.

He toured Oklahoma and on December 20 read from a play and some poems for the students at chapel at the University of Oklahoma. On January 5, 1927, he read *Lantern to See By* for the Oklahoma City University chapel. He spoke to the Oklahoma Authors League on January 10, and at the Hotel Tulsa on January 17, at a Little Theatre luncheon where he praised the unique work of the New York Theatre Guild. He read *Rancour* a few days later for the Tulsa Shakespeare Society's annual tea.[15]

From his father's home in Claremore, on January 4, 1927, he mailed Clark a revision of *Rancour* and repaid him a twenty-five dollar loan. A jubilant letter written New Year's Day began, "Herewith the scalp of Oklahoma City society." Placards all over the city were publicizing a performance of *Lantern* on January 10, and an article about him had appeared in approximately three hundred Oklahoma newspapers. *Big Lake* had been the "most in demand" book at the Oklahoma City Public Library in mid-December.

Rancour is about Dorie Bickel, whose husband, Ned, and son, Julius, neglect farming in favor of hunting and loafing. They fall in love with a mother and daughter, Maggie and

Loochie Williams, who are equally unambitious. While Dorie makes a successful living out of the truck farm and a restaurant, Julius drops out of business school to marry Loochie. The husband commits suicide after he is rejected by Loochie's mother. Although deeply hurt, Dorie realizes she has to keep going, to make it by depending only on herself, much like Riggs's earlier heroine Willie in *Sump'n Like Wings*.

Although never published in book form by French, the play (with the spelling changed to *Rancor*) was available in mimeographed form for many years and was performed by numerous amateur theatrical groups between 1928 and 1935. It made its debut at Hedgerow Repertory Theatre in Rose Valley, Pennsylvania, near Philadelphia. Located in a quaint old mill, this resident company of approximately thirty actors had been founded in 1923 by Jasper Deeter and was dedicated to presenting new as well as established playwrights. During the week of July 12, 1928, when it produced *Rancor*, Hedgerow was presenting a distinguished repertoire including *Mary, Mary*, by St. John Ervine, O'Neill's *The Hairy Ape*, and Ibsen's *The Pillars of Society*. Jasper Deeter, the eccentric and innovative director of Hedgerow, was interested in Riggs and produced many of his plays.[16]

Riggs sent Barrett Clark, along with the revision of *Rancor*, a letter revealing how difficult it was for him to acquiesce in the conventions of the theatre of his time or to tone down his plays' harsh revelations:

> Please don't dislike too much the "articulateness" of this piece. I've been recluse and hid away and perhaps subtle in some of the others. This time I want to be as clear as possible. I've read the play carefully again. It seems to me very moving. And for the first time, I believe I've written a play that lots of people will respond to. Of course, I believe, by its very acceptance of theatrical conventions it's inferior to *The Lonesome West*. But to have used them, with any success at all, is for me a kind of *tour de force* . . . and here's my thanks for your critical hand in this. What a relief! My 7th long play.

He explains the changes he has made in the play. Where, in the first act, Ned tells Dorie he has been seeing Maggie, "It is her jealous feeling about Ned, you see, that drives her to get ahead—for the sake of making him suffer, too." An added scene in the second act increases the conflict of Dorie's struggle to the point where she drives Julius away. The son's "rancor" adds to her problems. The second act makes clearer that "the bond between Dorie and Ned is one of those terrible ones—senseless, of course—that are so current in life: two people who love each other, but can't move or speak without causing each other pain. It's a kind of rebellion at the way they are held."

Love, in most of Riggs's plays and poems, is more a source of pain than pleasure. In his poem "Epitaph" he had said that he never meant to die at last unloved—"for such it is for such as I . . . unrewarded by the wizardry that love is." This "wizardry" caused people he knew to rebel at love, or to be crushed by the love, often counterfeit, which held them.

In his January 7, 1927, letter to Clark he wrote that he was using his visit to Oklahoma to check on people and places for his plays:

> I'm hoping to go tomorrow to the country to take pictures of the land of *A Lantern, The Lonesome West*, etc. I've some marvellous pictures of the originals of Willie, "Watt" Jim, Harriett, and Fanny of *Sump'n Like Wings*. My aunt tells me great tales— of the Chinaman hung in a sack from his ceiling, of an old boy-friend of my brother's and how he murdered his Osage mistress, etc. The town is still brutal and unlovely. The sky is the only thing here. [About *Rancor*] Yes, if all is well with it go ahead with Margaret Anglin. Just mention that this is the play Zoe Akins suggested I write for her.

Riggs goes on to say that the Tulsa Little Theatre is considering a performance of *Big Lake* and asks for review copies for the literary editor of the *Tulsa World* and for Miss Hopkins at Claremore Public Library. Accompanying pictures show the real set of *The Lonesome West*: the old Riggs farm, although the underground potato house had been filled, the kitchen and breezeway were gone, and the swept yard was "now littered with chickens, pigs, dogs, and washtubs." Another photo shows Main Street in Claremore, with his note that "The Domino Parlor is in a building 2 blocks down on the left."

Riggs said that he hoped to leave Claremore by January 15 or 20, but wrote a curious note to Clark on January 16, saying:

> There are so many relatives. Could you, would you—send me a telegram—something after this fashion, so I can leave without so much annoying "visiting"—
> Suggest you return as soon as possible about Rancour.
> Your immortal soul will not be jeopardized by this procedure! Here's a dollar. . . . I won't leave this week, anyway. Has Mac-Bride said 'No' to my poems?

His next letter, on January 19, expressed thanks for the telegram and said it "solves a lot of tiny problems about departure. I won't leave however until after the 27th—when I make my last appearance in Oklahoma." He enclosed photographs of Big Lake near Claremore and clippings. The Tulsa Little Theatre planned to do *Big Lake* in March, and Riggs was thinking about a new play called *The Domino Parlor*.

His half-brothers, Lee and Joe, were twenty and fourteen in 1928. His sister, Mattie, thirty-five, and his brother, Edgar, thirty-three, were well known and liked in Claremore. His father, Bill Riggs, had an uneasy truce with his wife, Juliette, which was to end in divorce the following year. Although Lynn was then a celebrity, and refreshing his mind and eye with local scenes was important to him, he still found home to be the source of destructive emotions. His desire to leave was countered by his father's wish that he stay, try to keep the peace though miserable, and become what his father wanted him to be.

The conflict threw him back again, gratefully, into the life of Greenwich Village and Santa Fe, where as a person he was accepted. He still felt that he had to earn his credentials among the artistic and gifted—and perhaps that is why many people said he "couldn't take criticism." In happier moods, however, he played guitar and sang, his sense of humor had free play, he gave unstintingly of whatever he had, and people often recalled him as "a prince of a fellow." He had many friends, although he had few or none in Claremore.

The aura of home remained with him as he returned to the Fraternity Club in New York, where he wrote *The Domino Parlor* in the next two months. His friend George O'Neil showed the play to the Pulitzer Prize–winning poet and playwright Zoë Akins, supervisor for the Shuberts, who bought it in two days and quickly went into production. Irene Fenwick (Mrs. Lionel Barrymore) played the lead, and Barrymore is reported to have said, "It's the best play I've read in twenty years," according to the *Oklahoma News* of May 29, 1928. The play had a preliminary showing at Springdale, Connecticut, on June 15 and opened in Newark at the Broad Street Theatre on June 18.

But this felicitous beginning came to a bad end because Riggs did not feel that the Shuberts understood the intention of his play. Barrett Clark wrote in *An Hour of American Drama*, "It was badly miscast, and because Riggs refused to let the manuscript be tinkered with, nothing more was done about it." [17] *Domino Parlor* was never published and was not copyrighted until 1930. Riggs went to Europe on the Guggenheim Fellowship with a burning resentment against the Shuberts as representatives of people who could distort his plays into something they were not and who could never understand what they were meant to be. He clung to his integrity as a playwright—just as the life and people and places he knew in Oklahoma clung to him.

The Domino Parlor takes place in a men's club of the same name, ostensibly in alcohol-dry Oklahoma, in the town of Blackmore, which "God and the oil boom forgot." The proprietor, Jude Summers, is reunited with his sweetheart of twelve years earlier, Toni Devereau, a blues singer. Now with hardened spirits, they find they cannot renew their love in the same way, but they recommend to two teenagers that they hang onto love, because "it'll make you decent about a lot of things. It'll make you face what you have to face." Toni kills the villain, Charley Troglin, in order to protect Jude, but the violence is the evocation more of sadness than of hate.

In an undated newspaper article in Riggs's scrapbook, entitled "Lynn Riggs, No Servant of Broadway," Betty Kirk wrote that Sam Shubert told Lynn that the heroine could not kill a man and that the hero had to be a bootlegger rather than the more odious bank bandit. Riggs refused, on grounds of authenticity of character, to make these changes.

When the offer of the Guggenheim Fellowship came, Riggs replied on March 14 that he was "exceedingly grateful—and incoherent" with joy. Although the tenure of the fellowship began May 1, he remained in the United States for the *Domino Parlor* production and sailed after July 21. He asked for the $2,500 one-year grant to be paid quarterly, beginning with $1,000 on April 23 (to arrange passage on an Atlantic Transport ship to London), then $500 per quarter. He explained that he expected to travel and see the theatres of England, France, Germany, and Italy in the first few months of his year. He was optimistic about his prospects: "Later, of course, when I settle down somewhere to write my new play, and perhaps plays, I won't need so much. By that time also, if prospects materialize, I'll be drawing royalties from two or more productions. The Guggenheim fellowship seems to have brought me luck, for as nearly as such things can be positive in the theatre, I'm to have two new plays produced in the fall in New York."

But on July 2, after *Domino's* unhappy closing, Riggs wrote to Clark:

> Would you think me utterly mad if I asked you if Samuel French, on the suspicion that I might really make money some day soon, would feel like advancing me, now, $1,000 in cool cash? I'd rather owe Samuel French than the people I do owe, and it would take a great easeful weight off my mind to get

this settled this week. And the sooner, the better—I don't feel myself to be a poor business proposition. And your firm has been so damned considerate of me in every way, that I'd like it to be them who profits in the end. At the moment it is myself who would profit, and profit greatly. And be sure of my gratitude.

Reckless is all but finished.

He wrote Hal Bynner on March 20, 1928, his thanks for "your share in its coming to me" (the Guggenheim):

It solves my future for a year—and perhaps it solves my future. I've been working hard. Besides a reading tour of Oklahoma, I've written two new plays since last October. And Harvey Fergusson wants me to dramatize *Hot Saturday;* and I've undertaken to make a survey of dramatics in the settlements of New York, for a month or longer, before I sail for God knows where—A theatre in Rome is producing *Sump'n Like Wings* in Italian.

On June 28, Riggs wrote a brief and, to him, painful autobiography for Barrett Clark: "I've made three (this is the fourth) attempts to do this biography stuff. Won't just the exterior facts do?" He told of spending school vacations riding after cattle with his father and brother or visiting relatives and friends in small towns. He also had worked in the glass factories at Sapulpa one summer. He read a lot—"trash, mostly" (Old Sleuth, Diamond Dick, and Horatio Alger)—and went to country play-parties, box suppers, pie suppers, Friday "speakings," and auctions. He sang in the spotlight of a movie house that was owned by his voice teacher.

He said that, after riding "the caboose of a cattle train" to Chicago in 1917 and working there and in New York, he went back to Claremore "a wreck" in 1919. That summer, while working for the *Oil and Gas Journal* in Tulsa, he "discovered poetry":

Read all the modern poetry, and wrote my first poems. Reams and reams. Very bad. I went to Los Angeles, played extra in many movies with the older stars. On a raft for a week in San

Pedro harbor while Hobart Bosworth made "Beneath the Sur-
face"; ten days, very much of a "dress-suit extra" on Universal's set of the Metropolitan Opera House, for Dorothy Phillips
in "Ambition" (a young man, just beginning, shot himself a
dozen times while the cameras clicked, and fell as many times
out of an upper box—Rudolph Valentino); spent a long night
on the Lasky ranch with a thousand others while James Cruze
directed Wally Reed in "Hawthorne of the U.S.A.", etc. Read
proof for the *Los Angeles Times* and nearly ruined my eyes.

He said he returned to Claremore in 1920 "a wreck again,"
entered the University of Oklahoma in the fall, where he
"never missed a dance or a football game." Mencken and
Nathan began to publish his poems and stories in *Smart Set*,
and the Chautauqua tour with the Southern Minstrels took
him to Iowa, Kansas, Nebraska, Ohio, Minnesota, Michigan,
Wisconsin, Indiana, and South Dakota. Then:

> 1923—November. Complete nervous collapse. Various rea-
> sons. Went to Santa Fe and worked on a ranch. Recovered.
> Went to work for Spanish and Indian Trading Company. Won
> Oklahoma poetry prize, for two sonnets. Wrote long poem,
> "Santo Domingo Corn Dance," which appeared later in *The
> Nation*. Published many poems in *Poetry*, etc.

He described *Knives from Syria*, his first one-act play, which
he said he wrote because of a "bantering bargain" he had
made with Ida Rauh, who directed it for the Santa Fe Players.
He went to New York in 1926, he said, as the result of a letter
from Kenneth MacGowan, who contracted *Sump'n Like Wings*
for Actor's Theatre. There, Riggs said, he wrote plays and
"many poems." While *Big Lake* was in production, he worked
in a bookstore in Grand Central. On his lecture tour of Oklahoma, he "checked up on the places and people I had been
writing about. Relieved to find I had been right about them,
and not romanticizing." Riggs concluded:

> P.S. Is there anything in the above that is usable? Or would
> you rather know that I've farmed, punched cattle, been night
> clerk in a small Oklahoma hotel, ridden a freight to Chicago,

worked for an express company, played extra in dozens of movies, clerked in Macy's, read proof for various newspapers, reported, sung all over the middle west one summer in chautauqua, taught English, published poems, worked on a ranch, etc.?

Before sailing, Riggs wrote a letter making Barrett Clark his literary executor until further notice, making his father, his brother, Edgar, and his sister, Mattie, the beneficiaries "of my enormous earnings (after all debts are paid)." His royalties from Hedgerow Theater during its first fifteen years (1923–1938) amounted to only $426.[18] He was discouraged and in debt—but during his next year, underwritten by the Guggenheim Foundation and experiencing the new sights and sounds of Europe, he would gain the distance and perspective he needed to write his greatest Oklahoma play.

CHAPTER 5

GREEN GROWS THE IMAGINATION
IN FRANCE (1928–1929)

But momentary—as a lightning flare
springs in the dark and harries like a hound
the fleeing shadow in that bowl of air—
so, in the night when there is little sound
of the wild discord that assails the ear
of present lamentation in the land,
a tone may rise, voluminous and clear,
drowning all others in its large command.

. . . . A molten planet splinters from the sun,
a golden music beats upon the face
of a man against a glory sharply stood
transfixed—a beacon and a burning wood.

—"But Momentary"[1]

WEARY AND READY FOR A CHANGE, a new perspective on his work, and a new creative environment, Lynn Riggs sailed for Europe, late in July, 1928. In later years he rarely spoke of the period in France, even to his closest friends, but his long, introspective letters to Barrett Clark reveal that it was a time of self-illuminating struggle out of which his greatest play, *Green Grow the Lilacs,* and an important long-term project, *The Cherokee Night,* were conceived and written.

Needing time to relax and separate himself from the strains of recent months, he spent three weeks in August in the Basque country of France, at St. Jean-de-Luz. He noted the

67

coincidence that another playwright, Lynn Starling, was staying in the same pension and working on a Basque play. Riggs
wrote that he was swimming every day and not working yet,
but he hoped to be rested soon. He saw the bull fights at San
Sebastian and Pamplona. He had snapshots taken of himself
lying on a beach—which he captioned "the idle rich"—and
one of him sitting by an adobe wall, playing his guitar. He
wrote Clark, "I am crowded with sensations—strange ones
for me. But I believe, after all, America is best." He began to
encounter other literary exiles. On August 14 he wrote: "Saw
E. O'Neill coming out of a patisserie yesterday in Biarritz
(Yes!) Small world, n'est ce pas?" [2]

Settling in a room at 12 Rue Kepler in Paris, as winter approached, he tried to take up the threads of his writing. He
sought the muse along with other intellectuals at the Cafe des
Deux Magots. At that time word had gone out that Greenwich Village was no longer the Bohemian center: Paris was
the display case for international talent, both for participants
and observers. As Morley Callaghan wrote:

> In 1929, the world capital for the novelist did seem to be in
> Paris, sitting at the cafe. . . . That year Paris was crawling with
> Americans wanting to see everything, and having the money
> to see it, not knowing that in a few months the stock market
> would crash and the year of Panic would begin . . . and the
> clients of those cafes who got money, no matter how little,
> from home, were to vanish, one by one. [3]

Callaghan said those who frequented that cafe, in addition,
of course, to Ernest Hemingway and F. Scott Fitzgerald, included two other Guggenheim fellows that year, poets Léonie
Adams and Allen Tate, with his wife, Caroline Gordon. Other
1929 fellows included the poet Countee Cullen, the fiction
writer Eric Walrond, the artist Anthony Angarola, and Riggs's
playwright friend Paul Green (who went to Germany). Riggs
was the first Guggenheim scholar from Oklahoma, to be followed the next year by his Oklahoma University professor
Walter S. Campbell.

As Paris's damp winter chill came on, Riggs wrote a one-act play called *On a Siding*, but it did not please him, and his records indicate that he destroyed it. Discouraged and ill, he wrote Clark at Samuel French, Inc., that he had lost ten pounds, did not sleep, and "looked like the devil." He added: "Many thanks for the kind words in *The Drama*. Some nice word from you is always arriving just when I've decided I'm no good, and that I might as well jump in the river." Clark had called Riggs one of the most promising young playwrights in America.[4]

The *Domino Parlor* failure of the previous summer weighed heavily on Riggs's mind. Since the play was based on his experience with an actual men's club in Claremore, where the much-criticized liquor and rough talk were commonplace, Riggs began to doubt his ability to articulate Oklahoma life in a way that Broadway would accept. Yet this was a goal from which he could not waver.

Money troubles pressured him. He had borrowed two hundred dollars from French Corporation just before sailing to repay a loan due his father, who had asked for it and, as Riggs said, "can't do the handsome thing at the moment." With three plays ready for production, but their future uncertain, he lived on the welcome but scant fellowship income.

Riggs wrote Clark that the Paris theatre he had seen was for the most part dreadful, the museums and people "embalming," but the "miracles" were the bars and German beer. One exception he made, Gaston Baty in *Hamlet*, reflected Riggs's continuing love for Shakespeare. The Bard's hearty characters and lusty action always seemed closer to his own ideal than most of the effete offerings of current Broadway theatre. He added prophetically, "And the more I see of Europe, the more clearly I see certain things about America."

At the time, however, even writing Hemingway-style at a table at the Deux Magots, saucers piling up beside him to tally the bill, failed to inspire him. Early in November he wrote Clark an angry outburst of frustration about struggling to

maintain his integrity as a writer while being pulled by others
in conflicting directions:

> I've been meaning to write you for a long time, but I've been
> lost in a drear void, not quite existing on any land, and cer-
> tainly loath to testify to that state, when I ought to be feeling
> assured, leisurely, more poised, more energetic than ever in
> my life. But it has remained for Paris to reduce me slowly to a
> sort of amoeba-like state in which I am grateful for even a
> twinge of changing proportions in myself which means solely
> that I'm alive, and not much else. The reason for this is of
> course, not Paris, maligned place, but the fact that when I
> came I was tired out. I'd written three plays in the preceding
> year as you know, and then that disgusting burden of the
> tryout of the play just about finished me. God slay me if I ever
> stand around and *Yes* dumb actors and mix with swine of the
> theater again. They make me dull, false as themselves, wrong,
> vain, slavish; but I'm not miraculously freed and absolved, as
> they are, from a species of reprimanding intelligence. They
> never suffer because of their defections and pretenses. It seems
> to me I do nothing else. I used to call it Puritanism. But now I
> believe it's something better, more exacting. I seem never to be
> able to approve of myself and my work, when it has become
> meat on a platter. And when it has to be fingered, and poked
> at, and flaked into morsels, it seems badly cooked, tough, or
> decayed, like the meat in "Potemkin."

A review sent because of Clark had challenged, then
humbled Riggs; and it moved him to articulate his vital goals:

> Charley Brustman has sent me, at your behest no doubt, the
> review of the new book [*One-Act Plays*] from the *Dallas Herald*.
> One ought to be pleased at the attention from a state so near
> my own, I suppose. And at first I was, because I care very
> much about Oklahoma's seeing some justice, and some truth
> in my work. But the more I think about it, the more I believe
> that this review is just as bad in its way as one written by Lee
> Shubert. Simply because, essentially, Mr. Rogers, meaning to
> be kind, but a little complacent, has not stated, really the
> thing that is truest about the plays, and so talks about their
> truth to the people on the hundreds of farms and along the
> railroads. No, the truth about those plays is that here is a germ

of *light*, a germ of *poetry* about a dark and sometimes fierce, and nearly always ignorant people. . . .

People are always asking me about Oklahoma. Sometimes they say: "I know a lot about Oklahoma, from your plays." This always makes me ill at ease. The range of life there is not to be indicated, much less its meaning laid bare, by a few people in a few plays. Some day, perhaps, all the plays I will have written, taken together, may constitute a *study* from which certain things may emerge and be formulated into *a kind of truth* about people who happen to be living in Oklahoma instead of South Dakota. But not now. The secret is scattered too widely—and, what is worse, hid away—in the breasts of too many people. Farm people, ranchers, lawyers, bankers, doctors, waitresses, bakers, tool dressers, school teachers—there, as everywhere, unite in a desperate concealment; the beats of their hearts are mysterious and faint; no pressure of hand or even opened vein may teach much about that guarded flow.

But I have felt a great deal about them. And I know that what makes them a little special, a little distinct in the Middle West is the quality of their taciturnity. They are voiceless, tongueless; they answer the challenging "Who goes there?" only by a flash of a lantern so quick, so momentary, that none but the acute guard sees more than a shadowy figure retreating into the darkness. There are two reasons for this: one— faulty education (or none at all); the other, the people who settled Oklahoma were a suspect fraternity, as fearful of being recognized by others as they were by themselves. Gamblers, traders, vagabonds, adventurers, daredevils, fools. Men with a sickness, men with a distemper. Men disdainful of the settled, the admired, the regular ways of life. Men on the move. Men fleeing from a critical world and their own eyes. Pioneers, eaten people. And their descendants have the same things in them, changed a little, grown out of a bit, but there, just the same. And so they don't speak. Speech reveals one. It is better to say nothing. And so these people, who had been much admired and much maligned, have been *not quite known*—a shifting fringe of dark around the camp-fire, where wolves, perhaps, and unnamable things lurked.

I happened to be born myself just outside the rush of light. And I know how it feels, and, I think, how those others felt. And it seems to me that if there was much ignorance in these people, there was also a minor wisdom; if there was much cruelty and darkness, there was also gentleness, and the singing of old songs. These people, human, were victims of a special and touching disinclination, and even inability, to publish their humanity. That's what I'm trying to do for them, and for their descendants, falteringly, imperfectly, incompletely, in the plays.

And now that I've said this, it all sounds pretentious, and wrong. It's better for me to say nothing, I'm coming to believe, except in poetry or drama.

On a lighter note, Riggs describes his current play in progress, about the rarer Oklahomans "who were not parsimonious of speech and ordinarily, not parched in their fruity enjoyment of life. These people were few and far between indeed; but they existed, uneaten, undisturbed, hearty, fertile, and gay. . . . The play is a great joy to work on, because it's rich and juicy."

On September 17, 1928, he wrote Alice Corbin Henderson in Santa Fe that her book had come, adding, "Now I'm so homesick for your bright hills, even Paris can not compensate."

At last, on a doctor's advice, Riggs fled the winter with everyone else who could, to the south of France, and settled in Cagnes-sur-Mer, seven miles from Nice. White, tile-roofed houses and small hotels crowded against the hillsides and looked out through trees at the blue Mediterranean Sea. Unpretentious rooms for writers and artists who wintered in this and other small "off-Riviera" towns were available (without bath) for only two dollars per day; two additional dollars bought meals.[5] Here Riggs wrote daily at a table in his almost illegible pencil scrawl. Working with characters remembered out of his childhood and youth, who took on a dramatic life of their own, he created the most authentic and immortal play ever to spring from Oklahoma soil, *Green Grow the Lilacs*. Revised later as *Oklahoma!* it became the best-known and most popular of native American dramas. It has played continuously for more than forty years, in all parts of the United

States and in many countries around the world. The original *Green Grow the Lilacs*, too, has continued to be performed regularly by amateur theatre groups.

Riggs's relaxed social life at Cagnes included informal visits with George Seldes at the nearby village of Bandol, with Anthony Angarola, and with other writers and artists whose lives, while far from affluent, nevertheless included some lively parties and excursions. Seldes, author and journalist, said Riggs's first title for his major play was *Shivaree*, a word derived from the French *charivari* meaning a mock serenade for a bridal couple on their wedding night. A New Englander, Seldes was surprised to hear that this old French custom, which often became a bawdy, villagewide celebration, was the same in Riggs's Oklahoma.[6] Although he later changed the title, Riggs obviously saw the shivaree as the climactic episode in the drama, when Jeeter, the rejected suitor, tries to take his lethal revenge on Laurey and Curly.

This play about a courtship set at a "play-party" (a house or porch party with music, song, and square dancing) became a vehicle for using the many old songs Riggs had sung from childhood—sung with his cousins and the railroad section hands on the front porch of the St. James Hotel, or sung to the accompaniment of his guitar for his friends ever since—songs that he feared would be lost forever unless written down. He wrote Clark, "Indeed the subtitle might almost be 'An Old Song,' for, like the old songs of its period, it tries to reproduce a gone age in the Middle West—its quaintness, its absurdity, its sentimentality, its pathetic and childish melodrama, its rude vigor, its touching sweetness. . . . I miss my guess if this one doesn't turn out to be the one of mine you like best." Like Curly in his play, the singer of the lyrics of the song "Green Grow the Lilacs" is haughtily rejected by his ladylove. He threatens to join the army (to exchange the green lilacs for the red, white, and blue) and thus win her favor by his bravery.

Riggs wrote to Joe Benton, then a well-known tenor on

Riggs relaxing in Spain on his way to France in July, 1928, during his Guggenheim fellowship year in Europe. *Beinecke Library, Yale University*

the music faculty at the University of Oklahoma, and to his female cousins, asking them to help him record the authentic words and music to many of these old songs. He listed the following titles to be used in *Green Grow the Lilacs,* either during the play-party or between acts in front of the curtain:

"As I Walked Out One Bright Sunday Morning"
"A-Ridin' Old Paint"
"The Miner Boy"
"An Owl in the Bresh"
"Sam Hall"
"The Little Brass Wagon"
"Weavilly Wheat"
"Custer's Last Charge"
"The Blind Child"

"Skip to My Lou"
"When I Was Young and Single"
"Barbara Allen"
"Drew a Knife from His Pocket"
"My Old Beaver Cap"
"Way Out in Idyho"
"There Is a Lady"

Samuel French, Inc., published most of these songs in 1932 in a small book called *Cowboy Songs, Folk Songs and Ballads from "Green Grow the Lilacs,"* the anthology that Riggs had begun at Yaddo. The themes, as he indicates, vary from maudlin sentimentality to patriotism, romantic tales of history, fun and nonsense, and rhythmic dance music.

Imaginative immersion in the life that he remembered from childhood was not without its hazards, its extreme mood swings. Rigg's impulse to write received much of its stimulus from his own remembered feelings of inarticulate helplessness during his growing years, feelings exacerbated by his father's derisive opinion that writing was not a proper occupation for an Oklahoma man, when compared with the solid rewards of ranching and banking. One gray French morning in Cagnes-sur-Mer, December 17, 1928, Riggs wrote of the playwright's struggle, fears, and frustrations. He conjured up scene after scene from the drama of his growing years, scenes that friends actually remember, scenes he could not forget and would like the world to understand:

> When I get like this—and I do often—there's nothing to do but bear it. Or forget it. Or pick on some kind person who will listen—and not hold it against me. It's this—I'm deep, deep down on account of the things I can't do in any way.
> I can't make—in drama or poetry—the quality of a night of storm, for instance, in Oklahoma, with a frightened farmer and his family fleeing across a muddy yard (chips there, pieces of iron, horseshoes, chicken feathers)—to the cellar, where a fat bull snake coils among the jars of peaches and plums.
> I can't begin to say what it is in the woods of Dog Creek that makes every tree alive, haunted, fretful. I can't tell you what

dreadful thing happened last Christmas—when a son and his
wife stumbled drunkenly into his mother's house; the words
that came out of brazen tortured throats, the murderous hints,
threats—and all the time a little sick child, radiant, great-eyed,
sat up in her bed and saw and heard and wept at something
foul in her presence for the first time, life with venoms beyond
her comprehension. And most of all—after sorrow, fear, hate,
love—I can't even begin to suggest something in Oklahoma I
shall never be free of: that heavy unbroken, unyielding crusted
day—morning bound to night—like a stretched tympanum
overhead, under which one hungers dully, is lonely, weakly
rebellious, and can think only clearly about the grave, and the
slope to the grave.

It seems to me more and more that I am haunted and driven
by pictures and pictures—ominous, gray, violent, unserene—
and this in spite of the fact that I become more and more sane,
more and more free of hysteria. So it begins to grow on me
that only in that borderland of life, that disjointed, slightly un-
focussed arena can we touch the pains of truth. And wouldn't
it be good to be felled by those feet, to be a good Christian in
those unholy playful jaws?

I wish I were writing a play about *Twilight*, or *Yellow Radi-
ance after Rain*, or even *More Sky*. There's verity in little else—.

Riggs depended on the loyalty and discretion of only one
or two friends, most often Barrett Clark, his sympathetic
sounding board and advisor. Clark understood that rejection
was a nightmare never far from Riggs's consciousness, that
Riggs sometimes felt it pursuing him like an assassin whose
aim was to erase even the evidence that he had ever lived.
Riggs's need to confess his frustrations, his feeling of martyr-
dom on the altar of the muse, and his guilt, which urged him
as a "good Christian" to throw himself to the welcome lions,
were spent in letters, which allowed him to get back to his
work. Then suddenly there would come a day when things
were going well, when the plucky people dancing and frolick-
ing from his pencil to the paper came alive and spoke their
lines, when he could again describe their motivations and de-
clare, "It's the best thing I've written yet!"

On December 28, he reported on his progress to Henry Moe of Guggenheim Foundation, expressed gratitude for the foundation's support and "stringless attitude," and asked for an extension of the grant for six months or a year past the May 1 deadline, since his scheduled play productions had been delayed and had brought him "hardly any money." He had completed three scenes of *Green Grow the Lilacs* and expected to finish it in February.

> The play itself is the most ambitious I've tried; and I hope it will be my best. It's a play about a vanished era in the Middle West—an era a little more golden than the present one; a time when people were easier, warmer, happier in the environment they had created. Song flourished. There were the usual human anguishes, of course. But there was *wholeness* in the people, there was great endurance. And in spite of ignorances and darknesses, there was a cool wisdom our radios and autos have banished forever. Even the speech of the people, backwoods though it was, was rich, flavorous, lustrous, and wise. And the songs are now forgotten, except for a few which have gotten into anthologies. In this play I am using for the first time in drama, I believe, many American folk songs entirely unknown to the world even of anthologists. . . . if the Committee sees fit to give me another grant, I shall only hope that my work may be meritorious and as honest as possible.[7]

Riggs outlined for the foundation his "folk play in Six Scenes, with Songs and Ballads of the period," and listed the seventeen songs he planned to include. He said that he had seen the theatres of France and Spain and that he hoped to go to Italy, back through Germany, and into England and Ireland. (In fact, since the grant was not renewed, he went home through Italy but missed Germany and the British Isles.) He told Moe that, if he were granted a renewal, he would use the time to finish his dramatization of James Gould Cozzens's novel *Son of Perdition* and write another American play, probably "one I have contemplated for some time, a dramatic study of the descendants of the Cherokee Indians in Oklahoma, to be called *The Cherokee Night.*"

On January 18, 1929, he wrote cheerfully to Clark, enclosing copies of the first three acts of *Green Grow*:

> My life is incredibly simple these days. I go on sitting at the breakfast table, while the maid potters about, and begin working. Sometimes I go for an afternoon to Nice, to Cannes, to Vence, or overnight to Monte Carlo, or Villefranche. Last week I went for three days to Toulon, and watched the town busy doing nothing on its curious and intimate quay. D. H. Lawrence was there.

Green Grow the Lilacs is set near Claremore in Indian Territory in 1900, seven years before statehood, at the white frame farmhouse of Laurey Williams. When some critics later wondered whether the farmhouse was authentic to the place—perhaps envisioning log cabins—Riggs said, "It ought to be, because it was where I was born." [8]

The characters were based on real people. Jeeter, in fact, was known as one of the meanest boys in town. Old Man Peck really did have play parties at his home with square dancing on the porch, and people came on buckboards and horseback (some in fancier surreys) across the prairie. Aunt Eller and Laurey may be composites of various individuals, but they contain much of Riggs's beloved Aunt Mary Brice and her daughters, the sources of fun and music in his youth. Aunt Eller's hardy pioneer spirit in the face of adversity is passed along to innocent but high-spirited Laurey as she assumes adult responsibilities. Laurey sees the excitement of life on the frontier, made ever sweeter by its danger and beauty.

Appropriately dedicating *Green Grow the Lilacs* to Barrett H. Clark, Riggs explained, in a lengthy preface published with the play, that his intent was solely to

> recapture in a kind of nostalgic glow (but in dramatic dialogue more than in song) the great range of mood which characterized the old folk songs and ballads I used to hear in my Oklahoma childhood—their quaintness, their sadness, their robustness, their simplicity, their hearty or bawdy humors, their senti-

mentalities, their melodrama, their touching sweetness. . . . It seemed wise to throw away the conventions of ordinary the-atricality—a complex plot, swift action, etc.—and try to ex-hibit luminously, in the simplest of stories, a wide area of mood and feeling.[9]

He said he thought of the first three scenes as "The Charac-ters" and the last three as "The Play," making the people known as they proceed to act out the destiny that is in charac-ter. He adds a declaration of independence of Broadway:

My beliefs anyway, I find, about the nature of true drama run counter to the current notions about it. Two people in a room, agreeing or not agreeing, are to me truly dramatic. The edges of their being can never be in accord; psychically, as well as physically, they are assailed by an opposing radiation. And the nature of the flow of spirit from each determines both the quality of their conflict, and the shape of their story. This flow may be violent or comic or tender; it may be one-sided, subtle, maddeningly recluse.

And the dramatist, it seems to me, has no business to inter-fere just for the sake of making a "play," in its present—and idiotic—meaning. That he may be tempted to do so is lament-able, but not surprising—the rewards are great. But if he takes his work seriously, he will face his problems in a limbo beyond the knowledge of applause. His role will continue to be humil-ity and abnegation.

And sometime, his characters may do stirring things he could never have calculated. And sometime, if he is fortunate, he may hear from the people he has set in motion (as Shake-speare and Chekhov often heard) things to astonish him and things to make him wise.[10]

When he wrote Clark on March 10, he was already looking toward the next play, outlining his plans to join together separate dramatic incidents to illustrate the plight of a people:

The play will be finished in a few days—perhaps three. And luckily. Since Spring is definitely upon us here, and the warm hillsides are too alluring. I'm a little tired, but happy, and after a little rest, I've plans for work popping right and left. You

liked the idea of the short plays—Now I have an idea that if
some solvent, some fluid, some technical means presents itself—I can write a most curious, most novel long play which
incorporates the short plays. This play will be called *The Cherokee Night*, taking its title from this:

> *The grass is withered;*
> *Where the river was is red sand;*
> *Fire eats the timber—Night has come to our people.*
>   —*from the Cherokee*

The play will concern itself with that night, that darkness (with
whatever flashes of light allowably splinter through) which has
come to the Cherokees and their descendants. An absorbed
race has its curiously irreconcilable inheritance. It seems to me
the best grade of absorbed Indian might be an intellectual
Hamlet, buffeted, harrassed, victimized, split, baffled—with
somewhere in him great fire and some granite. And a residual
lump of stranger things than the white race may fathom.

But the play will play itself out realistically, unpretentiously.
It will probably be about—a young man about to marry an
Osage girl, with tons of money (*The White Turkey*); a few
couples picnicking at Claremore Mound where the last battle
between the Cherokees and Osages took place (*Sixty-Three Ar-
row Heads*); three boys at the scene of a murder (*Where the Nig-
ger was Found*); a man in a cell for murder (*The Claw Hammer*);
two sisters and the irony of their first meeting in years (*Lini-
ment*); the last exploit of a desperado—as in my story of the
Cataloosie killing (*Panther Creek*); two children running away
from an early picture show in fright and sitting on the curb
eating a hamburger (*Nickelodeon*); none of which is positive
yet, of course. But this is the cloud out of which something
will come.

Then there's a long play—a farewell to an epoch, in a sense—
the play about the cowboys—*Get Along, Little Dogies!.* But I'll
have to go to Oklahoma for some things I've forgotten. No one
has done the Cowboy correctly yet—his romantic dash, his
drollness, his humour, his childishness, his stupidity, his
charm. Curly in *Green Grow the Lilacs*, if I may say so, is the
only step in that direction in American fiction.

Riggs speculated about who might produce *Green Grow the Lilacs*, saying he did not "quite like" famed producer Arthur Hopkins's attitude toward him. He warned prophetically, "I'll not have this play mangled, if it never gets produced, which is what you'd advise yourself." Fear of another *Domino Parlor* fiasco haunted him:

> I hate the idea, but I shall have to be around if this play ever goes into rehearsal, on account of the songs, and the dialect, and what is more important, the *rhythms of the speech.* Jewish ideas of this special speech would be pretty awful, I'm afraid. Now that I've written this, I've a sinking sick feeling that I don't want to be *inside* a theatre again. I really do hate it, I believe. More and more.
>
> I'm getting quite content to be here, where one can fly off to watch the poor wretches trying to amuse themselves—at Cannes, Nice, Monte Carlo, etc.—when the spirit says so. But the village itself is a presence, an old one that lets me alone; or if it says anything, does it with such tired negation that it doesn't take me the way Paris does.

He hoped to be on the new Guggenheim list coming out. "What on earth could I possibly do in New York this summer?" he asked. "If I don't get a renewal, and you can think of a way for a bright young man to make money, let me know." He asks for news: "Will you send me *Street Scene*? Shuberts, I judge (and pray) have lost the rights to *The Domino Parlor.* And is the Lab. definitely under, and is *Sump'n* free again? What a time that unfortunate play has had!" [11]

The American Laboratory Theatre, a short-lived group, had planned to produce *Domino Parlor.* Riggs enclosed pictures of himself with George Seldes and Anthony Angarola, the white, tile-roofed houses of Bandol crowding over a hill in the background, then the curve of the sea.

On March 13, Riggs answered a request from Walter Campbell for some statements on the drama for a *Southwest Review* article:

I honestly haven't any theories, any very definite aims (except to be a good dramatist), and I don't know any rules. All I am sure of is this: Drama to me, in full, is simply the effect of person upon person. Put two people in a room, and there's drama. . . . No one could be more surprised than I at some of their incalculable actions. In the play I'm just finishing, *Green Grow the Lilacs*, there are a dozen examples. The play is concerned with a more golden day in Oklahoma, golden in the sense that the people I'm writing about were magnificently adapted to their environment, hearty, vigorous, gay people. And their lives, being rounded and varied, were full of unpredictable choices. They have taught me a lot about the Oklahoma of thirty years ago. And made me regret the parsimonious and desert days that came to birth in my early childhood and which continue almost up to the present. Not only have these people taught me much about the Oklahoma of the past. But, what's more important, much about *people*. I feel almost that all I know about people I learned from writing plays. For once having started a scene between living people, the dramatist, it seems to me, must step aside, self-abnegating whether he will or no, and listen to his creations.

You know yourself how much concerned I am about poetry, and the rhythms of speech. That's the reason I continue to write about Oklahoma people, and especially backwoods or unlettered people. Or *part* of the reason, at least—for I find it difficult to give up using that flavorous, that lustrous imagery, that beautiful rhythmic utterance. The main reason, of course, is that I know more about the people I knew in childhood and youth than any others. But it so happens that I knew mostly the dark ones, the unprivileged ones, the ones with the most desolate fields, the most dismal skies. And so it isn't surprising that my plays concern themselves with poor farmers, forlorn wives, tortured youth, plow hands, peddlers, criminals, slaveys—with all the range of folk victimized by brutality, ignorance, superstition, and dread. And will it sound like an affectation (it most surely is not) if I say that I wanted to give voice and a dignified existence to people who found themselves, most pitiably, without a voice, when there was so much to be cried out against?

Riggs closed the letter saying: "I'm in a little 13th Century village, near Nice, near Cannes, near Monte Carlo, near all the places of tired gaiety. Once in a while I go there. But not for long. I've had a blissful, a completely happy, healthy winter, writing my best play. My plans for the future are in the mists."[12]

It seems that his gloomy days of frustration and haunting memories were forgotten as his work progressed and sunnier moods returned—or was it that he confided in Barrett Clark but put up a cheerful front for Campbell and others who knew him in Oklahoma?

On April 10 he responded to the Guggenheim foundation's rejection of his renewal application by saying," Of course. I quite understand. And anyway I suppose I ought to be back in America after all. So let me reiterate—how terribly grateful I am. . . ." On April 7 he had written to Barrett Clark:

This is a farewell letter. For, be it known . . . I am sailing April 11, from Villefranche for New York by way of Genoa, Naples, and Gibraltar, arriving in that mad city of yours April 22 . . . S.S. Augustus—Navagzione Generale Italiana. In a way, it's a good thing. I've had a good year, what with *Green Grow the Lilacs* finished and forgotten, much of France seen and known (I've just come back from a long trip by motor, stopping a day or two or three in many places—Martigues, Marseilles, Toulon, St. Tropeze [*sic*], Cassis, Draguignan, Grasse, Cannes, a healthy, though somewhat mottled, tan making me look like a Mexican, all the Riviera coast unforgettable in my mind, a new play—*The Cherokee Night*—fermenting rapidly, and a faint homesickness beginning to stir. Yes, I'm completely American, after all. Though after my quiet life, New York will knock me down and trample on me, I'm sure. I keep thinking that I ought to be on a farm this summer, and think I'll bend my energies toward making it possible. I may write and I may not. The final virtuous act in this fever, it seems to me, is to lie under a tree and be alternately spattered with sun and shade. This last statement, no doubt, being a present mood, which won't last very long. For I must really do that new play.

I regret leaving here without having your word on *Green Grow the Lilacs.* . . . I'm so afraid that all my talk about it has made it sound pretentious and grand, when as a matter of fact, it's the simplest kind of story about a boy and a girl, and a life that has passed away. . . . Well, where am I? With three contracts in my pocket when I came abroad,—no productions. Just where I was, eh? But I've a new play, and maybe that's something.[13]

CHAPTER 6

SUCCESS WITHOUT STABILITY: THE DEBUT OF *GREEN GROW THE LILACS* (1929–1931)

> *Oblation is beneficence to melt*
> *the heart of stone—or so I have believed—*
> *as pilgrim meek in selflessness has knelt*
> *at wayside altar and has there received*
> *august alliance with the crypt revered*
> *and risen in the gold and singing day,*
> *a mountain peak, who dwarfish had appeared—*
> *his rags a robe, his forehead green with bay . . .*
> —"Unless Oblation . . ."[1]

BACK HOME FROM FRANCE and living at the Fraternity Club in New York, Riggs found some old debts waiting, and he asked Clark in a letter on May 1, 1929:

. . . if Samuel French's patience with me about money is exhausted. I know I haven't broken them up; but I am sensible that they've given me money, and the returns are slow in coming. Their generosity about giving me Shubert and Laboratory advances has been one reason, the other being the incalculable bad luck of having three contracts for productions come to naught . . . the fact remains that I'm broke, as usual, again, and want to write my new play, and don't want to get a job (provided I could get one). Oh, I shan't starve for a week, perhaps two; but please tell me what you think about the matter. . . . Ida Rauh and her son are taking a house in Provincetown for the summer, and want me to come there. She assures me living is cheap. . . . My father would like me to come back to Oklahoma. But I don't want to, as I shouldn't be able to work there.[2]

A telegram followed on June 5 from Provincetown: "STAY WEEK END IF POSSIBLE PLENTY ROOM BRING BATHING SUIT— LYNN." An advance made it possible for Riggs to continue writing and, in spare time, attempt with Ida to reorganize a theatre group, with whom Riggs hoped to promote plays by newer playwrights.

Although the Theatre Guild was to sign a contract on October 1, 1929, to produce *Green Grow the Lilacs*, it was put off until the next year, due to casting schedules, and finally made its New York debut on January 26, 1931. Arthur Hopkins was opening his season with *Roadside* in 1929, and Doubleday-Doran had contracted to publish Riggs's book of poetry, *The Iron Dish*, but the blossoming works had yet to bear substantial fruit. Although *The Domino Parlor*, too, was again under consideration by producers, it was to be 1931 before things looked up for Riggs financially. Since the production of *Knives from Syria* in Santa Fe in 1924, he had written ten full-length plays and two one-acts and had seen eight plays produced and a book of poems published. Samuel French had published *Knives, Big Lake, Sump'n Like Wings, A Lantern to See By,* and the one-act *Reckless*.

Meanwhile, the *Domino Parlor* experience made Riggs leery about productions of *Green Grow the Lilacs*. He wrote Clark on June 21, 1929, "I don't see how anybody but the newest, most careful, most poetic kind of producer can touch it, so we must be very reluctant to give anybody but that kind of person any hopes of being allowed it, don't you think?" He considered a production by Irene Lewisohn of the Neighborhood Playhouse in New York, but it came to naught.

Upset by a proposal from Clark to try out a production with no pay at Rochester "to show its possibilities," Riggs exploded in a June 27 letter:

Surely we ought to know by now that no hurried production of any play of mine is going to show anything except a disgusting mess. We have only to remember *The Domino Parlor*, which of all my plays might have yielded to cavalier treatment. And so unshowy and poetic a piece as *Green Grow* will yield nothing but pain for me, a baffled audience, and the general air of lack of skill—if it gets a casual and hurried presentation. This I'm sure of.

Relenting a bit, he added:

We ought to get 5% at least, or certainly $25 a performance. . . . I insist on nothing being changed, not even a phrase, without my written consent. . . . I see no reason why Brian shouldn't take up the New York option one week after the last performance in Rochester. I see no point in being suicidally grateful to anyone for doing a play which many people would be glad to do, and pay for doing. . . . What about the songs?

Thus, although he was eager for success, Riggs's primary concern was that the characters who had so absorbed him in that small room in France be neither betrayed nor caricatured.

In a happier mood, on July 27 he wrote Paul Green, who with his wife and two children remained in Germany on a second-year Guggenheim fellowship. They were surviving amid desperate social and financial circumstances as communists and fascists struggled for power. From Provincetown, Riggs wrote:

I'm here for the summer, been here since June 1, and I find it an admirable place to be. Like you, I carry my own state with me—when I'm working at least—but I find the sand and the gulls and the boats something to ponder in this place. Some day I'm going to write a play called *More Sky*, after I've found a little more myself. I don't want ever to be in New York now for more than a month at a time. In fact, I'm asking for a semester job at the University of Oklahoma this fall. There's some pretty wide air out there, and more sky than is allotted to most sections of the country. You'll gather that I'm beginning to find out where I live. . . .

Green Grow the Lilacs, my first poem for the theatre, has attracted some attention. Three of the Guild Board are in Europe,
but the other three are enthusiastic, and have taken a $1,000
option until the others see it in September. *Sump'n Like Wings*
has just been sold again, the third time, to a new producer,
Ruth Benedict. I'm writing a new one, *Roadside.* The next one
will be *The Cherokee Night,* about the descendants of the absorbed Cherokees in Oklahoma. Come back, can't you?[3]

Apologetically, Riggs wrote Clark on July 29, saying that he
had not meant to imply that he wanted to change agents; in
fact, he regretted some dickerings with another agent:

It's too damn bad that I've let myself get mixed up in any way
with another agent, who may be, and no doubt is, enthusiastic, but who may go trying to get me tied up with the wrong
kind of producers. But I suppose if we don't *like* an offer the
other agents may procure about a play, we can always say *No.*
The point is, I wouldn't think of allowing anyone else to
handle what business may come up, if Samuel French will do
it for me. I'd certainly be an idiot to want anyone else. So that's
that, *alors.*
Lord, what news of heat in New York! I hate to think of you
sweltering.
By the way, if you can keep your hands on that clipping
from the *World* about that shivaree in Kentucky, will you hold
it for me, in case I see the Guild Board. You know, part of the
evidence.

Again, Riggs needed "evidence" to convince New York theatre people that reality was indeed behind the events in his
Oklahoma plays. In an August 4 letter he discussed with
Clark the possible publication of a new book of his plays, considering for inclusion *The Lonesome West, Rancor,* and *The
Domino Parlor.* But he hesitated: "I'm getting a little worried
about *Rancor,* and may change my mind about wanting it
printed. And I consider changing *Domino* to *The Blues.*"
Although he was excited about introducing new playwrights in the Provincetown theatre, the August doldrums
arrived before it was accomplished. He wrote Clark on Au-

gust 14, returning five plays that Clark had sent for consideration: "Production plans all off—this season anyway. Everybody is too busy. Susan Glaspell with her new novel; Ida
remodeling the house; myself with *Roadside,* etc. . . . Ida in-
vites you up again if you can make it."

Although he wrote on August 21 that neither the Oklahoma University job nor any other had yet materialized for
fall, he rhapsodized that "Provincetown is a marvellous place;
I've had a great summer. I hope you'll be able to come up still.
You could see Susan Glaspell and Frank Shay. Miss Glaspell
has just sold *Brook Evans* to Paramount for a talkie—$15,000. I
have a hunch it's for Ruth Chatterton."

On August 27 he wrote again:

> I've just mailed *Roadside* to you. I intended to finish the play by
> my birthday at least, but it got itself arranged before that date.
> Yep, on August 31, I'll be thirty. I grow ancient. And since a
> birthday is a good time to make plans, I'm brimming with
> them. In the first place, God help me, I feel committed to the
> theatre now. And if *Green Grow the Lilacs'* fate is a happy one
> finally, I'll be certain that there's room for my kind of play, or
> rather the kind I intend to write. Even if its fate turns out to be
> a little bleak in production, there's always publication—a book
> can be a noble thing.

He listed seven proposed projects and his hopes, then asked
forgiveness for "talking about drama and writing plays,"
adding:

> And while I think of it, I wish you'd throw away that chro-
> nology of my life. I don't like my life very well, after all, and
> there's no point in its being made public. I suppose I'm getting
> morbid about it—if any of my plays ever merited any public
> attention, I'd be terribly pleased if no one ever thought of the
> play except as a play, and forgot to inquire who wrote it.
>   I still think *John* is Philip Barry's best play. I hope it gets
> a fine production next time. The best thing in it, of course, is
> the off-stage Christ. I wish somebody would do a play about
> Christ—custom or no custom—and show him at his trade.
> His intelligence, his suavity, his diplomacy, his cool wisdom,

his towering rages, his simplicity, his cunning, his nobility. He
was a man, all right. And if those little (some of them) sham-
bling disciples could create him, why can't somebody else? I'd
like to try it. It would be a rewarding failure.

In spite of his reluctance to review his life for the public, on
September 16, 1929, he sent Walter Campbell the chronology
of June, 1928, discussed the uncertain status of his current
plays, and made careful suggestions about the kind of personal information he wanted publicized back home:

> The Theatre Guild has until October 1 to make up their minds
> [about *Green Grow*] . . . so please say nothing about it. . . .
> And while I think of it, will you please leave Witter Bynner out
> of the story. For years that poor man has been getting clip-
> pings about me, which somehow hoping to improve the story
> of me have dragged him in. And especially in Oklahoma, it's
> done to death—of course there are implications back of it
> which are slightly embarrassing, as you'll know. So do you
> mind killing this fictitious overtone by ignoring it.

Campbell (under the pseudonym Vestal) wrote of Riggs's
work in the autumn, 1929, *Southwest Review*:

> There is not a writer in the Southwest whose work is more
> deeply rooted in his native soil . . . an intimacy and intensity
> which might do credit to Thomas Hardy or some other literary
> lover of an English village. . . .[4]
> The old Indian Territory—east side of Oklahoma, is very
> different from the West, resembles Arkansas or Kentucky
> backwoods where life has in a measure stood still. . . . As he
> sees them they are not romantic figures of the frontier, but
> baffled, discontented folk struggling against hard conditions
> in a harsh environment. He insists that he has not falsified the
> picture. . . . No one has been more meticulously careful to re-
> produce precisely the actual rhythm and vocabulary of a spe-
> cific community than has Mr. Riggs. . . .[5]
> He has never shown the slightest desire to adjust his work
> to the current demands of Broadway. Time after time he has
> refused to alter his plays even in the slightest degree in order
> to placate those who might have showered rewards upon him.

This integrity and sincerity, I take it, is the quality which has enabled him to develop as he has and to produce plays of such fine and dramatic quality. His latest plays are not only good theatre and good literature, but authentic and Southwestern to the core.[6]

On November 4, Riggs wrote happily to Henry Allen Moe at the Guggenheim that the Theatre Guild had signed contracts on October 1 to produce *Green Grow the Lilacs*, the play he had written in Europe on his fellowship. He arranged to have lunch with Moe, and on his advice he wrote the Guggenheim Foundation again on December 20, 1929, requesting a renewal of his fellowship, since even "with these most auspicious things happening to me (including the poetry book contract with Doubleday-Doran) I am still the impecunious poet and dramatist." He proposed to sail for England, France, or Italy at once and to go to work on two plays, *Son of Perdition* and *Cherokee Night*.[7]

But New Year's Day, 1930, found Riggs railroading west on New York Central's Twentieth Century Limited. He wrote Moe:

This will surprise you as much as it does me—yesterday, late in the afternoon, Hollywood—Pathé Studios, to be exact, telephoned me an offer to come out for 6 weeks and do a talkie. So I'm on my way. Just before I left, Mr. Arthur Hopkins told me he might still do *Roadside* this spring, instead of fall. So, all in all, things are shaping so that the poor playwright can feed himself again—for a while, at least—I think I had better withdraw my Guggenheim Foundation application—and leave room open for someone else. . . .

He wrote again on January 13: "I'm liking it so far out here. The Pathé people are giving me a free hand. And the miracle is that they like, too, what I am doing. I rather like it myself. It's a picture, called *Beyond Victory*." He next wrote the screenplay for *Siren Song*, the first movie role for opera star Mary Lewis.

His enthusiasm continued in a letter to Clark on January 18:

I think of the damned thing (*Beyond Victory*) almost night and
day, rising often in the cold gray dawn—and before—to jot
down a note. . . . They gave me the scheme, of course. Five
men, desperate situation in the war, they reminisce about their
lives. But I'm trying to make them human; and the desperate
situation, my own invention, if I do say it, is a knock-out. It
would even be good on the stage—which is my standard.

I've seen Sidney [Howard], went to the theatre with him
once; and was about to dine with him, when Laura Hope
Crews called him up, so went to her house, and dined with
her and Gloria Swanson. Miss Swanson is quite marvelous in
many ways, intelligent, and intrigues me a lot. They all like
me; Miss Crews wants me to do Miss Swanson's story, to follow *Queen Kelly*. She may change her mind. Wayward impulses afflict the Hollywood air. . . .

I've got a beastly cold; I hate the climate; the studio people
are grand to me; give me a couch and a stenographer—(to be
used apart from each other, you understand); a noble office;
my office hours are whenever I like. Sometimes I come in at
ten, and leave at 2—or anytime for that matter. If I wanted to, I
could work at home. They don't care. I'm told Pathé is unusual
in that regard. The others seem to be factories.

In a note to Clark on April 1, 1930, he wrote: "Here's the
article Mr. Henry Roth has written for Mr. Botkin's forthcom-
ing *FOLK-SAY*. I think it's swell, and flatteringly swell. If you
agree, could you write the boy and tell him so? It would be
great encouragement of a genuinely brilliant talent. . . . I love
New York." And on April 21 he told Clark: "I ache for summer and a pencil. I shall go to Provincetown, that's settled."

Roth's article, "Lynn Riggs and the Individual," evaluates
the plays of Riggs's first five years. He finds a central theme:
social institutions that are "symbolic of restrictive and level-
ing forces in life against which the individual bent upon self-
development must contend. . . . it is this dominant theme
rather than the more obvious folk basis and cultural background of his scene that makes him important as a dramatist." This conflict, Roth contends, is the struggle to maintain
integrity, to live according to one's "natural and free impulses

and by no other standards." Tragedy results when either "warped convention" or "petrified morality" overcome the idealism and gentleness of fundamental innocence, or when idealism and innocence attempt to adjust to such demands for conformity and uniformity.

Roth finds in each Riggs play an individual different from the herd who resists subjection. He praises *The Lonesome West*, whose strange characters "exhibit that intense self-absorption and psychological isolation in the presence of each other which one finds only in the uncanny reality of Russian creations." The defeat in their lives of love, joy, and poetic imagination Roth terms "ironic and hopelessly pitiful," since it comes through craving after false and trivial things. *Roadside*, he said, shows laws, taboos, and mechanical procedures to be useful guides to the herd, but apt to collapse under joyous, free human impulse.

In *Green Grow the Lilacs,* Roth said, the tragedy lies in "the necessary passage of a glorious mood." Characters recognize change and valuable maturity in society and in themselves, but must sacrifice "a lyric sense of newness and freedom." Roth said that Riggs's characters, being spiritual without being religious, "never stand before the abysses of the contemporaneous mind with its search for emotional discipline, standards, and religion." Their attitudes are in fact directly opposed to the modern search. In summing up, Roth said it was Riggs's belief "that joy is the true nature of man, a sign of his true development, and tragedy the defeat of his true nature."[8]

On March 11, 1930, Riggs wrote his friend James Gould Cozzens about Cozzens's novel: "I left New York to come out and make the talkies safe for art. . . . Am staying on until June, and then to Santa Fe, and then to Oklahoma, and by July 4, I'll be in Provincetown, working on the masterpiece, 'The Son of Perdition.'"[9]

In a letter of May 13 he was still discussing with Clark the possible fate of *Domino Parlor,* since Riggs had rejected a possible production by "dabblers":

I really want it to be a fine and stirring play. It needs work. I
know now approximately what kind of work. . . .
    Have you noticed the gradual change in the tone of my
Hollywood spirit? A curious thing happens. Out here, Broadway, which we all despise there, becomes a sainted virgin, the
final mecca of all that is brilliant, beautiful, divine in drama.
That, of course, is silly, too.

Back in Provincetown, Riggs wrote Clark on June 23 and
recommended a room with bath, available there for twelve
dollars per week. He had received a copy of Phil Barry's new
play, Hotel Universe, with a note from the playwright. Also
there were some problems about casting Roadside, since Walter
Huston was available only for four months. Hopkins was
looking for another lead actor. Riggs added: "I've seen Susan
Glaspell and read her new play. I like it very much. The Guild
ought to do it. They probably will eventually, as soon as they
realize how important Emily Dickinson has become." Glaspell's play, Alison's House, was to become Riggs's competition
for the Pulitzer prize.
    The Iron Dish, a selection of the poems Riggs had written
from approximately 1925 to 1929, was published in September, 1930. On September 25, A Lantern to See By was produced
by the Detroit Playhouse, a group that would produce his
Sump'n Like Wings the following year. Green Grow the Lilacs was
to open in Boston in December. Playwright Sidney Howard
said in an interview in the New York Telegram of October 31,
1929, that Riggs was one of only two playwrights bringing
freshness to the American stage at that time.
    Still in Provincetown on October 19, 1930, Riggs wrote Hal
Bynner that the Guild expected to start Green Grow the Lilacs in
mid-November, and he was working on Cherokee Night. About
Roadside's short life on Broadway, starring Ralph Bellamy, he
bluffed:

    The Roadside fiasco worries me none at all. I was surprised and
    disappointed—but I'm hardened to the N.Y. theatre—and I
    know what I'm doing. It's perfectly easy to go on—making the

kind of drama I believe in. There are enough believers to keep me from working in a vacuum—and I can always publish. Indeed, *Roadside* came out Saturday: I believe (I haven't seen it yet)—with the handsomest foreword that has ever been appended to any book published in America, I'm sure. It's by Arthur Hopkins, that grand gentleman.

You're still faithful to my earlier poems, I see. The book is spotty, I know. It's appalling how many poems I've written—and how few I wanted in a book. Some of *The Iron Dish* could go now, if I were selecting again. I heard about your novel from Marie and Marjorie. It sounds swell. I'm making notes on one (have been for 3 years).[10]

Hopkins's introduction said, "It is my belief that Riggs's play will reach posterity. It has the feel of survival. I believe it to be the first American dramatic classic." *Roadside* has proved to be popular with amateur theatrical groups and was published in an anthology, *Twenty-Five Modern Plays*, edited by S. Marion Tucker and Alan S. Downer, in 1953.[11] It was still current in French's 1988 catalogue.

On October 20, Riggs crowed to Clark about his progress on *Cherokee Night*. Using notes on it dating as far back as spring of 1929, he found the play, a string of related but independent stories, was at last "hanging together":

What astonishes me and delights me now is that finally, by projection, the play has a meaning beyond the story, even beyond the theme. The last scene of all concentrates a statement about and covers the entire field of Indian-White relationships in one dramatic incident such as I could never have foreseen. And it's not a protest—but a triumphant comprehension by an old Indian, a real nobleman, which makes the whole play dignified and austere beyond my first feeble calculations. I hope it will be my best play. It can be.

I've sent off the again-revised script of Scene 6 of *Green Grow*. If they don't like it, they can hang from a sour apple tree.

Several times, he had worked over the events in *Green Grow the Lilacs* following the climactic shivaree and haystack fire to allow a swift denouement absolving Curly of crime in Jeeter's accidental death, and clearing the way for a happy ending. Unlike the later musical version, *Oklahoma!*, *Green Grow the Lilacs* ends with Curly returning to Claremore to be held for trial, with the implication that he will be absolved by reason of self-defense. The Rodgers and Hammerstein version has a swift, rigged, on-the-spot trial and "not guilty" verdict. In Riggs's plays, as in life, the happy endings were never quite so pat, so beatific as Broadway wanted them to be. This up-beat play, nevertheless, depicts people coping with the rough frontier life with courage, with conviction of life's worth, and with story-telling, music, and dancing.

Since his play was to open in Boston in December, Riggs returned to New York on November 6, 1930, for rehearsals and for job interviews with George Kaufman, playwright, and Gilbert Gabriel, critic. He wrote Bynner, "Good God! If only I were brave enough to be a dishwasher!"

He declined an invitation for Thanksgiving with the Clark family: to "stay with *Green Grow* these perilous days. And I've promised to go someplace with Ida and Dan—so I've been taken care of."

Too much was invested in this play for him to attend open-ing night. Instead, he spent that evening of January 26, 1931, in Chapel Hill, North Carolina, in the home of playwright Paul Eliot Green and his wife Elizabeth, safely returned from their two years' Guggenheim tenure in Germany. Playing his guitar and singing old songs, he passed the time, as he says in his poem "Man at Piano," "keeping the quarried beasts at bay" with music. Others present included Professor Frederick Koch, founder of the Carolina Playmakers; the fiction writer Wilbur Daniel Steele; and Samuel Selden.[12]

About midnight he received two phone calls telling him that he had a hit. The critics' responses were mixed, but for the most part favorable. The play was entering a substantial Broadway run of sixty-four performances, to be followed by a successful Theatre Guild company road tour of Cleveland, Pittsburgh, St. Louis, Milwaukee, Minneapolis, Chicago, and

Detroit. It had tried out in Boston, Philadelphia, and Baltimore for seven weeks before it opened for eight weeks in New York City. Clippings in Riggs's scrapbooks tell the critics' responses to opening night.[13]

Charles Darnton reported in the *Evening World*, "Lynn Riggs catches and reflects the spirit of the people in the Indian Territory of 1900, when it was turning from cattle into farming country. This he has done with the sympathy of the poet rather than the power of a dramatist."

Robert Littell praised the play highly and caught Riggs's intention. He wrote in the *Morning World*: "It is one of the most thoroughly satisfying evenings that the Guild has given us in a long time—full of rich, free humor, salty poetry, and some reckless tenderness that was America's before she was tamed and civilized by fences and mortgages and chain grocery stores. . . . It is a glorious breath of fresh air, making us who live beside subways long—for 'way down inside us we are still Americans—for something lost out of our lives, something long ago and far away."

Brooks Atkinson's haughty first reaction ridiculed "milkmaids" that he thought he had seen in beef cattle country, saying *Green Grow the Lilacs* was "less a play than a hale and hearty narrative of loves, jamborees, and neighborly skirmishes. . . . Riggs sets his cowboys and milkmaids to singing broad, swinging ballads." He said that the one distinctive thing about Riggs's play was the dialect—that its fresh lyricism caused the audience to listen and flow with its poetry. Otherwise, he said that the plot was a cliché, in the same sense that Noel Coward's dramas of modern manners were clichés, "But it has a warm relish of its characters. How alive they are!"

Atkinson apparently was softened by a letter from Barrett Clark (with a copy to Riggs), who ask him to clarify his dismissal of *Green Grow the Lilacs* as a "folk-play." Why, Clark asked, was not a folk play good in this instance, if it was good in Atkinson's reviews of *Porgy* and *Desire Under the Elms*?

Atkinson wrote more favorably about the opening night of
Green Grow the Lilacs in the introduction to a Limited Editions
Press reprint of the play just after Riggs's death in 1954:

> It was a lyric occasion. Mr. Riggs's rolling, cadenced dialogue
> and his robust story conveyed a joyous mood. In the program
> *Green Grow the Lilacs* was described as a folk-play. It was more
> than that; it was the uncalculated poetry of a middlewestern
> troubador and a piece of individual literature. Of all the folk-
> plays we have had, this one is the most jubilant.[14]

Few critics agreed with Gilbert Gabriel of the *American*,
January 27, 1931, who called the play a *Porgy* of the western
plains and proceeded to make fun of it as a melodrama about
"Nelly, the Beautiful Cow-Girl": "I'm just one of those over-
sophisticated grumps of the Atlantic seaboard set who will
have to wonder why so much nice writing and handsome
producing ever were poured into such a little kinderspiel."
He admits, however, that *Roadside* was surprisingly pleasant
to read in book form after its Broadway failure.

John Mason Brown, in the *New York Evening Post*, said: "It
has a racy vigor that is undeniable and a swing to many of its
finely cadenced lines which indicates that it is a poet who has
fashioned them. It likewise gives, as few of our plays have
succeeded in doing, a refreshing and authentic sense of having sprung from the earth, and of belonging to it."

Arthur Ruhl, in the *New York Herald-Tribune*, recognized
Riggs's independence of commonly accepted dramatic forms,
calling the play a mixture of the tenderly lyric and the melo-
dramatic: "The stuff with which the author is dealing is, however, so refreshingly of our American soil and his whole intention so interesting, that one was inclined to give him a
good deal of leeway in arriving at the generally unstagy end
which he had in view. . . . A novel attempt to transfer the
mood and flow of the pioneer folk-ballad to actual theater,
but its moments of excitement and of lyric beauty made it
generally interesting."[15]

As we have seen, *Green Grow the Lilacs* centers on flirtation and jealousy between Curly, the handsome, bragging, singing cowboy, and Laurey, an inexperienced innocent who lives on her farm with her wise, patient Aunt Eller. After she has put off Curly's invitation to go to Old Man Peck's play-party, Laurey is too frightened to turn down the invitation of the sinister hired man, Jeeter Fry, who lurks in the "dog house" (a small bunkhouse) with his lustful thoughts and pornographic postcards. Upset by Jeeter's behavior at the party, the independent Laurey appeals to Curly for protection and, once her guard is let down, accepts his proposal of marriage.

After the wedding the neighbors force the couple out of the upstairs bedroom of the farmhouse for a rowdy shivaree, and they place Laurey and Curly on top of a haystack. Jeeter appears, drunk, and sets fire to the haystack. As Curly attacks Jeeter to effect their escape, Jeeter falls on his knife and dies.

While the wheels of justice turn slowly, Laurey accepts her aunt's wisdom and recognizes that she has moved beyond young innocence and flirtation to assume adult responsibility on the frontier, and that she will need to be courageous to meet whatever hardships she and Curly may face. Underlying the love theme is the story of the free and open cattle range-land that is being changed rapidly and controversially by the advent of farmers and their fenced-in crops. Although Riggs's play is in the naturalistic tradition of hard fate, the characters' responses are courageous and optimistic, and the play ends with good portents for their future.

As previously mentioned, Riggs's original title was *Shivaree*. In the *New York World* of February 9, 1931, Robert Littell quoted Benjamin A. Botkin, president of the Oklahoma Folk-Lore Society, on some details of the custom, adding "thank your stars and the age of big cities and automobiles that the shivaree has gone the way of the buffalo." Said Botkin:

> It is the rough music that is the most constant and persistent feature of the shivaree. Indeed, the din and discord of the

mock-serenade doubtless gave rise, by onomatopoeia, to the word charivari, of uncertain etymology. The improvised concert . . . is provided by a medley of kettles, dishpans, boilers, cowbells, tin horns, etc. emphasizing the rustic and domestic lot, with additions perhaps of tick tacks on screens or windows, sticks rattling on fence palings, and the firing of guns (a colonial wedding custom), though guns were apt to be frowned upon in the not unlikely event of a fight in the course of the evening.

A running fire of horseplay and practical jokes, crude jests and off-color remarks, was generally kept up before and after the crowd had gained entrance to the house, the kind and degree of "orneriness" depending on how much deviltry there was in the party. Not content with waiting for the groom to open the door at the strategic moment when his patience and the crowd's impatience had reached their limit, many, hoping to get a glimpse of the couple in their night clothes, would be climbing the porch and peeking in at the windows. . . . While some of the party were entertaining the bride and groom (who incidentally were handing out drinks, cigars, candy, ice cream, etc.), others were up to mischief, such as hiding clothes, tying the bedclothes in knots, or placing salt, cracker crumbs, hair clippings or toads in the bed.

The advent of the automobile, Botkin said, had reduced the shivaree to chasing the bridal couple around town with horns honking and tin cans tied on behind.

Produced by the still-young Theatre Guild, *Green Grow the Lilacs* was obliged to go on the road after eight weeks in New York to fulfill advance commitments to member theaters. It starred Franchot Tone in his first important role, as Curly; June Walker, as Laurey; Helen Westley, as Aunt Eller; Ruth Chorpennings, as Ado Annie; Richard Hale, as Jeeter Fry; and Lee Strassberg, as the pedler.

Musical authenticity was easily preserved when the Guild hired real cowboys, from the rodeo that had just closed at Madison Square Garden, to stay on in New York with the production. They sang eleven of the songs that Riggs had se-

The opening scene of the Theatre Guild's production of *Green Grow the Lilacs*, 1931: Curly (Franchot Tone) arrives singing an old cowboy tune and comes in through the window, greeting Aunt Eller (Helen Westley) as she churns butter.

lected, either within the play or in front of the curtain during scene changes.

Burns Mantle commented in the *New York News* on February 1, 1931: "Cowboy songs lack the melody of the songs of the south, and the softer sentiments; they are prairie blues songs, many of them. But they are rough and rugged and pitifully simple in expressing the heartaches and longings of a people who conquered the west."

On the same date the *New York Times* published an excerpt from Dr. Isaac Goldberg's perceptive interview with Riggs in the *Boston Transcript*. Goldberg described Riggs as:

A soft-mannered youth, fairly tall, with blond hair and a light complexion; his eyes, behind horn-rimmed glasses, look blue; when his speech, after a cautious beginning gathers momentum and confidence, they become even dreamy. He is unmistakably the poet. Yet the softness of his speech may easily prove deceptive, for just as unmistakably there is, behind his mild exterior, a directing will that is not lightly to be shaken. . . . It is a great man, indeed who has the courage of his convictions; it is a rarer one who has the courage of his exaltations. This is the quiet but unshatterable courage that characterizes Lynn Riggs.

On January 24 the *New York Evening Post* published an interview for which the headline read, "Dialect in Folk Plays; Lynn Riggs, Author of the Guild's *Green Grow the Lilacs*, Has Not Tried to Idealize the Speech of His Oklahomans." The speech of Riggs's characters was described as follows: "If the language of the play is often poetic, and critics in Boston, Baltimore, Philadelphia, and Washington seem to agree that it is, it is not because it was written by a man who sometimes writes poetry but because the people whom he depicts naturally talk this way in their daily lives." Riggs explained:

> The fact is that far from idealizing the poetic quality of that speech, I haven't equalled it. I have an aunt—one of two or three who unwittingly "sat for" Aunt Eller in the play—who naturally speaks a much more highly charged poetic language than I can contrive to write in their vein. To listen to her is a delight. From morning until night she will comment on the affairs of the household, on the state of the weather, on the goings-on of the neighbors, in a language which would gladden the heart of any poet who loves apt and spontaneous word-images. And this was generally true of the Oklahoma folk of thirty years ago, whom I have written about. . . .
>
> There people talked poetry without any conscious effort to make beautiful language, but in the effort to make their meaning vivid. Because of the external poverty and sameness of their lives they felt the need of richness and variety in their thoughts. Besides, they all had something of the actor in them—not in the sense that they acted false parts, but that

when they spoke they were making a definite effort to put themselves, as one might say, over the footlights, to dramatize their meaning and their personality. Images have an importance for these unsophisticated folk which we of the cities can hardly appreciate. . . . Because of this personal relationship to things, the images in his [the Oklahoma farmer's] speech have an emotional existence and reality which things can hardly have in sophisticated daily speech. . . . I let my characters write their own speeches, the language which was familiar to my boyhood ears. Whatever poetry may be found in the play is to the credit of my neighbors, not of myself.

After *Green Grow the Lilacs'* success, Riggs wrote Hal Bynner on February 28, 1931: "I'm glad you and Santa Fe are pleased: I'm quite a lot New Mexican. And I intend to be back in April some time whether I make a 'grand pile' or not."

Soon there were rumors that *Green Grow the Lilacs* might receive the Pulitzer prize. An article in the University of Oklahoma's *Sooner Magazine* in 1931 said that it was one of eight current plays eligible: "No doubt about it, the play is a Broadway success. And the drawbridge is rarely down over the moat that bars access to Broadway to a provincial."[15]

The Pulitzer award for playwriting that year surprised almost everyone, however. Burns Mantle tells the story in *Best Plays: Year Book of the Drama in America, 1931*:

Alison's House, by Susan Glaspell, modestly produced by Eva Le Gallienne and her Civic Repertory Company on December 1, 1930, was received by a few critics with an assortment of polite phrases in praise of certain of its virtues, coupled with the familiar predictions that it might please the Repertory subscribers and fit comfortably into Miss Le Gallienne's list of plays, but that much could not be hoped for it in the matter of popular approval.

Miss Glaspell's eighth and last play, *Alison's House*, played on an average of once or twice a week, for a total of only twenty-five performances during the next five months.

In May the Pulitzer awards were made and, much to the surprise and a little to the distress of the experts, Miss Glaspell's drama was given the prize as "the original American play performed in New York which shall best represent the educational value and power of the stage." There was more disagreement than usual over the award. Philip Barry's *Tomorrow and Tomorrow*, Lynn Riggs's *Green Grow the Lilacs*, Louis Weitzenkorn's *Five-Star Final*, and the Kaufman-Hart *Once in a Lifetime* were generally preferred by the professional play-goers. As usual, their agitation sputtered briefly and subsided.[16]

Although Miss Le Gallienne had closed her season, she agreed to open the play another week. Revived at the Ritz Theatre on May 11, it was hugely successful its first week, but a second week, under a spell of hot weather and poor returns, was withdrawn. *Alison's House* was a literary play based on incidents in the life of poet Emily Dickinson. Glaspell had changed the name and locale to Iowa because she was unable to get permission from the Dickinson family to do otherwise. Glaspell always insisted she was a playwright "by accident" and a novelist by profession.[17]

Riggs, in Tulsa for a Tulsa Little Theater production of *Green Grow the Lilacs*, was interviewed at a luncheon in his honor. Told that Glaspell had just won the Pulitzer, he commented: "I am very glad for Susan, for it will mean that her interest in the American theater will receive a stimulant. Before this she had been primarily a novelist but she has the sort of creative mind that is needed for the theater. For that reason, it seems wiser to me that Philip Barry should not have been chosen, although *Tomorrow and Tomorrow* is a good play and his past record is commendable. Barry would go on writing anyway."

Sending this press clipping to Clark, Riggs regretted that he sounded "smug." In fact, he had played his part well, for this was the greatest of many near misses in his professional life. A Pulitzer prize and a few other lucky breaks might have brought him much earlier in life the recognition and financial return he deserved and needed.

There were occasional rumors and negotiations by Hollywood studios regarding making a movie of *Green Grow the Lilacs,* although none of them came to fruition. For example, a gossip columnist wrote in *Screen and Radio Weekly* on April 12, 1936:

> Lynn Riggs, brilliant young playwright, is the current white-haired boy of Hollywood. It was Franchot's ambition to portray this role [Curly] on the screen, but RKO beat MGM to the punch and purchased the play for Richard Dix. Now RKO has decided to allow MGM to have *Lilacs* after all. Franchot Tone is scheduled to bring his original role to the screen, and Lynn Riggs may do that adaptation.

Ironically, Rodgers and Hammerstein's *Oklahoma!* was given a special citation from the Pulitzer prize board in 1944, and it was made a movie in 1955, the year after Riggs's death.

Although panned by some critics, as well as praised by many, Riggs's burning desire to give voice to the ordinary, often inarticulate people of early-day Oklahoma did ring true to audiences. Their appreciation was the spark that made *Green Grow the Lilacs* and the later translation, *Oklahoma!,* a joyful tribute to the steadfast courage of countless unknown pioneers in different places and times, and these plays have continued to bring pleasure to audiences the world over. During the fifty years after its debut, according to M. Abbott Van Nostrand, president of Samuel French, Inc., *Green Grow the Lilacs* received about six hundred amateur productions, with gross royalties amounting to about forty thousand dollars.[18] It continued to be offered to theatre groups in the 1988 French catalogue, along with five other Riggs plays.

CHAPTER 7

BICOASTAL COMMUTING AND PAYING
THE BILLS (1931–1934)

> And telling myself that shreds and bits are best
> to throw the dogs of need; telling myself
> architectonics, even overdressed,
> are clear bare ground and firm supporting shelf
> on which the soul may build its regal flat;
> I am this moment telling myself this and that.
> —"Telling Myself This and That"[1]

IN 1931, RIGGS'S CAREER was in full swing—but so was the Great Depression. The blithe Americans in Paris had run out of money and come home. Riggs's successful play *Green Grow the Lilacs* was selected for an anthology, *Best Plays of 1930–31*, edited by Burns Mantle. Recognition was sweet, but there was a rocky decade ahead, financially, artistically, and emotionally. Riggs kept writing, and although sometimes discouraged, he never again went into the kind of deep depression that had sent him fleeing to Santa Fe from Norman.

He enjoyed many friends in the New York theatre, in Hollywood, and in his favorite home, Santa Fe. He often visited there and made trips into Mexico, writing during this period about the Mexican–New Mexican ambience. Now known as an established writer, Riggs, like his mentor Witter Bynner, helped some young, struggling writers and artists. He also made a considerable effort to organize a support network, a "theatre of the imagination" to free playwrights, directors, and actors from the tyranny of Broadway. He rejoiced in the growing college and little theatre movements.

But the decade was to end with the tragic death of George O'Neil, who was his own age and for many years had been his closest companion. In 1938 he also lost his beloved Aunt Mary Thompson Brice, who died at age seventy-seven.

On January 31, 1931, he wrote Betty Kirk at the University of Oklahoma Press that he had gone to North Carolina to finish *Cherokee Night*.[2] Except for a brief visit to New York to see *Green Grow the Lilacs*, he stayed in Chapel Hill most of the first three months of the year, working and on occasion speaking about the theatre. On February 1 he gave a public reading of *Green Grow the Lilacs* in Chapel Hill's Playmakers' Theatre and "sang delightfully some of the cowboy ballads," Frederick Koch said. Riggs presented on February 4 a play called *East Lynn: A Satire on the Modern Psychological Play*. On April 19 he read for the Playmakers his new Cherokee play. Koch wrote:

> In his nearly three-months' residence in Chapel Hill, Lynn Riggs has contributed much to our fellowship of Playmakers. He says he will come back to us in the fall to renew his associations, and to follow the forest trails on horseback as has been his daily habit here. We shall be glad to have him back, this playboy of Oklahoma![3]

While Riggs and George O'Neil were staying that spring at the Carolina Inn, beside the University of North Carolina campus, Riggs was corresponding with Barrett Clark to help assemble an anthology of short plays. He said that he and O'Neil thought their friends Susan Glaspell and John Dos Passos should be included. O'Neil was to ask for a work from Julia Peterkin, whom they had visited nearby with Paul and Elizabeth Green. Green was to contact Laurence Stallings, and Riggs, Wilbur Hastings—but as it turned out, not enough short works were ready for the anthology.

On April 23 a *New York Evening Post* columnist reported that Riggs and O'Neil attended DuBose Heyward's play *Brass Ankle*

in New York. The audience also included Sinclair Lewis, Owen
Davis, Dorothy Thompson, and Stephen Vincent Benét.
Riggs then returned to Oklahoma to visit Claremore, Tulsa,
and Norman. Speaking on the current state of the drama at a
Tulsa Little Theatre luncheon on May 5, he said that he was

> . . . in the throes of the most profound depression concerning
> the state of the drama. . . . its state is lousy. . . . The drama
> has been deteriorating since Shakespeare's time; then its expo-
> nents were passionately concerned with life but . . . now it
> would seem they are not concerned with life at all. Passion,
> honesty, truth and glamour have been lost in straining after
> smartness, after the commercial thing. . . . there is evident at
> least a beginning of a trend toward something better. I say un-
> blushingly that unless the drama does something for the soul
> of man it isn't justifying itself.[4]

He read from *Roadside* at Claremore's chamber of commerce
luncheon on May 21. French's Hollywood agent was attempt-
ing to sell the movie rights to the play. Meanwhile, Riggs said
in an interview for the *Tulsa World* that he was planning to do
more straight realism and that he felt as if he were only beginning to write.

Home in Claremore in May, Riggs planned to take pictures
of scenes to be used in *Cherokee Night:* Claremore Mound, the
towns of Nowata and Bartlesville, and the woods. George
Milburn, who had written *Oklahoma Town* and was working
on a play, planned to go with him and Bill Riggs. Riggs carried a simple box camera everywhere in his travels and accu-
mulated many photographs. He had written a hospitality
thank-you note to Paul Green on May 8, enclosing some pictures Green had left in his camera: "I've kept a set of them,
being much impressed by all of them, especially those of Marlene Dietrich."[5]

To Riggs's distress, Barrett Clark left the employ of Samuel
French, Inc., in June, 1931. Thereafter he and Riggs continued to keep in close touch, although French retained control over most of Riggs's work. He recorded his disappoint-

ment "with the firm and the Guild" in a June 18 letter to Clark: "It's just that in the most amazing depression of the century, St. Ignatius, or whoever, decided to let French make their biggest profits. I don't suppose it has come to that but if you could use $500, or so, this summer, Mr. Riggs is one that's got it, the bloated plutocrat."[6]

In August, Riggs read at a "Poet's Roundup" for charity in Santa Fe, along with Mary Austin, Roark Bradford, and Evelyn Scott. Betty Kirk reported from Santa Fe in the *Daily Oklahoman* in late August:

> . . . poetry has been the chief interest . . . during the summer months. . . . He [Riggs] recently appeared at the Poet's Roundup which is held on a ranch near Santa Fe, and despite the fact that such notables as Mary Austin and Witter Bynner were on the program Riggs got the "biggest hand" of the afternoon. He read several poems from his *Iron Dish* and sang three ballads from *Green Grow the Lilacs,* accompanying himself on the guitar.

Riggs began a decade of commuting from Santa Fe to work in New York and Hollywood. When Betty Kirk and her sister Dorothy came from Oklahoma City to visit in August, 1931, they found Riggs having a wonderful time with the local free spirits. He spent weeks that summer making a silent movie for fun with his younger friend Jimmy Hughes, son of banker Levi and Christine Hughes.

Titled *A Day in Santa Fe,* the film has been preserved in the Archives of the State of New Mexico because it shows so many of the scenes and people important in Santa Fe at the time. Blond, energetic Jimmy manned the camera, while Riggs directed and wrote silly poetic captions for the film. It is the story of two burros who wake and come into town with a load of wood, observing the town as a character itself, wakening and going through its day. A local columnist, Henriette Harris, advertised copies of the film for sale: "fiesta, siesta, rain, work and play, the cathedral and Palace, Indian dancers, and all the lazy or hectic life of Santa Fe between dawn and

Riggs with Betty Kirk, *left*, and her sister, Dorothy, at the Al Fresco
Cafe in Santa Fe, August, 1931. *Western History Collections, University
of Oklahoma Library*

moon. The chronometer is a little burro from the mountain
with wings of wood." Riggs and Hughes had to wait many
days to capture a little rainfall on film. Some scenes were shot
at a sidewalk cafe and at the swimming pool of the Misses
White. A typical caption read:

> *Again the sun beyond the hill wakes and stirs—*
> *Dawn silence fills the domed tremendous glowing sky,*
> *The veils of dark begin to die.*
> *And hill and valley, town and flower*
> *stir in the long-awaited hour.*

The film attracted attention when sent in for developing at
Eastman Kodak in Rochester, and the company published a
story about this early, but advanced for its time, home movie.
Eastman's *Cine-Kodak News* for January-February, 1932 describes the project and quotes Riggs's description of the film
as "a typical Santa Fe day, seen in purely lyric and visual
terms."

The film premiered for a large crowd of Santa Feans in an
auditorium at the famous La Fonda Hotel on January 6, 1932.

Among those seen in it were Mrs. Gus (Jane) Baumann and her daughter Ann, Mrs. Juan Sedillo and her Great Dane dog, Edwin Brooks (diving into the Whites' pool), actor Norman McGee, John Dorman, artist Josef Bakos, Raymond and Frances Otis (at breakfast), Joseph and Evie Stevenson, Betty Galt, and Jimmy's sister, Mary Christine Hughes. A party followed at the home of Ernest and Gina (MacDowell) Knee on Canyon Road.

Riggs wrote Clark on August 31, 1931 (Riggs's thirty-second birthday), that he had finished his dramatic adaptation of *Son of Perdition* and Jim Cozzens was pleased with it. Arthur Hopkins had told Riggs in a letter, however, that to do the play would take a great deal of courage and backing. A successful production of *Green Grow the Lilacs* in Brussels was reported in a clipping sent by Clark, and *A Lantern to See By* had had a successful production at Hedgerow Theater near Philadelphia. Hedgerow also produced *Roadside* and *Cherokee Night* that year. Santa Fe Community Theatre did *Rancour* in December, and in November the Detroit Playhouse did *Sump'n Like Wings,* the play that was optioned but dropped by Broadway producers three times.

Riggs wrote Clark,

> I met Jacques Cartier at the Cyrus McCormick ranch out here this week, and he did a terrific song and dance about Jasper's production of A LANTERN TO SEE BY. He says it is the best play I ever wrote, that Jasper ever produced, and practically that the world ever saw. Unfortunately, it isn't that good and I doubt if it should be produced in New York in spite of all. . . . That man [Jasper Deeter] certainly must know what my plays are about.

He said the clippings about the Hedgerow production were "simply swell."

Betty Kirk Boyer, Riggs's close friend from 1922 on, described him in a 1968 interview as tender and generous. She said he never made an effort to hide his own spontaneous

Riggs and Jimmy Hughes plan their film, *A Day in Santa Fe*, in 1931. *Western History Collections, University of Oklahoma Library*

emotional reactions to people: "He liked to share his affections with others very openly with no self-consciousness whatsoever and he did this with dozens of his friends. That's why they all loved him so much." Others said, however, that although he was open to people, especially in the open society of Santa Fe, he was supersensitive to criticism or to any injury to his self-esteem.

She continued, "In a way he was a homeless person and he loved the warmth and fire-side of a home. He had a great devotion to Oklahoma and a passion for Santa Fe. . . . His po-

etry throughout is a love song to the natural earth from which
he came." She said that, although he was idealistic and ambitious, Riggs never became a cynic.[7]

Spud Johnson, in the same interview, told Dr. Arrell M.
Gibson of the University of Oklahoma that Mabel Dodge
Luhan's association with Riggs was cordial at first:

> Mabel asked him to stay there and they had a cozy time to-
> gether. Then Lynn had a friend joining him, a boy from the
> University of Denver, who came to stay with Lynn for a while.
> Mabel took instant dislike to this boy and from that moment
> on, although Lynn stayed on in Taos and had a house, she
> wouldn't even speak to him.

Betty Kirk Boyer, an assistant to Joseph Brandt, director of
the University of Oklahoma Press, made business trips to
New York, where she sometimes saw Riggs. She once had
dinner with Ida Rauh Eastman and Riggs, who mentioned
that Mabel and Tony Luhan were in New York and staying at
the Gladstone Hotel. He called Mabel and took Betty up to
meet her. In Betty's words:

> Even with the legend of Mabel I had, I was unprepared for
> what I saw. Over at one side, completely stoic and silent, sat
> Tony, and seated before a long coffee table sat Mabel, and she
> was very handsome indeed, wearing long, flowing chiffons
> which seemed to be veils all over her. She was still very beau-
> tiful, with lovely soft, shining hair and skin and a charming,
> lyrical, gentle voice. She had twenty bottles of perfume on the
> coffee table, and after she spoke would pause and reach for a
> little stopper and pass it under her nose, taking a slight whiff,
> and then putting it back. It was quite a performance! When we
> got into the cab, I remarked how gentle and kind she seemed.
> "Gentle and kind!" exclaimed both Lynn and Ida. "She's a
> viper!" Both said Mabel was an extraordinarily dangerous
> woman.

Spud Johnson said, however, that Ida was fond of Mabel and
found her stimulating: "Ida would be very sort of in-turned
and not give out very much sometimes, but if someone turned

her on she was brilliant, very witty . . . and Mabel did that for her."

In the fall of 1931, Riggs enjoyed directing, along with Anna V. Huey, the Santa Fe Players in George Kaufman and Edna Ferber's *The Royal Family* and his own *Rancour* (as he then spelled it). Another pleasure was that six of his introspective sonnets, untitled but numbered, were published without comment, under the title of "Listen, Mind," in Franklin P. Adams's column, "The Conning Tower" in the *New York Herald-Tribune* of October 13, 1931.

Riggs had always been ready to help a friend when he had money. Soon he himself was again on the downswing of his fortunes. On October 4, 1931, he wrote Henry Moe to ask whether he could renew his Guggenheim fellowship: "The point is this—revenue from *Green Grow the Lilacs* has taken care of me for almost a year now—and will continue to until next spring. Then (unless I have a paying play on this winter) I'll be the penniless young playwright again—and should like to go to Germany and England—or Mexico possibly—and do another play or two. Do you think I should apply right away?"[8]

Paul Green's fortunes were rising. On September 28, Riggs sent him an opening-night telegram to the Martin Beck Theatre, and on November 25 he congratulated Green on *The House of Connelly*, of which he had just received a copy: "The play is a great beauty. The first draft, which I saw years ago with its skulking negresses and the fatal gunny sack, or whatever it was, didn't seem to me quite to come off. But this version does. It has your usual magic overtones and a beautiful symphonic music."

On December 4, 1931, he wrote from Santa Fe to Moe at the Guggenheim:

> As you suggested, I'm writing you before the first of the year. I'm just finishing my new play, *The Cherokee Night*. It is so complicated and will require so much preparation on the part of the producer, that I don't see how it could possibly be done before the season of 1932-33 or even later.

> And since about April, I'm sure to need help again, I should like to ask now about renewal of my fellowship. If I am granted this renewal, I shall go to London, Dublin, and Berlin, and study the theatre in those capitals. Near one of them, I shall settle down and write a new play—probably *More Sky* or *To Cheat the Winter.*

In spite of his troubles, Riggs wrote an exuberant letter to Barrett Clark on December 18 from the La Fonda Hotel in Santa Fe, saying he had found it too cold to stay in his apartment. He enclosed "swell stuff" on the production of *Rancour* in the Santa Fe Community Theatre, with critiques by the novelist Evelyn Scott and by Alice Corbin Henderson, the poet and one-time associate editor of *Poetry:* "The script is final now, much improved in subtle ways. . . . Pictures of *Rancour* soon. We took movies, too. . . . I like it here. Christmas Greetings—"

A report in the Taos, New Mexico, paper of November 22, 1931, had some fun with this serious drama. Miss Jane Barry had come to the Taos weekly market the day before to announce its production by the Santa Fe Players. While the crowd cheered, colored banners fluttered from the bandstand to the four corners of the park. Gaily draped wagons, loaded with apples, cider, wood, potatoes, jam, peanuts, pork and other goodies, were parked all round the inner wall, ready for barter.

> Miss Barry's talk in behalf of the Santa Fe Players came as a delightful surprise. . . . "The young playwright," said Miss Barry in part, "whose play is now in rehearsal in Santa Fe . . ." And at this point Miss Dorothy Stewart drove into the plaza in her new covered-wagon Austin coupe, on its maiden voyage. Instantly another cheer arose, so voluminous that all ten-thousand tissue paper banners swayed like a great tidal wave; and order was only restored when Mrs. Kate Chapman, carrying in her arms two dozen "Adobe Notes," emerged from the tiny covered wagon and, towering above it, shouted through the din, "Three cheers for Lynn Riggs!"

The cheers were lusty and long and then three cheers were given for *Rancour*, three cheers for the Santa Fe Players, three cheers for Austin covered wagons, three cheers for Jane Barry, three cheers for Dorothy Stewart, three cheers for Market Day and three cheers for President Hoover.

Then the 25-piece band played "The Star-Spangled Banner" and everybody went home, one by one, after signing a pledge to attend *Rancour* on December 16 in Santa Fe. Miss Barry left Taos the same evening for Raton where she plans to remain several days, resting her voice.

Spud Johnson described an evening with the cast before the opening in a tongue-in-cheek article for the Santa Fe *New Mexican*, entitled "'Rancour' Stars Tell About Their Art and Their Public; Intimate Touches Thrill":

. . . Miss Mildred Maxey, Mr. Riggs' leading lady. . . . "I always live my parts," she said, dramatically passing a forefinger over her troubled brow. . . . "Now!" she said in a harsh voice, her eyes flashing. "Now I hate and love simultaneously with such vigor that I am practically a psychic wreck!" She whirled on the playwright.

"I hate you!" she cried fiercely. "Why must I be tortured by this predicament you have plunged me into?" Then she softened: "But it's a beautiful part, really. Sometimes I feel so elated. I'm doing it all for lu-uve!" The interviewer then turned to George Gormly, the ill-natured husband of the play, who turned out to be very sulky indeed and only grunted in reply to even polite questions. . . . "Tell my public," he murmured sententiously, "that I am torn between my firefighting and my acting." And he stalked out of the room.

. . . Peaches Harvey [a schoolteacher] . . . "What will the young ladies of the seminary think," she objected bitterly, "when I say, 'Nope, I ain't got any' and things like that?" Mr. Riggs soothed her by saying it was all for art's sake.

On a loftier plane, Barrett Clark in the *English Journal* of January, 1932, expressed regret that circumstances had caused two or three hundred dramatists to take up writing for the movies: "I have no doubt that every one of the 'regular' playwrights in Hollywood has a perfectly good reason for being there, but I can't help regretting their absence from the theatre." He cited Riggs's *Sump'n Like Wings*, sold three times, as an example of producers' cold feet, and said if he chose twelve plays that ought to be produced on Broadway, they would include *The Lonesome West*. Instead, much of what was being produced was trash. He concluded, "You may say what you like about the theater being a democratic institution where all must compete in an open market; but unless production is made easier, unless the 'little theaters' and colleges serve the theater as a whole, with particular emphasis on the young experimenter, our drama will of necessity become little more than what it was during the nineteenth century."[9]

On January 27, 1932, Riggs received a telegram from E. C. Mabie of the University of Iowa asking him to be a guest and speaker at the National Conference of Community and University Theatres on February 18 through 20. Other theatre people invited to speak included Hatcher Hughes, Barrett Clark, Frederick ("Prof") Koch, Edith Isaacs, Marion Tucker, Gilmore Brown, and Glenn Hughes.

The *New York Herald-Tribune* reported another honor on March 14, 1932, when Riggs was guest speaker at the twenty-first annual spring luncheon of the Theatre Club, where Dame May Whitty, Marguerite Churchill, and Franchot Tone were guests.

On March 20, at 7:00 P.M., he was an honored guest of the Hedgerow Theater at an invitational performance of *A Lantern to See By*, which was followed by a public performance of *Roadside*. The *Philadelphia Evening Public Ledger* reported on March 11 that this was to be the first time that the author saw these plays staged. On March 26, Henry T. Murdick reported in his "Mummers' Parade" column in the *Ledger* that Riggs had said:

> The playwright is always right. If a play seems to have the merit to make production a fact, the author should have the final word on the interpretation. He alone—and not the direc-

tor or the producer or the actor—knows the exact shade of meaning he intends. Past experiences with "doctoring" have convinced the Oklahoman that he is correct. He believes that the day of the poet in the theatre is dawning and that realism as the stage has known it for the last few years is dead . . . being a poet, he feels none too kindly toward a restricted Broadway theatre. People in the highways and byways are hungering for a theatre that Broadway neither practically nor philosophically supplies. Decentralization of the theatre is the answer, and he believes that it will surely come.

Poet and journalist Carl Sandburg, traveling in Albuquerque, wrote in the Cleveland *Plain Dealer* on March 23, 1932, of discussing the financial plight of Indian artists with Lynn Riggs, and of the new Cherokee play Riggs was writing.

Riggs assisted Hedgerow's production of *Cherokee Night*, which opened June 18, 1932, to an overflow crowd. Although reviewers reported that the audience was baffled, *Billboard* reported on June 25 that it was the most important first night in Hedgerow's eight years.

Barrett Clark visited Riggs at Northwestern University during rehearsals of *Green Grow the Lilacs*, which was presented there July 18 through 22. Clark also championed non-Broadway theatre, saying in the Evanston *News-Index* of July 14, 1932:

> Here is the direction our theatre must take or cease to exist. . . . What Northwestern is doing in bringing Lynn Riggs to direct his own play is one of the most significant things happening in our theatre today. . . . What [Leverton] has started here . . . will be quickly followed all over the country.

After *Green Grow the Lilacs'* successful opening, the *Summer Northwestern* reported in July, 1932: "Those who have come to know this young American dramatist admire him and his standards, his quiet humility, his gentle personality unaffected by fame. Through the members of the cast and those who have otherwise come in contact with him, the influence of his high ideals for the drama will be far-reaching."

In addition, the *Chicago Tribune* society section gave full-page pictorial coverage to the Northwestern University students and Riggs preparing for the production. While he was being entertained at one of several private parties in Evanston, Riggs showed his film, *A Day in Santa Fe*. Harold Ehrensperger, of the Northwestern School of Speech, presented Riggs with gifts at a farewell luncheon. Riggs said, "The professional theater grows successively more commercial, more stultifying, less lyric, less poetic—less all the things I try to stand for in drama."

Riggs telegraphed E. C. Mabie at Iowa City on August 16 that he would come to the University of Iowa in November to do a play. He was then in Santa Fe, where he performed as the pedler in *Knives from Syria*. He added: "Northwestern wants me so please write Garrett Leverton. Importing a playwright will be cheaper for two universities than for one." He did *Cherokee Night* at Iowa City, where he worked with rehearsals for six weeks during October and November.

On November 16, Riggs spoke on "Poetry and the Modern Theatre" over radio station WSUI in Iowa City. He criticized the "slick photographic, swift-moving realism dominating the modern theatre." According to the November 20 *Cedar Rapids Gazette*, he said the American stage must be "a platform for fervor, eloquence and blinding revelation of man. It must be more than entertainment. . . . It must touch and illumine the spirit of striving man. When the poetic theatre comes to the American stage it will house only an audience of poets. The movies will take care of the rest."

He said that the poet-playwright must transmit a correct, sensuous impression, whether it was beautiful or not:

> These audiences of poets won't have an easy time of it, for poetry makes demands on the attention which most of us are not willing to accede to, finding it simpler to turn on the radio. . . . But when all the marshmallow moons are in eclipse and the intricate seduction of jazz is dead, poetry will still say its important say. For the word—as the Elizabethans knew and as

the early Jewish prophets knew—the word is God. No man is exactly a fool who bows before something really majestic and austere.

The burgeoning college and community theatre movement was supported by the country's leading dramatists and critics. Clark explained in *Intimate Portraits* his own plan to "persuade the professional managers and playwrights to give serious thought to the really important work being done in the best of our Little Theaters, colleges and universities . . . involving production of new plays by established writers at various focal points throughout the country, and the statements I brought together and published were by no means perfunctory puffs. O'Neill, Hopkins, Green, Riggs and Howard were my spiritual backers."[10]

In March, 1932, Sidney Howard wrote to Clark of similar concerns:

> I read your piece with interest and admiration. Lynn came yesterday [to Howard's house on Eighty-Second Street in New York] to talk at greater length about the plan and about what the Hedgerow people are doing for him. . . . What you are offering Lynn & Co. is what the Provincetown outfit offers O'Neill, with the addition of the personal note. . . . Your scheme, too, comes most happily in these days of Broadway bankruptcy. The youngsters are clearly going to have a harder and harder time, particularly those, like Lynn, who have a fresh way in dramatic story-telling. . . . The alleged native drama is going to become a great deal more native when it sees the light and takes its first steps in hardier neighborhoods and under a more selfless tradition. Lynn's superb new play perfectly demonstrates the rightness of your schemes.

Howard added, in an April 4 letter to Clark from Los Angeles: "There is to my mind nothing experimental, for example about Riggs' magnificent CHEROKEE NIGHT, and the point is—isn't it—that managers are apt nowadays to be afraid to take a chance on themes and departures which have not been tested."

A few more personal glimpses of Riggs were in an Iowa interview of December 4, 1932, preserved in his scrapbooks. He said that when he was nineteen he had been in a picture that Will Rogers was doing in Hollywood, and that he had met Rogers again in New York, but "didn't really know him." He had been "connected" with Rogers, however, when, in 1928, Andy Payne, also of Claremore, had finished first in a 3,422-mile "bunion derby" from Los Angeles to New York, for a prize of $25,000. As a result the exultant city of Claremore had placed an interesting mixture of celebrities on a bronze plaque on the courthouse inscribed:

Will Rogers, Lynn Riggs, Andy Payne
Wit, Wisdom, & Vitality

Vivien Milburn interviewed Riggs for an article in *The Bandwagon* in 1932, entitled "In Bold Relief":

> He is thin, slightly stooped, of medium height, with fine, fair hair receding slightly. Tawny brown eyes, full of laughter— though at first glance he seems serious and shy. Slightly suggests a college professor. Wears various shades of brown, with accents of green and yellow; buys clothes prodigally and with care, believing in the dramatic effect of clothes. . . . at his best playing host . . . likes good food, but never takes dessert. Fond of lounging informally with cronies, feet hung over the arm of a chair, wearing, if weather permits, his old yellow coat-sweater, which he admired so wishfully two years ago in Provincetown that the owner could not help giving it to him. . . . He is remarkable in his kindness in introducing friends or friends of friends to people whom he knows might help them get a start in New York. Dislikes writing letters and farewells—often being vague about his date of departure . . . dislikes inflicting sadness or pain. He is the only person I have ever known who really has no regard for money. When he is flush he spends it happily; when he has less he is content.

When *Cherokee Night* opened on December 7 with Riggs in the audience, the *Iowa City Press-Citizen* reported that "the play sets a new high standard for the University theatre. . . . [The author] was given a warm curtain call." He was quoted telling a Rotary Club luncheon the next day that seeing the play produced at Hedgerow had proved to him that it "has no experimental problems in the way of reaching the audience," although Broadway producers had told him that the non-chronological, episodic play was "five years ahead of the New York audience."

On December 9 he wrote Clark: "The Cherokees swell. Pictures later. I leave tomorrow for Santa Fe. Heigh-ho! Mabie and all have been noble. I'll be a good director yet. You'll see. . . . How are you? I'm swell, swell and on my way to Santa Fe! I *must* finish *More Sky*. And *Keats in New York* is boiling (title to be kept secret)."

Riggs was present in 1935 when *Green Grow the Lilacs* was presented on May 10 in a Festival of Southwestern Plays at Southern Methodist University, along with two one-act Texas plays by John William Rogers, Jr., and *Night over Taos*, by Maxwell Anderson. Calling Riggs's play "magnificent," Rogers prophesied: "We are more sure than ever our people will come to cherish it among our true heritages and will love it too well to forget it for a long, long time to come. It will be given among us again and again." The play's next performances were at the Dallas Little Theatre, at the Westport, Connecticut, Country Playhouse, and at Colorado College.

On February 25, 1933, Hedgerow Theater presented the premiere performance of the fifth play by Lynn Riggs in its repertoire, *The Son of Perdition*, adapted from the Cuban novel of James Gould Cozzens. At this time Eugene O'Neill led Hedgerow's repertoire with six plays, Riggs had five, and Susan Glaspell, four. Hedgerow had also produced five Ibsen plays.[11] The famous but unprepossessing Jasper Deeter, a snaggle-toothed, coarse-voiced character, according to Paul Green, admired Riggs's work and rated him high among the newer playwrights.[12]

The *New York Telegram* of March 18, 1933, reported that Riggs was one of fifteen sponsors to organize the Theatre

Union, which planned to produce plays in the fall of 1934 "designed especially to appeal to audiences of workers as a class, and written from the viewpoint of the working man and woman." This was to be a nonprofit professional theatre with cheap seats. Other sponsors included Sidney Howard, John Howard Lawson, Lewis Mumford, John Dos Passos, Edmund Wilson, Maxwell Anderson, Stephen Vincent Benét, and Waldo Frank, with the inspiration and support of Barrett Clark. A symptom of the country's troubled times, the Union said it did not intend to give propaganda plays, although, it did represent a leftist movement among playwrights. On December 5, 1933, *Variety* added other prominent names to the group of organizers, including Sherwood Anderson, Elmer Rice, and Paul Muni.

Riggs did not receive a second fellowship from the Guggenheim foundation. On receiving a report, he wrote on April 18, 1933, to Moe from the Hollywood Roosevelt Hotel, saying, "I've wondered what the Fellows were doing, had done, etc. My thanks and congratulations."

On his trips east Riggs frequently visited Elizabeth and Paul Green in Chapel Hill, often accompanied by George O'Neil, his close friend. O'Neil achieved much less than Riggs as a playwright and poet during his lifetime, but apparently lived on an independent income that was more than adequate. Dark-haired, congenial, handsome as a Hollywood star, O'Neil appears with his charming smile in Riggs snapshots from California, North Carolina, New York, and Santa Fe. O'Neil liked good clothes and steaks, spoke with a clipped expression, and was generally a genial companion.[13]

O'Neil's play *American Dream*, produced by the Theatre Guild in New York on February 20, 1933, and published by French, was denounced as degenerate, profane, and Communistic. Paul Green remembered O'Neil discussing the play with him and Riggs while working on it.[14] To the world the affable O'Neil presented a gay disposition and a comfortable, blasé life-style, but in his writings he was a surly malcontent

From left to right, Paul Green, Riggs, George O'Neil, and Elizabeth Green, during a visit by Riggs and O'Neil at the Greens' home in Chapel Hill, North Carolina.

who attacked what he perceived as the exploitative and hypo-
critical underbelly of American society.

O'Neil had graduated from Washington University in St.
Louis and received early recognition for his poetry. Like many
other Americans, after Navy service in World War I he lived in
Paris and wrote poems, short stories, novels, and plays. He
published two novels, *Special Hunger* and *That Bright Heat*.
The Theatre Guild produced his play *Something to Live For* in
1933 and *The American Dream*, three one-act plays inspired by
a cocktail party. He coauthored a western play with Dan
Totheroh, *Mother Lode*, which was denounced by Brooks
Atkinson: "This reviewer has only the foggiest notion of what
the authors intended to say. . . . *Mother Lode* is in desperate
need of crisp expression." O'Neil's published poetry books
were *The Cobbler in Willow Street* and *God-Beguiled*.

Many writers of the time felt a traditional responsibility to
criticize the status quo, but O'Neil and others made a mistake
that Riggs never made, that of overestimating the play-going
public's willingness to accept strong condemnation. Riggs
was always more at home with internal rather than external
moralities, and he knew it instinctively. In contrast, O'Neil,
heir of a St. Louis lumber family, never lacked for money and
enjoyed a good time, but his dabblings in plays and poetry
show a bitterness born of malaise. Since he could be indif-
ferent to monetary success, he could afford to be cynical.

In this period Riggs was branching out, writing plays and
film scripts and seeing his works produced in university and
community theaters. He himself directed *More Sky*, set in the
lost city of Atlantis, at Northwestern University during the
summer of 1934.

In May, 1933, Paul Green offered a story by Riggs to Darryl
Zanuck at Fox Studios but he reported to Riggs that the story
editor had advised steering clear of all kidnapping themes because "of the prevalent moronic type of mind in the American
Scene. But just the same it is a dern good yarn and I hope

somebody takes it . . . More when I see you at the Greek play."

On another note, Franklin P. Adams reported on June 23, 1933, in "The Conning Tower" of the *New York Herald-Tribune,* that Oklahomans were asking what New York thought of George Milburn and Lynn Riggs. He said, "New York considers them two first-class writers; also that they are a pair of Oklahomans whom New York seems to be unable to spoil."

Riggs lived at the Montecito Apartments in Hollywood, where he wrote Barrett Clark on October 23, 1933, about his hopes for *Cherokee Night*—"after being away from it for almost a year." It had been produced at Hedgerow in August and at the University of Iowa in December, 1932:

> I told Helen Westley about the production in Iowa and about my intention to direct my own plays in New York. She was very excited about both things and said I really ought to tell the Guild about it. I don't see any point in that just now—because I can't be in New York at the moment—but some day I'll tell Terry Helburn all about it.
>
> I've just come from ten days in Santa Fe. I'm going to build a house there in March or April if I have any money. . . . Paul [Green] has just moved into my apartment house. Elizabeth arrived Sunday. Paul is about to do a job for Paramount I believe. . . . I was up to my neck in Stingaree for RKO until I went to Santa Fe. P.S. I'm sending you my sonnets.

Riggs had worked for MGM Studios, collaborating on a film version of Oliver La Farge's *Laughing Boy.* Then he spent July and August on *Stingaree,* which was a light operetta set on an Australian sheep ranch. Starring Irene Dunne and Richard Dix, it was released in April, 1934.

When Emily Hughes and her niece Mary Christine visited Hollywood from Santa Fe in 1933, Riggs introduced them to Joan Crawford and took them to watch retakes of her new picture on the MGM lot.[15] As he expanded his circle of West Coast friends, his name appeared frequently in social news.

Reine Davis reported, for example, in the *Los Angeles Examiner* of March 1, 1934:

> Lynn Riggs, noted New York playwright, honored Mr. and Mrs. Paul Daughtery of Carmel with a cocktail party in his new early American home on North Crescent Heights Boulevard. The guests were Mr. and Mrs. Robert Tucker, Connie Schuman, Gloria Stuart, Jerry Asher, Dan Totheroh, George O'Neil and Galt Bell.

Always a popular escort and dancing companion, Riggs sometimes found himself the subject of gossip columnists, especially in regard to his rumored "romance" with star Bette Davis. Dramatic critic E. de S. Melcher of the Washington, D.C., *Star*, for example, wrote, on August 20, 1933, of meeting Riggs and other celebrities on a Hollywood tour: "Bette Davis gives us a dinner. Playwright Lynn Riggs is there. . . . He likes working for films. That comes as a surprise. . . . Franchot Tone calls up. 'Joan Crawford wants you for dinner tomorrow night. . . .'" This dinner party included Tone, who was Miss Crawford's "inseparable companion since her recent divorce," and Riggs, plus a visit to the brood of Scottie dogs she had newly acquired and a private film showing. On the next day Melcher was invited for lunch and a tour with Riggs of the RKO-Radio Studio, where numerous stars were in costume. He remarked that Riggs was not well known among other studio workers and was amused when Riggs responded that he was "just a writer."

A *Hollywood Reporter* columnist reported on September 1, 1933:

> Lynn Riggs and Bette Davis thought they were keeping their "keeping company" very quiet, and when the news leaked out, Bette just laughed, but Riggs, who is a very modest and retiring fellow almost collapsed when he read here [August 19] that he and Bette were "ablaze." That very day, Riggs walked into the commissary at Radio for lunch and four fellows stood up and with one accord, yelled at him, "ABLAZE, eh???" Riggs blushed and fled and hasn't been back for a bite to eat yet.

In November both *Photoplay* and the *Los Angeles Herald* of November 14 reported that Bette Davis was temporarily separated from her husband, Harmon Nelson, a musician working on the East Coast, and that Lynn Riggs was her regular escort for dining and dancing, although she avoided being photographed with him. A photograph in the December *Silver Screen* showed her attending a premiere with *eight* escorts, including Riggs. She commented, "Every time I go out with a man people talk, so I thought I'd give them something really worth while and then maybe they'll get it out of their systems."

Rumors subsided when the following item appeared in the March, 1934, *Screen Play*, along with a picture of Riggs and Davis laughing together at the Cocoanut Grove: "For those who are interested and perhaps a little worried, too, about Bette Davis' constant dates with Lynn Riggs the writer, we thought we'd better tell you that Lynn has been given authority by Bette's husband to escort her wherever she cares to go."

Riggs remained a topic, however, in interviews with several glamorous Hollywood women, and received not a little bantering about his "best friend" status with them. For example, in a *New Movie Magazine* article of March, 1934, "by Joan Crawford (as told to Nanette Kutner)," Crawford said that she made the mistake of being too secluded because she did not drink, rose early, and therefore did not stay up late. "I see only three people," she said. "They are Franchot Tone, Lynn Riggs, who wrote *Green Grow the Lilacs,* and a magazine editor. Every Saturday night I have those three to dinner. Then we sit and talk for hours on end."

Riggs helped her design for her remodeled home a theater with a tiny stage, eight by twelve feet, where she planned to rehearse, alone, in preparation for a stage career, should she leave pictures. She was photographed attending the opera with Tone and Riggs. In statements in April and May, however, she expanded her list of "best friends" to include Francis

Lederer, Douglas Fairbanks, Jr., Clark Gable, and actress Jean
Dixon (*Milwaukee Sentinel*, May 3; *Denver Post*, April, 1934).

Actress Jean Muir also claimed Riggs as a best friend. A
society column noted her presence with John Beal and his
bride, Helen Craig, Francis Lederer, and Jerry Asher on October 16, 1934, when Riggs was one of too many Montecito
Apartment residents celebrating the opening of the new com-
missary there. They ordered dinner at 8:00 P.M. to be sent
up, had cocktails, and waited—until 10:00 P.M., when Beal
knocked at the door, wearing an apron and bearing a huge
tray full of dinner. He served it and then returned to the
kitchen, continuing to help the harassed waiters.

In 1936, Helen Craig entertained at a birthday party for her
husband, John Beal, with the actress Margo, Jerry Asher,
Riggs, Jean Muir, and Joe Beal present. This travelling party
of Montecitans moved later to Riggs's apartment, and still
later to Larry Riley's apartment.

Joan Crawford and Franchot Tone in 1936 held a swimming,
tennis, and badminton party on a Sunday afternoon with best
friend Riggs and "a galaxy": Barbara Stanwyck and Robert
Taylor, Ginger Rogers and James Stewart, Mary Anita Loos
and Francis Lederer, Mr. and Mrs. Gary Cooper, Moss Hart
and Margo, Henry Fonda, Una Merkel, and others.

Society news in the Santa Fe *New Mexican*, reported Septem-
ber 30, 1936, that Jean Muir, after making three movies in ten
weeks for Warner Brothers, drove to Santa Fe to be Riggs's
houseguest for a week. For a year she had directed her own
theatre school in Hollywood, where she had produced *Green
Grow the Lilacs*. The report said that George Gershwin and
Riggs had agreed to do an opera set in New Mexico, which
Riggs was writing. Gershwin was fresh from the success of
Porgy and Bess. Helen Craig and John Beal also visited Riggs in
Santa Fe.

As Christmas approached, Reine Davies said in his "Hollywood Parade" column for December 19, 1936, that Riggs, the
"ace host" of Santa Fe, had "at last" entertained at a dinner

party in Montecito for some "self-invited" guests: Ida Rauh Eastman, Phil Huston, Bette Davis, Jerry Asher, and Thyra Samter Winslow. Riggs decorated the dinner table with holly and placed a beautiful cellophane-wrapped cigarette lighter at each place.

As the year ended, Joan Crawford was again publicly counting her "best friends." She told Ernie Pyle, in a feature article in the *New York World-Telegram* on December 29, 1936, that the list then included the Gary Coopers, Jimmy Murphy, Barbara Stanwyck, and Lynn Riggs. Commented Pyle: "I'll have to hunt up this fellow Riggs and see how he does it. He's also Jean Muir's best friend. Sounds funny to me."

An article followed in the December 31 *World-Telegram* about Muir, saying that she was well educated, intelligent, and socially "radical" concerning poverty—and that she was *knitting a yellow sweater for Lynn Riggs* [italics added]." Once women understood Riggs's lack of sexual attraction to them, they loved him for his gracious sociability, his gentle listening, graceful dancing, and enjoyment of music.

In spite of the social whirl, Riggs worked steadily on his plays—in addition to the hours spent writing the screenplays that paid his bills. On December 28, 1934, while he was an honored guest in Carmel, California, for the opening of three performances of *Roadside*, he gave an insightful interview to Winsor Josselyn, which was published in the *Carmel Pine Cone* on January 19, 1934. Commenting that *Roadside* was his only pure comedy, he said:

"The other interesting thing is the response to that speech of Texas where he bursts out with the legendary story of his birth. The audience always reacts to it. There have been times when people, especially collegians, have memorized the speech and recited it to me as though it served to release something in them." He repeated the word release, half to himself.

Then he was telling how he thought that release was a strong factor in his plays. Yes, and homesickness. Homesickness for an era lost, for a frontier vanished; homesickness for something that people might not have known, but, now knowing, they miss—almost as if it were a magic land, the key to whose gate they cannot have. Release and homesickness, admixed with a fantastic quality, an underlying rhythm and even the use of ancient forms, such as the Greek chorus as represented in *Roadside* by the lovable louts Red Ike and Black Ike.

"And yet so far as personal release goes for me," mused Riggs, lighting a cigarette with a tiny square silver pillar, "playwrighting never gives me the freedom that writing verse does, and in a little book called 'The Iron Dish' I had more complete outlet than through any of my plays."

On November 15, 1933, Riggs had written a "homesick" letter to Spud Johnson, who had made and signed a lamp for Lynn to give Bette Davis:

> The lamp is a knock-out. I'm sure you outdid yourself. It created quite a sensation with La Davis. . . . You may not be astonished to know that I own a lot in Santa Fe, that vigas have been ordered, that adobes are being made, that the water is in, that plans are complete and exact for my little house which starts actually ascending in April.
>
> What's happening to George [O'Neil]? The so and so doesn't deign to write me. . . . Paul is growling about his job at Paramount. Elizabeth is studying puppetry. We are all going to the Hollywood opening of *The Emperor Jones*.

The Greens enjoyed the Hollywood bonanza, too, although their hearts were still in the academic community at Chapel Hill.

Meanwhile, Riggs's *More Sky* was produced at the Cleveland Playhouse. He worked on the screenplay of *Family Man* at RKO Radio in January, 1934, moving in March to Paramount Studio to write the screenplay for John Evans's *Andrew's Harvest*. In mid-May he went to MGM to work on *Wicked Woman*.

On January 28 he wrote Johnson that he would be home by June 15 and wanted Johnson to stay and care for his garden. He asked Johnson (who worked in Santa Fe's Villagra Bookshop) to send him Thomas Mann's books, plus the plays of S. N. Behrman, who might collaborate with him on *A World Elsewhere*—in which case Behrman would also come to Santa Fe.

Answering an inquiry from Clark about what was happening to his "once active brain," Riggs replied on March 6, 1934, that he had almost finished the first act of a play and would certainly finish it when he went to Santa Fe. However, he wrote:

> At the moment, Paramount has given me a novel to do—which, if we can agree on method of treatment, I'm going to do. It's called *Andrew's Harvest*, and is by John Evans, son of Mabel Dodge Lujan, and a friend of mine. It's very grand soil stuff.
> When is Paul [Green] coming out? George [O'Neil] is still busy on *Sutter's Gold*. Dan [Totheroh] is doing some thing for United Artists, *Count of Monte Cristo*. . . . George hopes to go east in a few weeks and live in Connecticut or some place he can find a pleasant hut by the sea.

Riggs's close friendship with Franchot Tone had begun with Tone's role in the original production of *Green Grow the Lilacs*. The black-tie dinners he attended with Tone at Crawford's home often included such luminaries as the Fred Astaires, the Fred MacMurrays, Barbara Stanwyck, Frank Fay, Helen Hayes and Charles MacArthur, the Gary Coopers, Sam and Frances Goldwyn, the Irving Berlins, Joan Bennett, the Ray Millands, and the George Murphys. In magazines Crawford shared her typical menu with Depression America, including pineapple and strawberries with mint ice, roast squab with wild rice, and crepes Suzette with flaming brandy. The small-town Oklahoma playwright for some years enjoyed a world that was about as far from his beginnings as was conceivable.

Having also come to luxury from poor beginnings, Crawford relished her life as a star and included in it those of Hollywood's newcomers who she felt were sympathetic to her. Bob Thomas wrote that in 1933 she asked Riggs to invite to dinner his collaborator at RKO, Leonard Spigelgas. On this memorable occasion Spigelgas, who ate his first artichoke that night, joined Riggs and the other guests for a swim in the pool—along with their hostess, who wore a topless swim suit.[16]

Generous with gifts to people she liked, Crawford gave Riggs a Scottie dog, named Baron, who gave him great pleasure for many years. On February 21, 1934, he sent Clark snapshots of the house he had taken at 800 North Crescent Heights Boulevard and of Baron, six months old.

Actor Norman McGee, who had performed in *Knives from Syria* in the early days in Santa Fe, said Riggs "went Hollywood," wearing exotic clothes and even lightening his hair color. "I had several conversations with him," McGee wrote later. "He was a different Lynn." McGee remembered Riggs's fine sense of humor and thought Riggs took himself too seriously in Hollywood.[17]

Paul Green said too many fine playwrights, attracted by Hollywood salaries of $1,500 per week and more, got "mortgaged to the life" and left their art behind. Green soon returned to Chapel Hill to teach and write. He said that he did not fit in at Hollywood parties, but Lynn, being an excellent dancer, enjoyed them and went often.

From July 24 through 27, 1934, Riggs directed his new play, *More Sky*, at Northwestern University. This large-scale mythological drama attempts to express the nobility of the free human spirit in the legendary city of Atlantis. As the island city gradually sinks, and the surrounding walls are built higher and higher, the sky seems to diminish in size. Simultaneously, the despotic rulers build higher barriers to cooperation and human contact with other peoples. When he sent the script to set designer Lee Mitchell in March, 1934, Riggs wrote on the title plate: "I don't care what you do with it in the visualization, but for the love of God preserve the legendary character of the thing. Make it as colorful as you can; it can't be too boldly done. Plato's story of the Atlantis may give you an idea or two." Discussing this experience in an article, entitled "Designer at Work," in the November *Theatre Arts Monthly*, Mitchell said: "The play itself was a nearly perfect design show. A narrative of heroic range, in verse, with the locale the continent of the lost Atlantis. . . . It was a drama of design, broad line, and bold color, and as such it had many magnificent moments.[18]

Always fond of classic literature, Riggs explained his theme in an interview with the *Summer Northwestern* while he was there:

I see the American stage as a platform for fervor, eloquence and blinding revelation of man. The theater must be more than entertainment. . . . It must touch and illumine the spirit of striving man. . . . American theater goers today are revolting against the worn-out realism of Broadway and turning to old classics which have proven their value. This reaction is not accidental, but the result of a definite antagonism toward the present type of drama produced in New York.

Although he said, "My intention in this play is to make people examine the world we are living in now," Riggs was less successful in doing that with such grand-scale pageantry than in his microcosmic plays, those which examine relationships in small towns and families. *More Sky* was well attended, skillfully directed and performed, but never published. Riggs returned to his Santa Fe–Hollywood commuting and went to work on a play that was to be more successful, the New Mexican comedy *Russet Mantle.*

On November 7, 1934, he wrote Clark from Montecito Apartments that he was leaving for Santa Fe to write. Regarding *More Sky*, he said:

The scene designs came out very well, I think, and ought to help the play quite a lot. Sorry Paul's play couldn't hang on. I hope to God I have a play on this season! P.S. I'm lunching with Galt Bell [director of Theatre Mart] today about *Green Grow*. I imagine he wants to start right away. If it doesn't sell to the movies before, this production ought to clinch it.

On November 17 he wrote Betty Kirk, "I'm here—in the pictures—making tons of money—and hoping to make a good picture finally. . . . Going in April to Santa Fe to build

an adobe house (1 large room, bath, kitchen). There I expect
to stay in my own sunny patio for the summer writing a play
a few shades less than immortal."

On December 23, 1934, he wrote aboard the Santa Fe train,
recommending to Clark, as a client, playwright Paul Horgan,
a Harper novel prizewinner who had written two plays in
which the Theatre Guild was interested. He said, "I'm Holly-
wooding—for Christmas only. Have a letter out about you—
Hope to have something on it soon—Thanks for the Christmas
card with the handsome urchins. Regards to y'all."

And on December 27, 1934, Riggs was finally released from
the last of three mortgages on his Claremore property.[19]

CHAPTER 8

THE SANTA FE HOUSE AND
THE MEXICAN PLAYS (1935–1940)

> . . . *Given weak hands and only those least supple,*
> *given gray eyes and bodies—even so,*
> *bound to the flaking wall each puerile couple*
> *is flint, is loveliness, is golden glow:*
> *three times the combustion one had counted on*
> *to win a height and kindle such a dawn.*
> —"The Stair Ascending" [1]

LYNN RIGGS BEGAN 1935 inauspiciously. He wrote Barrett Clark
from Santa Fe on February 12, making light of his illness as
always:

> I haven't written you lately because I have been quarantined
> with diphtheria. Now I'm up and about—and Friday, Febru-
> ary 15, I leave for Hollywood to do a picture for Universal, *De-
> lay in the Sun*. . . . I'm delighted about the Oklahoma date. . . .
> The date was arranged through Ben Botkin turning over my
> letter about you to Rupel Jones, I believe, since Botkin thought
> the Dramatic Department ought to handle it. Success to the
> grand tour! [2]

While Clark was lecturing at the University of Oklahoma,
Riggs was planning to stay at the Montecito Apartments
again for five to eight weeks. He said that Arthur Hopkins
was considering *Russet Mantle* and thought it would be a good
play for Joan Crawford and Franchot Tone. Riggs went east
the following October 11, 1935, to celebrate the marriage of

137

Jerry Asher *(left)* and Riggs *(far right)* help Franchot Tone and Joan Crawford celebrate their wedding on October 11, 1935, in New York.

that happy couple, who were wed quietly in the parlor of Mayor Herbert W. Jenkins in Englewood Cliffs, New Jersey.

Always Riggs most enjoyed Santa Fe, however, where local hostesses held teas (often thinly disguised Prohibition cocktail parties) for literary guests such as Vachel Lindsay (in 1929), Thornton Wilder (1933–34), and Edna Ferber (1935). Robert Frost appeared at the New Mexico Museum auditorium on August 5, 1935, sponsored by the Writers' Edition organization, which included Alice Corbin Henderson, Haniel Long, Ben Botkin, Witter Bynner, Willard ("Spud") Johnson, Lynn Riggs, Erna Fergusson, Elizabeth Shepley Sergeant, John Gould Fletcher, Raymond Otis, and others. Riggs paid tribute to Frost, winner of two Pulitzer prizes for poetry, for the "compassionate, stirring things he says of the gracious earth and its people."[3]

On occasional trips to Mexico from Santa Fe, Riggs had met and begun to sponsor a new protegé. On October 17, 1938, from the Schuyler Apartments in New York, he wrote recommending to Clark two plays by Enrique Gasque-Molina, "whom you met last winter." They were *Empire in Durango*, Gasque's first play, and *Mexican Mural*, a work in process. He added:

> He has, in my considered opinion, an unusual and fine talent—so much so that I personally offered the play to the Guild. They turned it down with "very beautifully written," etc. Harold Clurman has just written him a fine encouraging note—"You are a true writer . . ." etc. He stated also to friends that he has never seen such rich writing, such real people, etc.—or so exciting a first play. . . . I had him apply for a Rockefeller fellowship—Paul asked to see *Empire*—and has it now.
>
> If there's anything more I could do in the matter, could you advise me? There aren't many talents in the theatre—and I know you have to help where you can. God knows *you've* done it all your life. It's high time the rest of us did. I've interested Audrey Wood in him—and I think she may want him. (She wants *me*, Barrett. Many thanks. She loved *The Year of Pilar*.)

It was not until three years later that Riggs completed *The Year of Pilar*, about a Mexican family in New York and Mexico, but he had finished a first draft in the winter of 1935, in spite of illness. He was also polishing *Russet Mantle*, which was entered for copyright on October 7, 1935.

On October 25 he wrote Paul Green from the San Carlos Hotel in New York: "Thanks for your kind words which reached me two days ago via Franchot Tone at the Waldorf! (It was in his stack of mail.) We're about to cast *Russet Mantle*. John Beal is signed but no one else."[4]

This play was not ready to go into rehearsal until Decem-

ber 16, however. Then he found himself shopping in Santa Fe
for props and costumes that the producers could not find in
New York: the denim work jackets from the J.C. Penney Company that everyone wore in Santa Fe, which he bleached;
chillis from the Spanish & Indian Trading Company for the
set; and a skirt for Helen Craig, as the servant Manuelita,
from the McCrossen Weaving Company.

Riggs disliked driving, but often went by car between California and Santa Fe. Spud Johnson said when interviewed:
"I'd stay at his house when he was in Hollywood and take
care of his dog, and then drive his car out and we'd come
back together. He preferred not to drive. One year Ida, Lynn
and I went to California together. She had the greatest influence on his work and was very helpful in suggesting
rewriting."[5]

Joseph Benton recalled, in "Some Personal Remembrances
about Lynn Riggs": "In the fall of 1935 we met in New York.
One day following lunch as guests of George Gershwin, Lynn
and Gershwin went over their plans to collaborate on a folk-
opera, something similar to *Porgy and Bess* which was then
playing in New York City, but they never concluded these
plans before Gershwin's death in 1937."[6]

While Benton was in New York preparing for his debut at
the Metropolitan Opera on January 10, 1936, Riggs was attending every rehearsal and revising right up to the January 16 premiere of *Russet Mantle*. A sophisticated comedy set
in New Mexico, it ran successfully on Broadway for 117 performances. Critics praised it highly, and more than one suggested it was a contender for the Pulitzer prize. The comedy
is in the contrast between the wealthy but unrealistic older
Anglo generation and the poor, earthy New Mexican Indians.
A high-spirited, beautiful heroine and a poor but proud poet
revolt against pressures from their elders and resolve to make
a new beginning—like many of Riggs's young characters. The
play's humor is overriding, however, and its message emerges
merely as denouement. Perhaps the extensive rewriting dur-

ing rehearsals enhanced the comic values and contributed to *Russet Mantle's* success—whether or not it fulfilled Riggs's intention. Robert Benchley wrote in *The New Yorker* of January 25, 1936: "Whether he wants to be or not, Mr. Riggs is one of the best writers of comedy in the country, and he would do well to go to it, hammer and tongs, and leave the message-bearing to less gifted playwrights.[7] Brooks Atkinson called *Russet Mantle* "wise, fresh and incorrigibly ridiculous, and by all odds, the best thing Mr. Riggs has done." Again in line for a Pulitzer, Riggs was again to be disappointed.

On April 12, 1936, a column in *Screen and Radio Weekly* reported that "Lynn Riggs, brilliant young playwright, is the current white-haired boy of Hollywood" and that both MGM and RKO studies were negotiating to do the movie version of *Green Grow the Lilacs*. The article added, "Lynn Riggs may do the adaptation. Meanwhile he has been brought back to Hollywood by David Selznick to to the dialogue for *The Garden of Allah*."

Strangely, *Green Grow the Lilacs'* potential failed to catch the imagination of movie producers, in spite of all this ball-tossing, five years after its stage production. It was not translated to film until long after its 1943 stage success as *Oklahoma!*

On June 1, 1936, Riggs wrote Betty Kirk that he was delayed in California while *The Garden of Allah* was filmed, with Marlene Dietrich and Charles Boyer. He stayed on location in the desert to rewrite as needed. He commented: "Dietrich, the bitch, is sometimes ravishing. Boyer (at least in the rushes) is superb."[8]

Although some of *The Garden of Allah* was filmed on the same lot where Riggs had been an extra sixteen years earlier in Valentino's first big film, *Ambition*, most of it was filmed outside Yuma, Arizona. According to the *Ford News* of September, 1936, regular temperatures of 120 degrees in the shade and 140 degrees in sun caused many to succumb to heat prostration, including Miss Dietrich on two occasions. The crew performed prodigious feats, among them transport-

ing water six miles in tank trucks for the pool of a constructed
desert oasis. Boyer killed a rattlesnake and got seasick riding a
camel. The sifting, blowing sand harassed both actors and
equipment, and *Newsweek* (November 21) reported that crews
had hauled eighty tons of it back to Culver City for the shoot-
ing of the final scenes. Richard Boleslawski directed the movie,
which was cowritten by Riggs and W. P. Lipscomb. Reviewers
declared it a technicolor triumph.

After completing *The Garden of Allah* for Selznick-Inter-
national, Riggs moved to Paramount, where he did the screenplay for another highly praised film, *The Plainsman,* starring
Gary Cooper as Wild Bill Hickok and Jean Arthur as Calamity
Jane. Written with Waldemar Young and Harold Lamb, and
compiled from stories by Courtney Ryley Cooper and Frank J.
Wilstach, the film dealt on a grand scale with the history of
making the West safe for settlers after the Civil War. The
Hollywood Reporter of November 21, 1936, called the writing
"keen, clear, and admirably direct."

Betty Kirk said that Riggs was also talking to Aaron
Copland about making an opera of *Cherokee Night.* She
thought that he and Gershwin had quarreled about their
planned collaboration.[9]

When he did return to Santa Fe after *Russet Mantle*'s launch-
ing, Riggs said in an interview published on February 1 in *The
New Mexican:* "I'm pleased at having a new kind of feeling
about me in New York. I never wanted to be known as a "folk
playwright," and I myself didn't consider *Green Grow the
Lilacs* that, but it was called that. I'm out of the groove. Right
now I'm known for my comedy."[10]

Samuel French, Inc., telegraphed Riggs on January 29,
1936, that Paramount would probably pay him fifty thousand
dollars for the movie rights to *Russet Mantle* if he would revise
the play's illicit love affair to suit them (the heroine becomes
pregnant). The *Tulsa Tribune* said that RKO wanted it for
Katharine Hepburn, Universal wanted it for Margaret Sulli-

van, and Sam Goldwyn wanted it for Miriam Hopkins. Yet
the play never became a movie.

The February 1 *New Mexican* also reported,

> Mr. Riggs has been working on the script of *Russet Mantle*
> since arriving here, preparing it for book publication. It will be
> published with *The Cherokee Night* next month by Samuel
> French. He has the entire structure of a new play worked out.
> It is to be called "A World Elsewhere" from *Coriolanus*. Mr.
> Riggs plans to go to Mexico to write it. However before that he
> is supposed to go to Hollywood for more picture work.

Riggs dedicated the published volume of two plays to Ida
Rauh.

Delayed in Hollywood, Riggs wrote Spud Johnson on June
26, 1936: "I've hired—at last—a permanent secretary, Marvin
Clarke. I've known him for years. Used to be on switchboard
at Chateau Elysee. Has to brush up on shorthand and typing—so tell Henri I still need him for *Big Lake* while Marvin
straightens out my complicated mass of papers, organizes the
house-running a little, etc." [11] Riggs added that he was looking for a room for Clarke, and he mentioned also "Moises"
among those who worked for him at the Santa Fe house. On
July 1, still on Paramount stationery, he wrote that, though he
was not leaving by July 5 as planned, he would leave soon
and would bring Marvin.

Riggs went to Albuquerque on July 23, 1936, for the University of New Mexico's summer lecture series, where he read
act one of *Russet Mantle*. The *Albuquerque Journal* of July 25
said, "Riggs is writing the script for one of his early plays, *Big
Lake*, to be produced by Syracuse University's motion picture
production classes." The *Journal* said also that *Cherokee Night*
was Riggs's own favorite among his plays.

On September 19, 1936, Oklahoma City's *Daily Oklahoman*
published an article entitled "An Oklahoman in Santa Fe
Leads Enviable Existence," by Frank Dennis:

Riggs is 36 years old, has no office hours, quits work when he wants to, lies in the sun or shade as he prefers and when he prefers, lives alternately in Hollywood, Santa Fe, and New York as the season and his state of mind dictate, and otherwise has an enviable existence. . . .

Just now Riggs is engaged in three tasks that require considerable preoccupation: the training of a black German shepherd puppy named Franz; supervising of construction of an addition to his pleasant home and the writing of a new play.

First, the dog: He was given Riggs by Francis Lederer, the actor, is now 3 months old and is both awkward and graceful, an unbelievable combination. He insists on playfully mauling Riggs' other dog, The Baron, a 3-year-old Scottie given Riggs by Joan Crawford. . . .

Second, the house: Riggs has been building it for several years as he got enough money to make additions. It's a man's house. Riggs is unmarried and his house is built to suit his needs and tastes, without compromise. It is the home of a poet and playwright and dreamer, too, in case you wonder if it is beautiful.

Third, the play: Its title is "World Elsewhere," and it is a play about Americans in Mexico—chiefly Mexico City and Vera Cruz. More than that, Riggs will not divulge because he has found that telling another the plot of a play not written lessens the zest of writing. . . .

"The spoken word is God on the stage, but it is only secondary on the screen," he pointed out. "In the movies, it's what you see that's most important. . . . But they can do almost anything within reason on the stage now," Riggs reminded. "The New York stage today is the best technically anywhere in the world and in history. . . ."

[On writing without having much money:] "Such struggling probably is good for a youngster if it doesn't break his spirit," he decided. "I don't suppose it would break his spirit if he really has something to write. . . ." The play most satisfactory to him from all angles—financial, artistic, reception—was "Russet Mantle."

Riggs works hardest at his writing in the morning. . . . He has pleasant blue eyes, rather thick-lensed horn-rimmed glasses, and thinning blond hair. . . . He has written 14 plays, of which 10 either were produced, bought for production

Riggs on his sunny Santa Fe patio in 1936 with "The Baron," the Scottie dog given to him by Joan Crawford.

but not produced, or published. . . . He expects to visit his old home at Claremore and the University of Oklahoma next spring.

Santa Fe was still where Riggs felt the healthiest, happiest and most free. He wrote Clark on October 6, 1936, "See Santa Fe—and us all, probably in very silly poses, in the October 15 issue of *Vanity Fair*." The *Vogue* magazine of October 15 also featured an article by Spud Johnson describing the Bohemian life in Santa Fe, with two photos of Riggs and other people:

You will find the more successful or the handsome-though-poor ones at the smart tea-parties and the scornful young poets, the more determinedly "modern" painters, and the

"proletarian" artists and writers renting a plumbingless mud
house at ten dollars a month, with a yellow rosebush beside
the well or plum-trees along the irrigation ditch, while the
fashionable portrait-painter, the writer of best-sellers, or the
blue-stocking may have the house next door, which has three
bathrooms and a Spanish garden, and rents for two hundred
dollars. . . . Chummy, that's the word for Santa Fe social life!

Riggs reviewed Margaret Larkin's *Singing Cowboy: A Book of
Western Songs* for *The Nation*. He called the booklet especially
"happy" because Larkin knew the cowboys: "vainglorious,
simple, mildly passionate, chivalrous, whimsical, gay, sentimental, unafraid. . . . about one-half actor." [12]

In his own adobe home at last at 770 Acequia Madre, Riggs
was working on his play and still talking to Gershwin about
a plan for an opera. On October 6, 1936, he wrote: "Listen,
Mr. Clark, Riggs is ensconced in his new study—and is it
a beauty!——and writing *A World Elsewhere*. I'm still in the
planning stage—but I've assembled the right people now to
tell the tale, and the first act plan is approximately settled. . . .

My God, it is beautiful here! I hope you are happy, I hope
the family is happy. When *are* you coming to see me? Because
now I can put you up."

Meanwhile, Mayor J. M. Davis issued a proclamation making Monday, December 14, 1936, Lynn Riggs Day in Claremore. Riggs did not attend. In the assembly at the high school
celebrating the day, a teacher told anecdotes about him. Family members were introduced, and W. G. Riggs said that he
had launched his son in the world by giving him fifty dollars
before his trip on a freight train to Chicago after his high
school graduation. According to the Claremore *Daily Progress*
of December 14, Bill Riggs said that "he had never had any
real positive ambition for his son, but that he had more or less
expected him to follow in this father's path of cattle buying
and selling. But at Norman, Lynn began to show signs of his
abilities and his father decided then that his son was to be-

come a teacher." Lynn was not present, nor is it likely that he was impressed by the occasion.

On January 2, 1937, Riggs wrote Johnson that he and Ida Rauh had gone up for New Year's to Rancho Yucca Loma at Victorville, California, and were going back Sunday. "Did you have a good Christmas?" he asked. "I bled and died for Jesus—and I want to go home." On January 26 he wrote from B. P. Schulberg Paramount Productions, asking Johnson to come out by train or plane and drive him and Ida down to Ensenada for a few days, then back to Santa Fe.

Doubtful at this time about French's handling of his works, Riggs wrote Clark that he would like to give the Theatre Guild rights to those of his plays to be produced within five years and that he was looking for another New York agent. French acted as both his publisher and his marketing agent; a full-time agent, he felt, might secure better backing for his future plays. French had rights as agents for all of them up to and including *Russet Mantle*.

In Hollywood, Rosalie Stewart of Edington, Vincent & Stewart handled his work, "and they have fulfilled all my rather special demands very expertly and with great consideration," he wrote to Miriam Howell of Leland Hayward, Inc., on March 17, 1937: "I won't sign a contract—except for one picture at a time; and they have been very understanding of my desire to run like hell for home the minute I have finished a job. So I couldn't decently leave them, as you will understand." [13]

But French had been generously supportive also, and it was not until the late 1940s that Riggs put his plays, as well as his poems, short stories, and other works, into the hands of another New York agent, Lucy Kroll. He had few works produced or published, however, during that last decade of his life.

In the spring of 1937, Riggs and Johnson made a long visit to Betty Kirk in Mexico City, where she was foreign corre-

Ida Rauh Eastman with "The Baron."

spondent for several American newspapers. Kirk said that
this was the happiest time in her life and that her visitors
loved Mexico, too.[14] Riggs finished writing *A World Elsewhere*,
set in Mexico City and the Yucatan.
He returned on a leisurely ship to New York City, then
went to Santa Fe. He worked to promote Gasque-Molina's
works, as he had earlier. Riggs described the Mexican playwright in a letter to Hal Bynner on June 12, 1937:

He was born in Merida, Yucatan in 1912. . . . He was educated
till the age of eighteen in the United States. . . . I want him to
stay here as my guest as long as he wants to, and he wants
very much to do so. The house runs pleasantly, he has a studio
to paint in—and it's a good arrangement for us both, because,
as you know very well, it's a hard job for one person to inhabit
a house entirely *solo*.

He came in at Laredo, Texas, on May 13, 1937, under a bond
of $500, which I supplied. . . . His permit says he must leave
on or before November 12, 1937.

Hal, can anything be done to allow him—not only to stay
for another six months—but indefinitely?

I'm not going to tell you, Hal, that the American drama
(whatever of it is represented in me) will die on its feet if Enrique has to go back—but I'd like you to know that—in the most
literal fashion he's a big help to me. My new play is laid in
Mexico—and the next one beyond this is about the Mexicans
in and around Lamy.[15]

Bynner wrote a letter on Gasque's behalf, and their efforts
must have succeeded, since Gasque lived with Riggs for some
time. Riggs built a studio room over his garage in Santa Fe for
him and helped arrange shows of his paintings in Santa Fe
and Hollywood.

On July 15, Riggs wrote Betty Kirk, thanking her for a good
time in Mexico, adding:

Enrique is ensconced in a studio and painting like mad. He's to
have a show here and one in Hollywood. . . . We really have
lots of pleasure in the household. Hazel (the Negro girl)

Enrique Gasque-Molina (Ramon Naya) in the studio that Riggs built
for him over the garage in Santa Fe.

brought in her husband to live with us—he's the gardener—
and they're both swell. Next week we go to Central City to see
Ruth Gordon in *A Doll's House*. Then Aug. 1 to Hollywood.

Gasque also enclosed a note. One of his paintings was a por-
trait of Hazel.

Johnson wrote Kirk on July 13 that Riggs had given his
German shepherd dog to Walter Campbell, whose homestead
was near Santa Fe, since

Enrique doesn't like dogs, but does like perfume. . . . Lynn's entire life and habits have been completely changed since our return from your charming but upsetting adopted country. Among other things, they've turned into hermits, see very little of Lynn's old friends, including myself, don't go out socially at all, have stopped drinking and smoking—and even writing and painting as far as I can make out. All very odd indeed.

Although this may have been an exaggeration, it illustrates Riggs's enthusiasm and possessiveness in this new relationship. He was determined to help Gasque advance his career—and he somehow felt that the easy-going spirit of Santa Fe could seduce and absorb them. Once he and Gasque left Santa Fe—at odds with Riggs's old friends—they stayed in California or New York and did not return. Much later, when Gasque was out of the picture, Riggs expressed yearning again for his favorite old home, Santa Fe.

In the *San Francisco Chronicle* of October 17, 1937, Riggs, vacationing, again expressed concern on the state of the theatre:

The theatre is an excellent medium through which to attack or embrace the world. Any play which makes no attempt to realize this function is bad. It is intellectually shoddy to use the theatre for entertainment alone. . . . I am interested in pictures and do not ridicule them as do so many playwrights in Hollywood. After all, they are a medium of drama which you can only hope to use properly.

Riggs wrote Paul Green on October 26 that he was back in New York, at the Schuyler Apartments, with Enrique Gasque, who was writing a new comedy. Riggs said: "I've renounced Hollywood, too—I think forever. I'm now trying to establish a continuous—if not permanent—alliance with the theatre—and things look promising for me to do it." He added, "George O'Neil is in Hollywood. What doing I don't know." Green proposed a tryout of *The Year of Pilar* in Chapel Hill, which they did early in 1939.

In 1938, Riggs was elected to honorary membership in the University of Oklahoma chapter of Phi Beta Kappa. Responding to his election, Riggs's secretary wrote the alumni office on April 29, as follows:

> He flew to Yucatan, Mexico, at the year end—1937, to finish *A World Elsewhere*. Then early in 1938, he took a boat up to New York, stayed a while, then came out to California to write a new play, not a comedy, which is almost finished. . . . He may write a picture here, or finish another play he started some years ago, on an American subject. . . . He is of course greatly honored by his election to Phi Beta Kappa.[16]

Joseph Benton said he and Riggs both were honored to take part in "The Night of Stars" at the 1938 Los Angeles convention of their fraternity, at the Cocoanut Grove of the Biltmore Hotel. He wrote, "It was my pleasure in 1921 to pledge Lynn to Pi Kappa Alpha and he wore his pin with much pleasure. . . . My mother was Lynn's first literary mentor and critic."[17]

In September, 1938, Riggs wired Paul Green from Hollywood to inquire about the deadline for the Rockefeller dramatist fellowships on behalf of his "young candidate," Gasque. Responding immediately, Green asked that Gasque send a copy of *Empire in Durango* to him in North Carolina. Riggs had completed *The Year of Pilar*.

A short story by Riggs, "We Moved to Pomona," appeared in the summer, 1938, issue of Spud Johnson's magazine, *Laughing Horse*. In it Trimble, a restaurant owner, tells of his troubles with Elsie, his daughter and waitress, who attracts men customers too well. After finding out too much of the way Elsie was developing, both physically and morally, he moves his family to Pomona and observes, "Sometimes I can't help wishin' I'd gone on ignorant." The issue reflected Johnson's continuing loyalty to *Laughing Horse*'s regular authors. Besides Riggs's story, he published in it an unfinished play by D. H. Lawrence and a statement by Mabel Dodge Luhan: "Indians are like glowing coals, and the white people like ashes."

French published Riggs's Mexican plays, *A World Elsewhere*

and *The Year of Pilar,* in 1947 in a volume called *Four Plays.* The others were *The Cream in the Well,* an Oklahoma play completed in 1940, and a 1944 play, *Dark Encounter,* set on the eastern seaboard in wartime. Originally a one-act play, *A World Elsewhere* was published by the Dramatists Play Service in 1940 as the lead play in a volume of the best one-act plays of 1939, edited by Margaret Mayorga. Riggs directed the three-act version himself when it was produced from April 8 through 13, 1940, at the San Diego Community Theater. Its other performances were in 1948 at New York's Tamara Daykarhanova School for the Stage, with Andrius Jilinsky directing, on February 5 and 6, and at the University of Iowa from April 23 through May 1.

Enrique Gasque-Molina had adopted the pseudonym Ramon Naya. He was best known for his adaptation of the early seventeenth-century Spanish playwright Lope de Vega's *Peribanez.* Renamed *Peter Among the Horns,* the adaptation was optioned by the Theatre Guild but not produced.[18]

In 1939, Riggs and Naya collaborated on *A Cow in a Trailer,* with music by Jerome Moross. Riggs read this play in 1940 for the benefit of the New Mexico Association of Indian Affairs, and CBS Radio presented the first half of it in April. *Roadside* also was adapted for radio by the Columbia Workshop of CBS and was published in *Best Broadcasts of 1940–41.* Riggs also wrote a one-act play about the Depression, called *The Hunger I Got,* which was published in 1939.

He wrote Paul Green on March 5, 1939, that he had returned to Santa Fe from New York, "still anxious to keep out of Hollywood if possible." He added that he and Ramon Naya felt that the theatre establishment stifled and distorted the creativity of "poetic" playwrights, as well as the directors, dancers, musicians, and other artists. Artists were stifled and "maimed" by backers and producers, and their talents wasted:

> You yourself—your vigorous and lyric talent—have no continuous life in the theatre. It's a disgrace and a loss. It's true that you've had productions, it's true that your name is re-

spected. But you have never been truly seen or even moderately realized. They begin, those little people, to chip you down, blur your edges, resolve your dissonances, rechannel your extravagances, confine your song—even before they deign to put your work in rehearsal. This should not be.

Riggs and Naya had met several times in New York with his old friend Mary Hunter and Andrius Jilinsky to design a more free theatre. He wrote in this same letter to Green, "We want you to know what they [the foursome's points of agreement] are because we unite in a common love for Paul Green; you are the only other American playwright we feel could possibly belong to such an enterprise." He praised Green's innovative dramas, then, in a torrent filling fifteen typed pages, Riggs listed thirty-five points around which a "theatre of the imagination" should be organized. The list, condensed in the following paragraphs, reflected both the frustration of many theatre people and the tenor of the times.

Riggs and his collaborators sought, more than a theatre of amusement, a "vital experience of life." People would come to their theatre not to be educated but to share. From a poem by Pushkin, "The Prophet," the collaborators named it The Vine, because it was to be upward, affirmative, resilient, and "thrusting toward the sun."

Positive, not destructive yet revolutionary, The Vine was to change the world by drawing people to life instead of death: "Our theatre will attack nothing. . . . It will lean, by its very nature to the affirmative principles of goodness and truth. It will be aggressive in the way an oak is aggressive; not as the cannon is."

The Vine was to remind people that theatre is "not a racket; it is an art." Yet it would not be an "ivory tower" theatre, aimed only at producing good plays; it would "attempt to fix and comprehend the world and its forces."

Vine productions were to be artistically innovative but not photographic nor journalistic. "It is not enough to reproduce the color and smell of life. Let the movies do that," said Riggs.

Vine productions were to travel the country, playing in small towns and colleges, learning and drawing vitality from "the dominant, joyous creative spirit of a wide land." Naya said that the plays should remind people of the best in their experience, make them feel stronger, better able to cope. They would not aim to startle people.

The Vine Theatre would have to be both visionary and practical, and there would be no place in its organization for "small egos with their machinations and duplicities." The actors, directors, and backers would have "spiritual stature," humility, and dedication to their ideals. No dilettantes would be allowed.

The Vine building would have to feel warm and homelike to audiences, who would be "the young, not entirely in years, but almost completely so." Jilinsky said all public statements about the theatre should come from the playwrights, "poets, with the habit of eloquence." The Vine would not copy any other theatre, nor compete with Broadway. "Lenin believed in the perfection of the spirit in the right kind of state. We must keep our eyes on, and believe in, the perfection of the spirit in the Theatre State," said Riggs.

Riggs said that he was too eager to rewrite all these notes before mailing. "We feel that the 'body of theory' I mentioned can be built eventually from our correspondence while we are all so widely separated—our Russian and our Irish-American [Hunter] being in New York, our Mexican in Mexico [Naya], our white man in the south [Green] and our red Cherokee in New Mexico."

Riggs described Jilinsky, who had been with the Moscow Art Theatre before coming to New York with Richard Boleslawski on an acting tour. He and his wife taught at Madame Daykarhanova's School of the Theatre. In the spring of 1939, Jilinsky had in rehearsal the American Actors' Company production of Riggs's play *Sump'n Like Wings* that Riggs said was "a thrilling experience—completely and faultlessly realized."

Mary Hunter, Riggs's friend from many years earlier in

Santa Fe, had organized the American Actors' Company. At this time she acted in *Sump'n Like Wings*, and Riggs said that she had a "great interest in the problems of the world, and such a warmth and a sense of justice as one seldom encounters. . . . [She is] extremely practical and has great executive ability." Later, in 1948 and 1949, she directed his plays *All the Way Home* and *Out of Dust*.

Naya's talent, Riggs said, was creating excitement at the Group Theatre, founded in 1931 to produce socially activist plays. In 1939, Naya was working with Riggs on a new kind of musical play. Most of the ideas, Riggs said, owed their inception to Naya, "because of his fertility and purity and real taste."

Green responded enthusiastically to the Vine proposal, but Naya suffered some kind of breakdown and Riggs wrote on March 21, 1939, that he had returned to Mexico to stay "until he is well. Also, his money—what little there is—holds out better there. . . . I'm finishing tag-ends here of our collaboration."

Gasque's play *Mexican Mural* was a finalist in a Group Theatre competition. On June 11, Riggs said that he and Naya had finished their collaboration on *A Cow in a Trailer* in Mexico: "You will like it, Paul. The music is being composed at present." He asked Green to permit Jilinsky to work on Green's *Shroud My Body Down*, and proposed a Vine meeting for fall. Riggs enclosed a copy of a letter from Jilinsky of May 14, 1939, showing his mistakes in English "because they have for me a curious charm": "June month will be my vacation. I'm going to Main. Far, far north. I will have 8 acres island, wind, sea-gulls, and some salted water. July-August again School for the Stage in M. Kisco N.Y. September back to New York." Jilinsky proposed to start a studio for actors and directors, using the plays of Riggs, Green, and Naya, plus classics such as Cervantes, Molière, Calderon, and Shakespeare: "I call you now: the big three. . . . I want to be ready to show you these three plays in September. After you will see you will tell me what do you think: wether it's O.K. or to the hell! . . . I would give very much to have a chance to look at new Ramon's play even through key-hole."

Green stated in a 1980 interview that Riggs's idea of evil was "self-waste" and that his motivations were psychological rather than sociological. The social aims of the Vine proposal came from the others. Riggs was a mystic, sensitive and somewhat self-enclosed, although he was open to all possibilities and set a value on independence in his plays as in the Vine proposal: Riggs's values in his plays and poems showed a "Western and Indian echoing of the rugged American, the sturdy warp, woof and grain of the American spirit," according to Green.

Green mentioned that, paradoxically, Riggs did not do hard physical work, "hated gardening as well as farming, and had an almost Parisian, effeminate quality in his physiology. Equally at ease at a corn-shucking or a soiree, Lynn turned away from the Oklahoma environment that he often wrote about. . . . His lambent mysticism, his communion with the uncaused," Green said, "showed at times in the weakness of his story line." [19]

Although concerned for justice for minorities and for peace, Green was solidly patriotic and did not go along with the leftist leanings of the Group Theatre and similar organizations. Nevertheless, aided by the Theatre Guild, the Group had opened its productions with Green's *House of Connelly*, and near its close in 1941, it produced his antiwar play, *Johnny Johnson*. Both Green and the Guild objected to the Group's Russian Communist influence and withdrew their support. Green outspokenly opposed what he regarded as sordid themes that were surfacing in plays at that time, such as homosexuality. The sexuality in Riggs's plays centered not on homosexuality but on problems in relationships caused by a castrating female, an evil, domineering woman whom Riggs often matched with a father figure interested only in his own physical comforts and sexual satisfactions, not in the needs of his children.

While the theatre world was in transition, so was the world of international politics. The Vine Theatre never materialized, although the decentralization movement to little theatre groups did continue.

In July and August, 1938, Riggs corresponded enthusiastically from Santa Fe with Samuel French, Inc., about a contract with Arvid Englind to produce *Green Grow* in Stockholm. He said, "I think it very important for me to have some kind of international reputation." He asked French to put no obstacle in the way of these negotiations, being willing to let the Swede's contract run for ten years clear of competition.

At the end of 1939 he moved to La Jolla, California for six months, until July, 1940. Again in financial straits, he wrote Barrett Clark on February 7, 1940: "Do you know I've had nothing but rotten luck since you left French—and thus me? . . . The simple truth is that since last May, when I stated my willingness to go to work, there has been no job for me in Hollywood. I don't understand it at all. I know Rosalie is on the job, but it's simply that I've had no play on Broadway since 1936, and no hit picture since *The Plainsman*."

He asked Clark for advice on a lecture tour:

> I've got a lot of new and to me pretty exciting ideas about what the theatre should be—and surely my record ought to be good enough over the country to get small audiences. Sidney [Howard] used to say I was ten times more well known all over America than he was. . . . I've got to do something, and I've got to do it soon. I'm tired of the wolf baying.

He added cheerfully that he was feeling wonderful, in spite of it all. "Meantime, I'm writing a new play," he announced. "Lord, it looks promising! I hope it works out."

Responding with an undated handwritten note on the back of Riggs's letter, Clark discouraged him from the lecture circuit, but suggested instead an offering of appearances at college drama departments for short periods, to direct plays, meet playwriting students, hold a course, or appear publicly to discuss his theories, choosing especially colleges that had done Riggs plays. He stated: "I feel that Garrett [Leverton at Northwestern University] had better do this for you. It strikes me that French would be glad: it is good advertising for them and more dignified for you. This I see as the quickest and best means of raising dough. Likewise it would give you a chance to go on working on your plays."

On April 26, 1940, Riggs answered Clark from La Jolla,

I just came back from Santa Fe where I finished selling my house (even with mortgage I had a little left over to pay debts with!). . . . Part of the reason you know the pictures aren't interested in me, is that I'm not interested in the pictures! It makes a deadly aura about me.

Lord, I think I might be of some value in an up to date university. . . . You may gather that I'm simply bursting with energy these days, so full of plans for work—and actually working!—that I hardly recognize myself. The doldrums I was in are long past. I've never felt so ambitious—or so competent. So you call that a lecture? I call it sense!

After losing his long-sought Santa Fe house after only six years, Riggs spent the rest of his life dreaming of getting back to a *casa querida* in Santa Fe—the one place where he felt completely free, completely accepted by the community, completely happy.

Things began to look up, for a while. French wanted to publish *The Hunger I Got,* a play that was dropped by a Mr. Hagedorn, who differed with the playwright about its structure. Riggs asked Clark on May 9, 1940: "Lord I wish you could get a look at this beautiful place! Any chance? . . . I may have a try out or two East this summer. And I want to see you. Love—and to the family."

While Riggs was trying to work out his financial problems in La Jolla, his friend George O'Neil was stricken with a cerebral hemorrhage in Los Angeles. He had been working for Universal Studios, but was found wandering in a daze in a downtown park. He died in the hospital on May 24, 1940, at the age of forty-two. From their early days at Yaddo, he and Riggs had been close companions, and they had often travelled together. The death of his contemporary reminded Riggs of his own mortality—but he avoided all discussions of death or sickness, and he hid his grief.

Riggs stated his ideas for improving the state of the theatre in an address to the San Diego Community Theatre, entitled "A Credo for the Tributary Theatre," which was printed in the February, 1941, issue of *Theatre Arts* and reprinted in the *Theatre Arts* anthology in 1950.

On June 5, 1940, he wrote Clark from La Jolla—on the beach—that he was still surviving on the proceeds from his Santa Fe house and that he had revised the controversial *Domino Parlor*, now titled *Hang On to Love*. Arthur Hopkins wanted to try it out in August at Locust Valley,

> Also, he plans to try out the opera [*Cow in a Trailer*] this summer—part of it has been broadcast on CBS—*twice* in fact. Enthusiastic demand. . . . If the college thing works out, I'll be damn glad. I'm interested very much—*no matter how these matters go I want to stay in the theatre*. . . . Good Lord, what a world we inhabit! I think I know what *my* job is, however.

CHAPTER 9

NEW YORK YEARS:
SHELTER ISLAND HOME (1941–1950)

. . . If I am human, if I am even less,
save me, my mind, from easy wickedness:
it is so easy to be chill and dear,
fanged and resentful. Rather let me be
like every oak in every wood or year,
spacious with leaves and rooted majesty.
—"The True Seducers"[1]

WHEN HE WAS WRITING *Green Grow the Lilacs*, Riggs had his willful characters Curly and Laurey decide to eat some of the thick, sweet cream that they found in the cool depths of Old Man Peck's well. Riggs knew that they would find it there, since that was where country people in Oklahoma chilled and preserved their cream.

However, in his play *The Cream in the Well*, completed in 1940, the well does not perform its preserving function; instead, like the woman of the house, it sours the things that it is meant to preserve. This story of the incestuous, murderously possessive love that a woman holds for her brother is mild by today's standards, but it soured on Broadway, too. Critics neither understood the custom that was the play's central metaphor nor believed in the characters. They ridiculed Riggs's concept, pummeled his artistry, and severely bruised his confidence. Although he resided again in New York, he

161

no longer felt at home in the commercial theatre there. He began to cut back in the theatre and to send out attempts at growth and fruition in other literary areas: a novel, short stories, television plays, and more poems.

The Cream in the Well was copyrighted on August 16, 1940, from La Jolla, California, and opened in Washington, D.C., on January 14, 1941, with Riggs present. It moved to the Booth Theater in New York on January 20 and closed February 8 after twenty-four performances. Scathing criticism in the January 21 New York papers labeled the play a dramatic failure. In the *World-Telegram*, Sidney B. Whipple called it "a drab and unmoving story." In the *Journal and American*, John Anderson ridiculed it with a one-sentence summary: "Moral: Use refrigerators and avoid incest."

Riggs's attempt to dramatize some of the darker Freudian passions was denounced almost unanimously, but kinder and more thoughtful criticism came from the distinguished critic Joseph Wood Krutch in *The Nation*. After acknowledging Riggs's sincerity and competence, he said, in an article called "Tragedy Is Not Easy":

> . . . . we demand most of all of the author who invites us to a high tragedy. We resist it as we resist all things which are even superficially unpleasant or painful.
>
> What's Hecuba to us or we to Hecuba? As the tired business man says, we have troubles enough of our own. We must, if the tragedy is really to succeed, be caught up and carried away in spite of ourselves. We must find ourselves concerned whether we want to be or not, too moved to ask why we should care. And if Mr. Riggs commands respect and holds attention without quite stilling question or complaint, the reason probably is simply that though his play is good it is not quite good enough to meet the requirements of the most difficult and exacting of dramatic forms.[2]

On February 7, 1941, Riggs wrote from New York to Paul Green, giving as his return address 792 Camino del Pomiente in Santa Fe:

Thanks for your nice note. Well, the play staggered on through its 3 weeks Guild subscription—and closes tomorrow. Audiences still seem spell-bound—but there you are.

I'm leaving for Santa Fe—to stay at Ida Eastman's—and am hoping to get a Hollywood job (a brief one) to keep the wolf from the door. But I don't much trust Rosalie Stewart's ability to get me one any more. I'd much rather pay my bills some other way—but just what way has [not] opened up yet. Anyway, I have plays to write—and somehow they get written.

Robt. Edmond Jones who was mad about Cream insists that I ought to publish all my back plays and get in the position he thinks I deserve in a book. . . . It seems to me a good idea—does it to you? Garrett [Leverton] is taking it up with Random House. . . . I'm in a marvelous good humor—and looking forward to the Sun of New Mexico—I wish I could see you—
Ever, Lynn[3]

Samuel French, Inc., published The Cream in the Well in the collection of Four Plays by Riggs in 1947. Returning to the healing New Mexico sun in 1941, Riggs nevertheless kept his pleasant apartment at One Christopher Street, Greenwich Village, as a permanent address. On February 20 he read the infamous Cream in the Well to a group of his Santa Fe friends, who sprang to its defense. Ida Rauh Eastman and others wrote letters to the "Drama Mailbag" of the New York Times, which were published on February 2 and March 9. Ann Webster's letter said, "Incest is obvious by innuendo during the play and bursts forth at the end in a staggering climax—not an anti-climax as Brooks Atkinson said."[4]

Riggs had left Santa Fe in 1938 with some estrangement from many of his old friends, according to Spud Johnson. But now that Enrique Gasque-Molina was no longer with him, old ties could be renewed. He had sold his house there, but always had a warm welcome from Ida. She was often in New York also, ready to come when he needed her.

Johnson said Riggs longed to sit on a sunny patio and write plays: "Always so convinced that it was worthwhile, he had no kind of modesty about that." He had methodical and neat

working habits, with a handful of sharpened pencils nearby
and nothing to distract his almost illegible scrawling. Whether
he was visiting or at home, he always excused himself from
company for a couple of concentrated hours of writing.

Johnson said that by this time Riggs had changed, burned
from superficial relationships in Hollywood and brutal rejec-
tions in New York; he was more serious than ever in associa-
tions with people:

> If he liked a person, he loved him; he wasn't interested in
> causal associations. . . . [With Gasque-Molina] he was so de-
> termined that . . . their friendship should not be tainted as it
> were by the sort of social life here, which always does exist in
> any art colony. So he withdrew himself—didn't want all this
> social life, becoming more and more complicated—quite dif-
> ferent from when he first came, when it was a small town. It
> was a kind of rejection of what was happening here. He re-
> fused to go to parties. . . .[5]

This possessiveness of Riggs, who was then in his late thirties, reflected his fear of alienation, rejection, and loss. Although he and Gasque were together for a few years in New
Mexico, California, and New York, that relationship, like so
many others in his life, ended too soon. In 1941 Gasque was
back in Mexico. O'Neil was dead.

A break in his fortunes came in late July, when the Santa Fe
and Waco, Texas, newspapers announced Riggs's appointment at Baylor University as a Rockefeller professor. He was
to teach a course called "Drama and the Playwright."[6] While
in Waco, he served as an advisory director of Shakespeare's
Macbeth, which was presented at the university on November 13, and he directed his own play *Borned in Texas* (formerly
Roadside), which opened December 8. He said in an interview
in the *Waco Tribune-Herald* on September 21, 1941, that his
course was going to teach students not how to write plays but
prewriting skills: "Its purpose is to direct the student in the organization of his qualities and the evaluation of his experience
for creative art. You may call it a course in self-examination.

Most people are deplorably lacking an awareness of their own potentialities resulting from episodes in their own lives."

Paul Baker, the young director of the school of drama at Baylor, had invited Riggs on the recommendation of Witter Bynner. The plays opened in a new, modern studio theater which Baker had designed. Although he took leave for Army Special Service in 1942, Baker was to return to continue a distinguished career at Baylor. He produced Riggs's *Green Grow the Lilacs* there in 1947 and 1952. In July, 1952, he took the production to France, to the Baylor Arts School in Paris, for four performances.

Baker described Riggs in an interview in October, 1979, as an inspirational lecturer, more creative than academic, who had good rapport with students. He often talked with students, even though he was "rather reclusive, since he was writing at the time also." Students came and brought food for Sunday evening dinners at Baker's house, where Riggs would sit on the rug, smoke his pipe, and talk for hours in his slow, thoughtful way. "An intelligent speaker, he never forced his ideas on anyone." He dressed informally in a sport coat and short-sleeved shirt and was much admired by students. Baker commented that "*Green Grow* stands as the best play on Oklahoma, in atmosphere, plot and dialogue."[7]

One of Riggs's students, Gene McKinney, later of the drama department of Trinity University in San Antonio, said in October, 1979, that Riggs seemed rather shy and that he spoke in anecdotal ways, using no prepared notes, telling stories about early days in Oklahoma. He said that Broadway was provincial and had difficulty accepting the regional writer. "I admired his good ear for the sound of the region—his authenticity captured the flavor of the region so beautifully in dialogue," McKinney said. "He had no pretense, all very honest both in his plays and his person. Comfortably informal. He and Waco society paid no attention to each other."

Another former student, Virgil Beavers, said that Riggs, a charming lecturer, stressed "abnegation"—the need for the writer to get out of the way and let the material speak. "He read often out of his own journal and urged the student to explore himself by writing in a journal."[8]

Riggs had dedicated *Roadside* to his father, who came to Baylor to see it for the first time on opening night with his third wife, Minnie. Paul Baker described W. G. Riggs as "a short, soft-spoken man in a big Stetson hat."

When his semester as visiting professor ended, Riggs returned to California, where he registered for the draft on February 14, 1942. He was drafted in July, while working on a picture for Universal. In an interview in the *Fort Ord* (California) *Panorama* the former writer of antiwar poetry, forty-two years old, sounded a clear call of dogged patriotism: "Here— in the Army—is our opportunity to become new men. We are sharply related to our time, and responsible to our time. Most of the soldiers I've talked to are feeling that the skies may crack and hell may freeze—but they'll be damned if they'll let themselves or their country down!" On November 23, 1942 he was transferred to the 846 Signal Service Photo Battalion at Wright Field in Dayton, Ohio, where he worked on training films.

In that same year, Aaron Copland composed "Rodeo," which was choreographed for the ballet by young Agnes DeMille. DeMille was preparing for her big step to fame in 1943, when she choreographed the dances for *Oklahoma!* According to Jacques Hardré of Chapel Hill, Riggs had played folk tunes for Copland and other friends in New York and thus had some influence in inspiring the music for "Rodeo."[9] Later, in 1950, Copland arranged and published *Old American Songs*, featuring a number of songs from Riggs's boyhood that Riggs had sung to the composer, including "The Boatmen's Dance," "Long Time Ago," "Simple Gifts," and "I Bought Me a Cat." Copland, along with many other theatre people, autographed a panel which decorated the bar in Riggs's New York home.[10]

While at Chanute Field in January, 1943, to make a training film, Riggs visited the theater director at the University of Illinois, his friend Wesley Swanson. Interviewed for the *Daily Illini*, Riggs said eight of his plays had been under contract for production in Scandanavian countries, starting in Stockholm, but they were postponed for the duration of the war.

Riggs teamed up with another famous writer-soldier, Private William Saroyan, to write a show called *The Gay Nineties*, which was produced from March 18 through 20 in Dayton, Ohio, for the benefit of the Soldiers Service Club. Both writer-soldiers were stationed at Wright Field and writing for Uncle Sam.

Numerous show-biz careers, like Riggs's own, were suspended for the duration of the war. But when the Theatre Guild opened Riggs's step-play, *Oklahoma!*, a version of *Green Grow the Lilacs* set to new music by Rodgers and Hammerstein, on March 31, 1943, Technician Third-Class Lynn Riggs sat quietly in the audience. When he wrote Moe of the Guggenheim foundation on May 15 about *Green Grow the Lilacs's* relationship to the new musical, he added: "I've been in the Army ten months—I'm here [Wright Field, Dayton, Ohio] in a Signal Corps Co. attached to the Air Forces, making training films. But I'm getting out in a few weeks—over-age—to work for the OWI." He signed "S/Sgt. Lynn Riggs." [11]

On June 2, 1943, he was separated from the service and went to New York to write for the Office of War Information. That May his half-brother Joe married his wife, Edrye, and took a Greenwich Village apartment around the corner from Riggs's place at One Christopher Street. They went together to plays and restaurants and became, for the first time, close friends. [12]

His OWI films were documentaries for the purpose of making friends for the United States in occupied and allied countries. For example, one narrated by Ingrid Bergman, intended for showing in Sweden, showed how some Swedish-

168

Americans were faring. He used some newsreel shots, narration, and commentary.

He collaborated with dancer José Limon to write a dance poem which the Army had requested for use in a war-bond–drive show in September, 1943. He was present when *Fun for the Birds*, a soldier revue, was given in Richmond, Virginia, on September 5. It featured a short work by him, *We Speak for Ourselves*, portraying the thoughts of a soldier faced with the radical change of living experienced in the Army. It starred Limon, then a private, and Private Diane Roberts of the Women's Army Corps. *Theatre Arts* published the poem with a full-page illustration in December, 1943.

Riggs, then forty-four, wrote Betty Kirk Boyer on December 20 from his Christopher Street apartment, kidding her as usual: "Did you know I was in the Army for 11 months—and a damn good soldier too—machine gunner." [13]

Visiting Ida in Provincetown, Massachusetts, Riggs wrote on July 27, 1944, replying to a work proposal from Barrett Clark:

> The answer is Yes, yes, yes.
>
> So here you are, as always, looking out for that rare and impossible breed, the playwright. It's just like you. And I don't know how anybody has ever gotten anywhere—in themselves or publicly—without your generosity and kindly attention.
>
> I'm up here working. I started a novel—but it turned out to be a play (I guess I'll *never* write a novel)—and it looks highly promising. It's called *Dark Encounter*, and it's just that. It begins on June 6 this year and ends the next night. I'm three-fourths through it now. No one can fail, at this juncture, to want to see the rest of it—so in the last quarter, I hope to deliver. Pray for me. . . .

Copyrighted October 6, 1944, this wartime play set on Cape Cod in anxious times was published in Riggs's *Four Plays*, but never produced. Riggs defended it in an interview reported in the *Daily Iowan* on April 22, 1948:

Scenes which begin naturalistically, he says, dissolve into a psychological treatment which is partly non-realistic. When he wrote the play in 1944, frightened producers had the "audacity," he says, to think he pleaded for a soft peace for Germany. "But your Americans are such heels," they told him. To which Riggs replied, then as now, "All people involved in wars are heels and the human race is the grand heel."

In 1945 he completed his twenty-first play, *Laughter from a Cloud*, a sophisticated comedy about Americans, which Eloise Wilson later compared to T. S. Eliot's *The Cocktail Party*, which it preceded by five years:

> In each of these society problem plays, a highly intelligent, socially prominent person is in marital difficulty; in "Laughter from a Cloud," the "trouble shooter" is the ex-husband, who understands his artist wife and simply recommends that they renew their love and marriage. The artist, Lisa Walker, has "curtained out" the mountain which symbolizes for her, as the ex-husband says, the majesty, awe, danger, and rapture of life. This mountain symbolizes evil and fear for the superstitious New Mexico primitive. In this play, Riggs acknowledges, for the first time, that an artist loses his worth when he withdraws from the world.[14]

The lead character was based on his artist friend of Santa Fe, Gina Knee, just as Enright in *Dark Encounter* was based on a German-American friend. In 1946, Riggs worked on a Georgia play that was an adaptation of Erskine Caldwell's novel *Tragic Ground*. It was to have had music by Copland, dances by De Mille, and sets by Oliver Smith. Bert McCord reported in the *New York Herald-Tribune* of July 5, 1946, that the play was finished. Copland was teaching at the Berkshire Summer Festival and had promised to do the score by September 1. Smith, a codirector of the Ballet Theatre and set designer for *Rodeo*, had begun sketches for the production. This play appears to have been lost.[15]

In June, 1945, John Golden announced the appointment of Barrett Clark to head a committee to administer the Golden

Fund for Drama Writing, set up at Columbia and New York universities and New York's City College. Other members were Riggs, Betty Smith, Otto Harbach, and Kenyon Nicholson. The fund was to lend money without security to selected dramatists. However, claiming Golden's aim was self-serving publicity, Riggs backed out in a letter to Clark on August 7: "Riggs is damned mad if you want to know."

Riggs also worked in 1945 and 1946 on a dance drama, "The Oedipus Story"; a short story, "Eben, the Hound, and the Hare"; and a television script, "Do I Have to Cross the River?" plus more poems. His attendance at plays was frequently mentioned in the "Gossip of the Rialto" column in the *New York Times*. *Borned in Texas* was performed in Connecticut by the Stamford Associates during the week of June 4, 1945, with Celeste Holm as Hannie, directed by Victor Jory. Riggs and other celebrities attended the opening, which was an unsuccessful tryout for Broadway.

In March, 1946, Riggs attended Gilmore Brown's production of *Hang On to Love* at the Pasadena Playhouse in California. *Laughter from a Cloud* was in casting, and *Tragic Ground* (now lost) was almost finished, after which he resumed work on *Verdigris Primitives*, which later became *All the Way Home*. On November 26, 1946, he came to Oklahoma City to see the travelling production of *Oklahoma!* He and Richard Rodgers, Oscar Hammerstein, Rouben Mamoulian, Agnes De Mille, and Theresa Helburn were greeted by a snow and sleet storm. A parade was cancelled, and both the celebrities and the celebration were chilled. Riggs quickly returned to New York after the production to resume work.

On November 27, 1947, he responded to Marion Starr Mumford of Claremore about his characters:

> How out of the past your note comes to me! I find it hard to answer such questions as you ask me—but for you I want to try. . . .
> Aunt Eller is based on my wonderful Aunt Mary—(Mrs.

John Brice)—and some of the things I vaguely knew about my mother—who died when I was two—(Her name, too, was Ella. "Eller," as people called her). . . .
     Laurey was my cousin Laura Thompson, who died some time ago. She was glowing and lovely—and made a deep and tender and lasting impression on me. Curly was a cowboy who used to work for my aunt. . . .
     I'm happy you heard your father's name. I knew him only slightly—but his name had for me as a boy great glamor—Best to you, Marion—and I hope this will do. Hastily, Lynn.[16]

In 1947 and for several years after, Riggs's companion was a young artist and dancer with José Limon's troupe, Gui Machado. In April they travelled to New Orleans, Taos, Chapel Hill, and Williamsburg. On April 8, Riggs telegraphed Paul Green from Taos: "HEADING YOUR WAY EN ROUTE NEW YORK ARRIVING CHAPEL HILL APRIL SIXTEENTH PLEASE RESERVE ROOM FOR TWO AT COLONIAL INN OR SOME PLACE. WANT TO SEE YOU AND FAMILY REGARDS. Green arranged reservations at the Colonial Inn and also at the historic Williamsburg Inn for "the well-known American playwright and his companion."
     On April 18, Riggs wrote the Greens from Williamsburg: "The map was perfect—and so is this place. We saw the hole in the ground by the lake—it'll be quite beautiful. Mr. Green [Inn manager] really came through. I feel like Mme. Recamier—who *never* went to the privy. . . . It was nice to see you even briefly. Come to New York soon."
     On May 20 he wrote Spud Johnson jubilantly that he and Gui had bought a "farm house" on Shelter Island and would take possession on June 14.[17] Gui was studying ballet and modern dance with José Limon, and Riggs was rehearsing *Laughter from a Cloud*, which opened in Falmouth, Massachusetts, on June 3, 1947, starring comedienne Ilka Chase. It did not proceed to Broadway, however.
     At last financially comfortable after *Oklahoma!*'s big success, Riggs had bought a two-story white frame house, surrounded by lilacs, on St. Mary's Road on Shelter Island, off the tip of

Long Island. He called his retreat "the farm," but this was more nostalgia than reality.

The house was often filled with New York theatre and arts people. According to Betty Kirk Boyer, it was "said to be filled with young men friends who exploited him for his great wealth earned from *Oklahoma!*"[18] But his good friend Nathan Kroll said in a 1979 interview, "If that's true, it was all right with Lynn. He might have known some were taking advantage of him, but he generously welcomed their company."[19]

Riggs wrote Johnson on October 5 that José Limon and his wife, Pauline, were visiting him and Gui on Shelter Island. In a convivial mood, they had painted in bright letters on one of the cabinets that served as a bar, "La Borracho de Isla Refugio—Cantina & Pulqueria—Riggs Y Machado, Props." Gui continued to paint pictures, and he created Christmas cards for the two of them to send to friends.

Riggs completed two great Oklahoma plays in 1948, *All the Way Home* and *Out of Dust*, both of which departed from his earlier works to show love in its finer aspects. Based on photographs in a family album, *All the Way Home* (formerly called *Verdigris Primitives*) opens with characters appearing two by two in spotlights, and throughout the play at important moments characters freeze into tableaux like photographs, with music supporting the mood. The seven women portrayed are those Riggs loved as a child: his Aunt Mary, her cousins, and her five daughters. Eloise Wilson noted the parallelism between generations: "In each generation there is a woman who loves deeply and is loved tenderly; in each there is a frolicsome Wife of Bath. A picture in the family album haunts the story and helps foreshadow a dream sequence that occurs while the family seeks refuge in the storm cellar. The dream gives Mary courage not to repeat her father's selfishness."[20] Riggs wrote Spud Johnson on February 14, 1948, that Engel, a musician, had written good background music for eight *a cappella* voices, but the financial backing was lost when the play was ready for New York.

On April 11, Witter Bynner, in residence in his beloved Mexico, wrote Riggs after reading his newly published book of *Four Plays:*

> I am instantly struck by your phenomenal growth during the six years. . . . Though I liked the themes in both Mexican plays, I had an odd feeling that they were translations, that the dialogue—at least in English—was overcharged, failing at times to make the people seem natural. The best study of a Mexican, for me, is the General, not only in characterization but in his insolent and yet jealous bantering of Americans. . . . No wonder our New Mexican neighbors throbbed over THE CREAM IN THE WELL. It is about very live people and done with sure strokes. But the book culminates with DARK ENCOUNTER, one of your finest and written throughout in telling idiom. . . . a fatalistic irresponsibility which grimly echoes the currents of men at war, the clashes of unthinking vanity and greed, this morbid embracing of death. Congratulations.[21]

On April 27, 1948, Riggs was among the first five alumni of the University of Oklahoma to be honored with a citation for their merit "in advancing a better contemporary society and their efforts to make Oklahoma a better known state." The others chosen by the secret alumni committee were Everette Lee DeGolyer, noted geologist; Mike Monroney, Democratic senator from Oklahoma; Major General W. S. Key, the Oklahoma state adjutant; and Lieutenant General Raymond S. McLain, former comptroller general of the United States Army. Riggs did not attend, but wrote Walter Campbell on April 17:

> Thanks for the good word. I'm very pleased about the citation thing, as anyone would be. Unfortunately, I can't be there April 27, so I won't get to see you and talk a lot of things over with you—after how many years! (I go to Iowa U. for 10 days next Monday for a kind of Festival—three Riggs plays—two of them new). And I start rehearsals June 5 for *Verdigris Primitives* here—so I can't make the Conference. I'll be out yet sometime however—it would be pleasant to see you.[22]

The citation in the Achievement Day Program said Riggs created a "vivid embodiment of the daring spirit of the pioneer in all his work" and praised, ironically, "his dynamic promotion of the state through the distinctive American musical, *Oklahoma!*." Riggs made a brief and humble reply: " . . . Actually, I have done little in life except try to discover who I am and what my relation to the world I know consists of. In the world itself I have never really felt at home. . . . [My achievement is] pitiable and it's puny—and it's all I know." [23]

Verdigris Primitives, renamed *All the Way Home*, opened in Ridgefield, Connecticut, on August 3, 1948, with Bambi Linn in the cast, directed by Riggs's long-time friend Mary Hunter. It played at two summer theaters in New Jersey and Connecticut, but did not go on to New York. The Theatre Guild was to produce *Out of Dust* at the Westport Country Playhouse in Connecticut late in the summer of 1949.

All the Way Home is similar to *Green Grow the Lilacs* in setting and cultural material, but it emphasizes female characters, and its structure Riggs called "Impressionistic." He hoped to immortalize in drama for the audience's enjoyment the women who had most brightened his own life. *Out of Dust*, although set in the American West, reflects Riggs's lifelong admiration for the lustiness of Shakespeare. Eloise Wilson wrote:

> Old Man Grant is the King Lear of the Shawnee Trail, denied by and plotted against by his older sons but loved by the youngest. In every respect this is Riggs's greatest play: the growth of the plot from the dust and envy of the trail to the final betrayal is strong and steady. . . . In "Out of Dust" three great influences upon Riggs—the Bible, Shakespeare, and folk song—have been combined into a three-dimensional drama. [24]

After these plays failed to achieve recognition, Riggs turned to a novel, *The Affair at Easter*, a play, *Some Sweet Day*, and a second television play, "Someone to Remember." *Some Sweet Day*, set at the time of Halley's comet's pass close to the earth in 1910, praises courage instead of fear, and looks toward the "sweet day" in 1986 when the comet will return and find

Riggs in 1949 at age fifty.

mankind's desperate needs for food, freedom, and love will have been supplied.

"Someone to Remember" looks back to the spiritualist "Mother Lake" of his 1922 Chautauqua troupe. It is set during that memorable summer in Riggs's life and occurs partly at Red Cloud, Nebraska. Riggs characterizes the spiritualist, Mother Latham, as "a woman who made life large, not mean and empty. Someone who made a difference, you see, just by being."[25] During the last five years of his life Riggs dabbled in spiritualism, recalling in spirit the women who gave him love in his childhood and youth, including the faintly remembered mother of his infancy.

CHAPTER 10

REFLECTED GLORY:
GREEN GROW THE LILACS
RETURNS AS *OKLAHOMA!* (1943)

> . . . . *Morning forever when you know it least—*
> *Alaskan men turning to greet each other;*
> *Bolivian giant and Madagascar beast*
> *one and the same—and European brother,*
> *with the dazed look of children at the breast,*
> *of morning long forgotten with the rest.*
> —"It Will Be Morning"[1]

AS THE GLOOMY UNCERTAINTIES of World War II hung over the country, the Theatre Guild, having played an important part in the flowering of American theatre in the twenties and thirties, was struggling for its life. In 1942, when it was considering producing *Oklahoma!*, it had only thirty thousand dollars in the bank, and its energies were invested in the Stage Door Canteen, where stars entertained servicemen passing through New York. The group wanted, like Riggs, to do "not a musical comedy in the familiar sense but a play in which music and dancing would be aids to and adjuncts of the plot itself in telling the story."[2] Convinced that *Green Grow the Lilacs* was what they were looking for, they searched for an investment of ninety to a hundred thousand dollars and were met with the same kind of opposition Riggs had with the original play. "I don't like plays about farm hands," one person said. An-

other asserted, "You can't kill people in a musical."[3] But the
money was found, and theatre historians agree that the resulting play changed the face of American musical theatre.

Playing for five years and nine months, *Oklahoma!* held the
record of 2,248 performances on Broadway before Frederick
Loewe's *My Fair Lady* surpassed it a generation later. It grossed
over $7 million dollars before it toured for ten years in 250
cities, where it was seen by ten million more people and
grossed another $20 million. In London it had the longest run
in the history of the Drury Lane Theater, and it has played in
translations around the world: in Germany, South Africa,
Sweden, Denmark, Australia, France, and Italy. It toured the
Pacific with the U.S. Armed Forces. For the first time the
entire score of a Broadway musical was issued on records,
by Decca, which sold over $1 million worth of *Oklahoma!*
Then the movie, released in 1955, grossed over $8 million—
and both the movie and the play continue to be shown to
this day.

Investors who reluctantly shelled out $1,500 to back a "cow-
boy" show earned more than $50,000 in return. *Oklahoma!* re-
ceived the first Pulitzer citation ever awarded a musical play.
All this from a folk play that lacked the traditional chorus
girls! A scorner said in the beginning, "no legs, no jokes—no
chance!" Although Riggs did not get rich on it as he probably
should have, his royalties of $250 per week provided him a
steady income—for a change—for the rest of his life.

On May 15, 1943, Staff Sergeant Lynn Riggs of Company C,
846th Signal Service Photo Battalion, at Wright Field, Dayton,
Ohio, wrote to Henry A. Moe of the Guggenheim foundation:

> You must know by this time that the sensational hit *Oklahoma!*
> is just our old friend *Green Grow the Lilacs* in a new dress. It's a
> great delight to me, you may imagine, to see that play which
> has been kept alive all over the country through these inter-
> vening years by numerous productions strike out to make a
> new kind of dimension again. I just thought I'd like to thank
> you and the Foundation herewith—for of course *Green Grow* is
> a Foundation baby.

The noncommittal title of *Away We Go!* in the New Haven tryouts was changed to *Oklahoma!*—retaining the exclamation mark—before the musical opened in New York at the St. James Theater on March 31, 1943, an instant and overwhelming hit. Arminta Langner of the Theatre Guild, daughter of a Pawnee, Oklahoma, sheriff, had wanted to name the play "The Cherokee Strip," but was voted down because of the obvious connotations.

The Guild saw that *Green Grow the Lilacs* was genuine Americana, rich in pioneer history and lusty with grit and humor. Theresa Helburn, coproducer with Lawrence Langner, said, "We thought this was an ideal time to do a musical play about America, and we wanted to recapture that special American flavor in the original script. We wanted to keep the gaiety and freshness, the poetry and humor of the people in Lynn Riggs' play."[4]

Rouben Mamoulian came from Hollywood to direct the show, and Agnes De Mille left the Ballet Russe to do the choreography. De Mille's creation of the "Dream Ballet," in which Laurey acts out her ambivalent feelings toward her rival suitors, Curly and Jud, elevates the play above any ordinary Western.

Oscar Hammerstein said he had been planning to do a musical version of *Green Grow the Lilacs* for two years when composer Richard Rodgers asked him to write the script and lyrics. Rodgers began by throwing out the old folk songs so loved by Riggs, but Hammerstein acknowledged that his script is Riggs's, with very few changes from the original. He told the *New York Times* after the opening that he and Rodgers

give credit where credit is due. . . . Mr. Riggs' play is the wellspring of almost all that is good in *Oklahoma!* I kept most of the lines of the original play without making any changes in them for the simple reason that they could not be improved upon—at least not by me. But more important than this, *Green Grow the Lilacs* had a strange combination of qualities—lust, melodrama, authentic folk characters and a sensitive lyric quality pervading the whole story. I feel that in some measure we were able to preserve these values in the musical version and they compose a very important contribution to its success. Lynn Riggs and *Green Grow the Lilacs* are the very soul of *Oklahoma!*[5]

In a similar tribute, Rodgers said he "just put the lyrics on the piano and the music wrote itself." As an example, consider Riggs's poetic stage directions introducing his first scene in *Green Grow the Lilacs:*

It is a radiant summer morning several years ago, the kind of morning which, enveloping the shapes of earth—men, cattle in a meadow, blades of the young corn, streams—makes them seem to exist now for the first time, their images giving off a visible golden emanation that is partly true and partly a trick of imagination focussing to keep alive a loveliness that may pass away. And, like the voice of the morning, a rich male voice outside somewhere begins to sing: "As I walked out one bright sunny morning, I saw a cowboy way out on the plain. His hat was throwed back and his spurs was a-jingling. . . ."[6]

Similarly, in *Oklahoma!* the handsome cowboy Curly, coming on stage to meet Aunt Eller, who is churning butter, sings, "There's a bright golden haze on the meadow. . . . all the cattle are standin' like statues, the corn is as high as a elephant's eye. . . . All the sounds of the earth are like music." Hammerstein commented, on the Decca record album,

That was for Dick and me—to set the mood of the show for us. And to set the mood for the audience, too. When Curly begins to sing offstage as the curtain goes up, and then wanders into the front yard of Laurey's farmhouse singing: "Oh, What a Beautiful Mornin'," you can feel the audience relax and smile, and settle back; you can feel them knowing the show will be fresh and easy-going and charming.

They understood that the star of the play was not a particular character, to be played by the traditional Broadway big name, but Oklahoma life itself, at the brink of statehood—the courageous, rowdy, innocent, sometimes vulgar yet hopeful culture of recent pioneers in the unique region called Indian Territory. Said director Mamoulian:

> To sustain the reality of the play properly balanced with the elements of song and dance was a difficult problem. But we didn't mind the hard work because we believed very much in *Oklahoma!* We believed in the spirit of it, so warm, so American, so sturdy. That is a good spirit to put on the stage today; we wanted to do it justice.[7]

Theresa Helburn said, "New York took *Oklahoma!* to its heart, and a new kind of play with music had been created. It is my great pride the critics have claimed that in this type of musical America had made its greatest and most original contribution to the theatre of the world."[8]

Hammerstein enhanced the part of comic Ado Annie. He changed the play-party to a box social and Jeeter's name to Jud. Instead of Jud setting fire to the haystack on which Laurey and Curly have been placed by the rowdy shivaree mob, the drunken Jud tries to kiss Laurey; in both cases, he struggles with Curly and falls on his own knife (the later movie version restored the fire). In the troublesome last act, instead of returning Curly to Claremore's jail, Hammerstein added a quick on-the-spot trial and acquittal, and thus a happier ending.

Both versions preserve Curly's visionary speech to Laurey on their future:

> Oh, I got to learn to be a farmer, I see that! Quit a-thinkin' about dehornin' and brandin' and th'owin' the rope, and start to git my hands blistered a new way! Oh, things is changin' right and left! . . . They gonna make a state outa this, they gonna put it in the Union! Country a-changin', got to change with it! Bring up a pair of boys, new stock, to keep up 'th the way things is goin' in this here crazy country! Life jist startin' in fer me now. Work to do! Now I got you to he'p me—I'll mount to sump'n yit![9]

Riggs's original dialogue, the authentic voice of early Oklahoma, can be traced almost word for word in the Hammerstein version. Both, for example, keep widow Aunt Eller's prescription for "heartiness" as Laurey mourns the disastrous events of her wedding night's shivaree and Curly's subsequent arrest: "Oh, lots of things happens to a womern. Sickness, bein' pore and hungry even, bein' left alone in yer old age, bein' afraid to die—it all adds up. That's the way life is—cradle to grave. And you c'n stand it. They's one way. You got to be hearty. You *got* to be."[10]

Ashamed of herself for being "sich a baby," Laurey replies, "I want to be the way you air." Aunt Eller responds: "Fiddlesticks! *Fat*—and old? You couldn't *h'ar* me to be the way *I* am. Why, in a year's time, you'll git so t'ard even of lookin' at me, you and Curly'll run me off the place, 'th a tin can tied onto my tail."[11]

Riggs told a Dayton audience in April, 1943, that Hammerstein had asked him if he had suggestions to make about the adaptation, but that he had had few and was generally pleased with the show.[12] Ida Rauh Eastman told Charles Aughtry, however, that Riggs preferred the simplicity of his own more authentic rendering of Oklahoma life.[13] He was sad, of course, that the old songs and ballads he hoped to preserve in the play were lost. Nevertheless, Rodgers and Hammerstein created some immortal melodies. Not least was the rousing title song, added to the last act during the Boston tryouts, which was adopted in 1953 by the Oklahoma legislature as the official state song.

Many theatrical reputations were enhanced by *Oklahoma!* As Curly, Alfred Drake won the award for the "best male performance in a musical comedy" from the New York Drama Critics Circle; Joan Roberts, a newcomer, played Laurey; screen performer Howard De Silva played Jud; and Celeste Holm, Ado Annie.

On the frontier families were extended and valued. The hazards of territory life; its boisterous celebrations, vigorous dances, and sentimental songs; the brash innocence of young people in their mating scurry; their early and eager entry into

adult responsibilities; the hard life that matched their desti-
nies with a spiritually unbounded environment—all these
make *Green Grow the Lilacs* and *Oklahoma!* more than simple
Westerns. Indeed, they are not about cowboys versus Indians, although both the original play and the musical version convey some feeling of cowboys versus farmers. Nor is
the plot simply a showcase for music, whether folk songs or
popular tunes; nor simply a love story, but a preservation in
drama of a life lived not so long ago. "A trick of the imagination focussing to keep alive a loveliness that may pass away,"
like Riggs's introductory golden morning, this drama stirs the
Jungian racial consciousness of people everywhere who have
weathered hardships to survive as a nation.

Still touring the United States, the cast celebrated the musical's tenth anniversary in 1953 in Washington, D.C. And still
looking back in a nostalgic glow of amazement and appreciation, members of the original cast, led by Celeste Holm, celebrated *Green Grow the Lilacs'* fiftieth anniversary in 1981 at the
Plaza Hotel in New York, where a revival of *Oklahoma!* was
playing on Broadway. They placed there a plaque commemo-
rating the cast party on the first opening night of *Oklahoma!*,
given at the Plaza by Oklahoma's unofficial ambassador, Perle
Mesta.

Oklahoma!'s enthusiastic reception in 1943 surprised the
critics and brought a breath of fresh Oklahoma air to the New
York stage. The twenty-five standing-room spaces were filled
at every performance, and as many people were turned away
as admitted. In "The Theatre" column of the *New Yorker*,
Robert Benchley called the play "completely enchanting, gay,
stylish, imaginative, and equipped with some of the best music and dancing in a long time." He said the musical avoided
distorting its original, as so many had in the past:

> After rereading Mr. Riggs's drama (a very fine and original
> one, by the way), I can't see that the version at the St. James
> has omitted anything of consequence. Naturally, there is no

special definition of character—though the villainous Jud . . .
is still a complicated and repulsive piece of work—and there
has been some tampering with the facts, especially at the end.
On the whole, however, it seems to me that Richard Rodgers,
Oscar Hammerstein II and their associates have heightened
rather than diminished their material.

Another influence of *Oklahoma!* on current theatre was that
it depended on no jokes that would have ired a censor, yet it
played to sold-out houses. Not since *Show Boat* had a play
been so completely enjoyable in this way.

Critic Richard Watts, Jr., reminded the play's admirers of its
source, in the *New York Herald-Tribune*, August 8, 1943.

> I think there should be a word about Lynn Riggs, an interest-
> ing playwright who has never achieved the success or the es-
> teem he has so frequently been on the verge of receiving. In
> "Green Grow the Lilacs" he wrote what he intended as a sort
> of singing folk tale of American pioneer life and managed it
> with charm and freshness. It is pleasant to note that this best
> of his works now has reached its proper niche as one of Amer-
> ica's best loved musical narratives.[14]

On seeing the play again a year later, Watts wrote: "There
has been a surprising minimum of applause bestowed upon
Lynn Riggs, who wrote "Green Grow the Lilacs" and who
seems to be the forgotten man of the musical show based
upon it. I was struck by this when I looked over the original
play once again and noted how much of Riggs's text has been
used in the new version."

Robert Garland said in the New York *Journal-American* in
July, 1945, after his "annual visit" to see *Oklahoma!:* "Few
combinations of words, music and dance have ever been as
good as this . . . a practically flawless combination of all the
theatre arts, to which have been added a rich humanity and
the endearing quality of true nostalgic Americana. . . . Lynn
Riggs's "Green Grow the Lilacs" is a fine, firm foundation."

Burns Mantle's book of *Ten Best Plays* for 1942–43 included
Oklahoma!, an unusual honor for a musical. John Chapman

said in reviewing the book for the New York *Sunday News* on November 14, 1943, "it is interesting to discover that Riggs was responsible for more, even than plot and atmosphere." He quotes Riggs's original description of the time and place, describing it as a "song cue" for Hammerstein's "Oh, What a Beautiful Mornin'": "Only by reading the new Mantle volume does one realize that Playwright Riggs rates a bow for this number."

Sellout demand continued as the national company toured, and even three years later in Los Angeles. Patterson Greene in the *Los Angeles Examiner*, May 7, 1946, told how the play relieved the nation of its war-weary blues:

Throughout the performance, there is a certain tidal pull of nostalgia. The show presents an era that, like the Wild West of the films, has become a racial memory in the American mind; a mythical period before world wars, before the idea of One World was neatly counter-balanced by the idea of One Bomb. An era of incredible peace, all of 40 years ago. My, my—we have come a long way since then!

The state, too, claimed a rebirth in *Oklahoma!*, which showed a counter-image to that created by Steinbeck's *Grapes of Wrath* in 1939. Steinbeck's portrayal of poor Okies with mattresses on top of flivvers, fleeing to California from Oklahoma's dust and depression, had rankled with Oklahomans. Several joyous celebrations greeted the play and later, in 1955, the movie, when they came to the state. Much genuine goodwill and humor was shown, in some cases, as amusing as the play itself.

In November, 1946, the touring company came "home" to Claremore. The city's leading promoter, dentist Noel Kaho, had gone to St. Louis personally to present invitations to the Theatre Guild national company for a Claremore party when they came to Tulsa the following spring.[15] The company was to come a few days later to Oklahoma City, where the longest parade in the city's history was planned, with a stagecoach, cowboys, and Indians. Riggs came and other celebrities, including Rodgers, Hammerstein, Mamoulian, De Mille, and

Helburn. However, an ice and sleet storm caused the parade to be cancelled an hour beforehand, and the visitors felt lucky to get safely across the glazed streets to their hotel. Riggs returned with many of the guests to New York the next morning, saying he planned to be present for the April showing in Tulsa—but he was not.

The following April 7, 1947, the company came for a ten-performance run at Convention Hall in Tulsa. The Theatre Guild director of publicity, Samuel Weller, wrote Kaho thanking him for offering hotel arrangements at the Will Rogers in Claremore, but said he had arranged for rooms at the Adams Hotel in Tulsa. He left some doubt about the cast's cooperation in the Claremore celebration, saying, "I cannot guarantee that each person or couple is really going to be at the hotel assigned. They do some strange things sometimes." Kaho forged ahead, even though John Joseph Mathews wrote from Ponca City that he probably could persuade the Ponca Singers or Osage Indians dancers to come, but that they, too, tended to be temperamental and go where they pleased.

The road show cast, with John Alexander as Curly, had been praised the week before by John Rosenfield of the *Dallas Morning News:* "On Monday night the champion musical show of stage history had its first of eight performances in Dallas at Fair Park auditorium. . . . The first of what will be eight capacity audiences cheered it to the echo. Four thousand of the 4,300 made a point of telling somebody that they had seen it in New York and that this company isn't at all bad. It isn't. It is very good."

"Claremore Night" was Monday, April 7. Dr. Kaho arranged for a bus to meet the cast at the train from Fort Worth on Sunday afternoon, take them to their hotel and then thirty miles northeast to Claremore Country Club, where each would be assigned a host couple.[15] By this time the cast had begun to feel like Oklahomans. They shared memorable experiences. Hi Anzell (Jud), for example, remembered waking up in Sioux City, Iowa, at 2:00 A.M. one clear night after a snowfall. The cast pulled their luggage in a hand truck to the train station, singing on the way, "Oh, What a Beautiful Morning." When the cast walked into the Adams Hotel in Tulsa, the clerk asked expectantly, "Oklahoma?" and one of them answered, "Yeah, home at last!"

Bob Foresman described the Claremore party in the Tulsa Tribune. Departure was delayed because Patricia Shay (Ado Annie) accidentally locked herself in her hotel room and had to wait for the management to free her. Before they all boarded the bus, Tulsa police shook down the actors for weapons, partly for realism and partly to be sure they would not react too violently to what was to come. Escorted with sirens, their bus was stopped east of town at the traffic circle, where a policeman handed the driver four bags labeled "gold" and said, "That's $60,000 there and I want a receipt."

Predictably, just inside the Claremore Country Club grounds a half-dozen mounted men, their faces covered by bandannas, halted the bus. While five hundred or so Claremorites watched from a nearby hill, the passengers were forced to leave the bus, hands above their heads. The robbers kidnapped the Tulsa bus hostess, Dorothy Jean Ballard, and dashed away with her on horseback toward the clubhouse— but forgot to take the "payroll" in the bags!

When they reentered the bus, Kaho introduced William Grant Riggs, Lynn's father, and said, "If it weren't for Lynn, you folks wouldn't have the jobs you have." They were to ride in surreys into Claremore, but since no surreys could be found, they were boosted with squeals into a battered old stagecoach, several buckboards, and a hay wagon. They made a quick tour of the Will Rogers Memorial, where they were interviewed for the local radio station, then went on to the Oklahoma Military Academy across the road, where they were introduced to a packed crowd. Some cast members joined in square dances with Leonard Lee and his Tulsa dancers. Chief Goodnight and the Pawnee Indian dancers performed.

Meanwhile, out on the old Alton farm three miles south of

town, the hands had been barbecuing a pig on a wooden spit for two days. Just as about a hundred guests had arrived, the juicy pig gave way and fell into the ashes in the pit! Undaunted, Kaho sent out for a very large order of steaks, which they quickly barbecued in modern Oklahoma fashion. Several of the stars worried about what the cool night air might do to their voices and left soon after supper; many of them lingered until 10:00 P.M., however, and then went to another party at the country club.

Oklahoma had royally welcomed home its long-awaited namesake. And if there was chagrin at the "cussedness" of some of its characters, there was also pride in the heroism of its ordinary people and a recognition of truth in its history.

CHAPTER 11

FACING TOWARD THE WESTERN SKY

(1951–1954)

> . . . But only note, beyond a shadow
> another room not lyrical
> whose air is something else than meadow
> bright with sun and madrigal.
>
> The wall is hardly there to see
> within that inner utmost lair.
> Step in, and if you will, with me,
> or if alone no one will care.
>
> Alone you must be in the end;
> the inner room appends unto
> whatever wood or mud you bend
> to shape of room whose shape is you.
>
> —"The Shaped Room"[1]

WHEN HE BOUGHT his 1860 farmhouse on Shelter Island in May, 1947, Riggs described it thus: "It's a dream, solid, all-year, with trees—locust and apple and fruit—and shrubbery and lawn and raspberries and strawberries and it looks at the sea, and it's quite ravishing." He spent the last few years of his life there alone, except for some extended visits to Chapel Hill.

Reached only by ferries, from Greenport, Long Island, or from the Hog Neck above Sag Harbor, the island was forbidding in winter weather. But although he kept his Christopher Street apartment, Riggs wrote in November, 1950, that he

lived "permanently now in the country," on St. Mary's Road.
On February 22, 1950, he wrote Witter Bynner,

> I'm tired of this endless need to keep working. I'm saddened
> when not sickened by the world's state—as who isn't. Bad
> times, hombre. Anyway, I'm not *always* cast into fits. There are
> jokes to crack and lifting things still. . . .
> Gui isn't with me anymore—He's with a design unit and
> they're making hand-printed fabrics (beautiful)—mostly Gui's
> design. He's painting well—and will be a very fine painter, I
> predict. I'm sure he'd send greetings and love.[2]

The Korean War was boiling. The United States and other
United Nations protective troops had withdrawn from South
Korea in 1949, and the new Republic of Korea was quickly
overrun. When on June 25, 1950, Communist North Korea in-
vaded, the U.S. and other U.N. countries responded to the
call for troops in a "police action" to halt the aggressor, and
the bloody three-year struggle began. The winter spirit of the
world reflected Riggs's own lonely winter.

He was rewriting *Out of Dust*, which had played for two
weeks in Westport in August, 1949, but had not gone on
to Broadway for the Theatre Guild. He was also reworking
Borned in Texas, which opened on August 21, 1950, with
Anthony Quinn playing "Texas" at the Festival Theatre on
Broadway. But it closed early.

Late in 1950, on Paul Green's recommendation, Western Reserve University in Cleveland commissioned Riggs to create a
musical drama, entitled *Toward the Western Sky*, for the celebration of their 125th anniversary in June, 1951. Riggs discussed the play with Green in March while visiting in Chapel
Hill. Green had had great success with the "symphonic dramas" that he wrote, beginning with *The Lost Colony*, which
has been presented annually in summer on North Carolina's
Roanoke Island since 1937. He used music, dance, and visual
arts with broad strokes in these dramas to dramatize the history of a place or the biography of an important historical figure. Among his annually recurring outdoor dramas are *The*

Stephen Foster Story, in Bardstown, Kentucky; *Cross and Sword,* in St. Augustine, Florida; *Texas,* in Palo Duro Canyon, Texas; *The Lone Star* in Galveston, Texas; *Trumpet in the Land,* in New Philadelphia, Ohio; and *Wilderness Road,* in Berea, Kentucky. Green hoped Riggs's pageant for Western Reserve would be presented annually there in summer and would support a scholarship in Riggs's name, although this was not to be.[3]

On this March, 1951, visit Riggs became close friends with Jacques Hardré and Bill Baskin III, French professors at the University of North Carolina. Hardré's home became for him a peaceful and pleasant retreat on several visits during the following years—a much-needed haven where he could work comfortably and escape the harsh and lonely northern weather in the company of good friends. Their warmth eased the chill of his nightmares: "December," he wrote in a poem, "claws at the gate and will not keep back. / This is the song and you have to sing it. / Citizen of snow and the bitter lime, / rise from the table—rise and sing it / . . . 'tis time!"[4] The clock was ticking for him.

Riggs made his last visit to Oklahoma in the spring of 1951 before returning to New York to finish *Toward the Western Sky.* He did not go back for the funeral when his father died at the age of eighty-two on September 6, 1951.

Nathan Kroll said that Aaron Copland originally was to do the musical score for *Toward the Western Sky,* but turned it down when he received an important offer to conduct an orchestra in Europe.[5] Subsequently, Kroll, a distinguished musician also, agreed to collaborate with Riggs on it. According to the foreword of the printed version published by Western Reserve University Press at the time of the Cleveland performance on June 11, 1951:

> *Toward the Western Sky* memorializes the early development and the pioneer spirit of that section of the Ohio Country from which the University derives its support and its name. Mr. Riggs was chosen for the task because of his identity with the folklore and traditions of the Mid-West as well as for his im-

pact on the American dramatic scene. The University has thus stimulated an additional creative contribution to the growing literature of the Great Lakes Basin—the heartland of America.

Riggs spoke at the commencement exercises and was awarded the honorary degree of Doctor of Letters. His graduation address to the Adelbert College of the university was titled "The Road Not Taken." Although he was increasingly bothered by the stomach ulcer that was to become cancerous, Riggs also gave a high school commencement address the same week.[6]

His income was sufficient for him to maintain the Shelter Island home, to send a monthly allowance to his sister Mattie, and to consider buying the old Carolina Inn at Chapel Hill. He kept up a cheerful front, not mentioning his illness to friends, and he continued to write and search for new outlets for his work.

Hardré, who described Riggs as "one of the princes of this world, good, sincere in friendship, and not a publicity seeker," said that Riggs did not express discouragement. His bantering letters to Hardré and Baskin called them "kiddies."

On July 4, 1952, Riggs cut short a visit to Chapel Hill, "a welcome retreat from the heat," saying in a note that he "bowed to the dentist" and would return to New York.[7] On August 27 he sent his new manuscript of poems, which he titled *Hamlet Not the Only*, to Paul and Elizabeth Green at Chapel Hill:

> (I could revert to an earlier title: *Of Oak and Innocence.*) Would you see what you think of it—and if well enough, would you submit it to . . . the Univ. of N.C. Press? I don't want you to have to endorse it—but I would like your own private word to me on it.
>
> I'm toying with dramatizing *The Friendly Persuasion* by Jessamyn West. It's rich and warm and humorous and elevated somewhat. Other than that I'm swimming and sunning. Wish you were here![8]

Green responded September 4, 1952 with congratulations, saying that he and Elizabeth (also a poet) thought the manuscript good and had turned it over to editor Lambert Davis. Green warned, however, that the University of North Carolina Press had issued only four books that spring, and it had pretty much stopped publication of poetry. Green said, "We are all looking forward to having you back with us in the fall." The press chose not to publish the poems. Although some of them had seen publication in magazines, the complete manuscript was not published until long after his death, in 1982.[9]

Riggs was to spend six months in Chapel Hill during the winter of 1952–53 working on his plays and poems, but he revealed little of himself to his friends there. In fact, he never discussed his personal problems nor his difficult childhood with Paul and Elizabeth Green, saying only that he had had "three nervous breakdowns." And although he was a frequent guest of Jacques Hardré, who was born in France and retained dual United States and French citizenship, Riggs never discussed with him the time he had spent in France on the Guggenheim fellowship. Hardré said that Riggs was so far from boasting that he did not mention his connection with the musical *Oklahoma!* till it came up by chance, commenting only that it "kept me in bourbon all these years."

On March 17, 1953, Riggs wrote a newsy letter to Spud Johnson. Ida Rauh Eastman and a new Boxer dog, Rebel, were keeping him company on Shelter Island. No doubt, she alone realized how much his health was failing.[10]

A short story in *Gentry*, "Eben, the Hound and the Hare," about a man very much like himself, came out in May. He describes himself wryly in this autobiographical tale: "a thin long somber man named Eben living there alone in the house that once was a farmhouse. But now, though he still called it The Farm, it was actually three acres of lawn and apple trees. . . ." Eben was a man who had had trouble with "his psyche" and who wanted a dog. He had had other dogs, but

he travelled so often, to New Mexico or to the "tumultuous aching spring of North Carolina" that he had given them away to better homes. They were "The Baron," a brindle Scottie, and "Franz," the shepherd. But lonely Eben "wanted, needed a dog again, and hoped this time he was done with wandering."
Eben had been

> mutilated by love. Shucked and tortured, desolated and gone dry with pain and desertion—how many times? . . . And yet such love was in him ready to spring and burgeon (and envelop if not watched) and there is no real stopping a man who has in him such a tenderness and desire and capacity for giving and receiving joy and hurt. But at this stage, a dog would help, he knew that, he had known it before, and survived darkness thereby.

Eben takes joy in his new, magnificent Great Dane—but finds in him betrayal too. He finds a latent, savage violence in "Skol"—a cruelty the more repellent because it reflects some basic violence in himself. Is he still talking about his former dogs when he says near the end: "(Foregone, fragile loves, lost groping hands of need, who is it murderously with the axe chops off the fingers clinging to boats on what seas, who stuffs the agonized mouth with nightshade and oblivion?) Was he, too, he asks, to be "mangled and ended . . . as one dies by the hands and teeth of love?"[11] The descriptions in this narrative of outer and inner scenes are powerful prose poetry.

Riggs had started a novel, about an old murder in Oklahoma in which the primary suspect had been acquitted. He told Johnson on March 17:

> This may really work. . . . I have felt like the very devil for about a year but am coming alive again at last. . . . Ida was here for 2 months, now back in New York. Will come out in spring. . . . Saw Gui last spring in Alabama. He's doing well— unhappy—sold paintings—doing over houses and apart-

ments. . . . Do you know that incredible *Oklahoma!* is still touring this country and England? Do you know that I'm still solvent?

Ever the New Mexican, Riggs, in spite of his stomach, asks Johnson to send some authentic New Mexican roasted green chillis and red chilli powder. On April 7, 1953, he wrote again: "Spud, you are an angel. The chillis came—and tonight I'm having some. Ida is here, too. She sends message: 'How is the state of malice in Taos?—Also, when are we going to see you?'"

A loose poem to Hardré on May 2 served as a letter from Shelter Island, following Hardré's spring visit there. Still a heavy smoker, Riggs perhaps used doggerel to avoid mentioning the gloom growing within his lungs and throat, the premonition of death that sent him on a mystical quest into spiritualism.

I know some folks who don't do any better
At writing a letter
Than I do.
I wish I didn't know people like this but as you go along you
*   have to know somebody, you can't just live in a*
*   shell. Or maybe I can at that, can you?*

The burden of this note is this: all kinds of things are in bloom here—
Cherry and pear and quince
Long since
Forsythia has come and gone, likewise the jonquils and all such trivia.
In Bolivia, I'm told
Old
Men and young men for that matter sit under giant blossoms and
*   drink juleps*
(It's better than tulips)
(It's better with your shoes off too, an old song says)
But you're not as tropical as that, you don't even wear a sarong
Long.
I'm doing all this straight on a typewriter with my Boxer pup sitting
*   at my feet curious.*

Are you coming to see me this summer or have you given me up?
Oh, so that's it? Well, I've still got my pup.
He isn't helping me any writing my novel, he's furious
At being neglected. Fifty pages I've done on the book and it's going
     very well.
In the meantime—what the hell—
I've got plenty of time, I wrote and sold my first short story called
     EBEN, THE HOUND AND THE HARE, *and it's coming out in May*
     in Gentry.

Tonight, to tell you the truth, it's wintry
With a gale from the East, and in the kitchen my week-end cook busily
     cooking chicken in wine.
I'm not going to eat, I'm going to dine.
Wish you were here. How about coming up again.

A respite from work in Aspen, Colorado, followed by a
brief visit to Taos, brought a cheerful letter to Hardré written
August 20, 1953:

My boys (New Music String Quartet) are in residence at Aspen
this summer—and that was fun. I stayed with the Walter
Paepches—Founders of the Festival. Frieda Lawrence arrived—said "You *must* drive back with us to Taos—even for a
minute." So I did. She will give me land on the Great Mesa
north of Taos to build on if I will. And I will! Perhaps next
year. I'd hate to give up Shelter Island (the house at least) but
I may. . . .

I'm writing a novel—and toying with a play I'm asked to do
for the Ford Foundation TV *Omnibus*—so you see. . . . Let me
know if there's a chance of your coming up? It would be fun!

If I close the house in late Nov. or Dec. I may come by to see
you. It will depend on (oh invitation, yes! but) the state the
novel is in. Dying to see you all—and your estate, too. As
ever, Lynn.

Busy, he wrote this note two days later, working on the
novel:

Jacques—What are the trees that grow in that glade—park—
that begins about where the outdoor theatre is? And goes on

and there are picnic spots. You know it goes along the stream, high up trees they are, and there are acres and acres of them. I have to know for the novel. Or haven't you ever been in that place at dawn, as I have? Find out for me, like an angel. And what are those trees—shrubs—that bloom redly in Spring all along the main streets of Chapel Hill?

About the issue of *Gentry* with his story in it, he adds: "In the ads, there's a mink ice bucket for $150. You'll want at least six. . . . Love, Haste,   Lynn."

But instead of going to Chapel Hill for Christmas, he went into the hospital because of a hemorrhage. He wrote Jacques and Bill on December 16:

> I am desolate, myself. But when this ridiculous thing happened, I thought it best to wire you in case you had made some plans that would have to be cancelled.
>
> The fact of the matter is that I had a concealed ulcer evidently, and it made its presence known very dramatically last Saturday and sent me to the hospital by ambulance. I'm back home now, still in bed but all right. I just have to eat very carefully, and of course, no drinking, no smoking, and so forth, so forth—all that boring concern.
>
> I'd like nothing better than to convalesce with you. I may have an even better idea. A stringent winter long in abeyance has been promised us. Sometime in January I have expected to close the house and go to Chapel Hill if I can find a house. I have an extra requirement this time. I will have to have some kind of place to keep my dog from getting run over in the streets. If your real estate man knows of a small house not too expensive for me and my dog for two or three months, I'd like to know about it. Failing this likely idyll—perhaps I should just drive down there when I am able to do so and place the dog in a kennel while I shop around for a place.
>
> The doctor is coming this afternoon, and I'll have a clearer notion about how long it will be before I can drive.
>
> My good friends, the New Music Quartet, will be there in Chapel Hill for some kind of musicologist conference (I believe)—be sure to see them and hear them—they're the best in the business, I think, and especially see Walter Trampler, a

very dear friend of mine. I spent Thanksgiving with the Tram-
plers in Connecticut. Incidentally, DARK ENCOUNTER in the
book of FOUR PLAYS is more or less based on Walter.
    I *hate* not being there for Christmas.

Love, Lynn

Riggs stayed several months with Hardré and Baskin in
Chapel Hill in early 1954. He worked steadily at least two
hours daily, at a card table set up in his room, with his dog,
Rebel, at his feet. He had the yard fenced for Rebel and enjoyed the house in lush, green Carolina woods. He continued
a cheery bantering with his friends, although his strength
was waning. An example is this undated note left behind
when he was away visiting the Greens for a day:

Pappy—would you consider letting Rebel out for a moment to
pee before you go to bed, giving him contents of Yummy box,
telling him (in English please) "He'll be back. Go to bed." The
"He" refers to me, who—in case you didn't know it—is GOD.
God bless you and all Swedish athletes.
                      —Rollo [The first use in writing of his first
                      name, Rollie, in many years.]

Saying only that he was going to Duke University Hospital
for a minor matter, Riggs underwent an operation there for a
stomach ulcer. If he knew that it revealed a cancer, he mentioned it to no one.
    On May 25 1954 he wrote to Hardré and Baskin from New
York:

Well, Kiddies—I haven't waited a year this time to write—I
don't know how I'd ever have got through that gloomy misery
of feeling so downright awful if I hadn't been there with you
all. How you stood it would, if told, be a saga of heroism, re-
silience and pure French-Georgian toughness.
    Anyway, next time you see me I promise to be absolutely
unbearably Bernar MacFaddenish. . . . I've had a bad week—
my chart hadn't come yet—so I've been patiently suffering,
just taking Codeine—but this morning—and a real gold-
plated one it is—I feel pretty damn good.

Our trip up, in the arms of sanctity, was pleasant. That's a sweet lad, and so is his friend. Tall, dark and handsome, too. Baby must bring him up to see you this summer. My friends who met W.B. were enchanted. . . . The farm is still in dogwood, lilac (finishing), dark purple iris and apple bloom and— is it baby's breath?

Why, William, thanks for finding those things. I had missed the ring. And so far I haven't found the Camel bill—but I'm not quite unpacked. . . .

Let me know when you're coming up, hear? I miss you all— Say my best to the perfect neighbors—the dark and the fair— and Buddsky—and Warner Baby—

Love, Lynn

Ida and Al are here with me—and Mrs. Sabal cooks every day. Don't forget to send me my bill for part of May. And the telephone bills.

Riggs's final note to Hardré and Baskin was written on June 18, 1954, from Memorial Hospital, 444 East Sixty-eighth Street, in New York:

Babies—I've been in Memorial Hospital, a sick lad, mon vieux— But now the Tide's moving again. They see ahead I'll yield to cure—So you see I wasn't kidding. —It's a nasty vicious tumor they've learned since '44 to control. Only don't go spreading the tidings—it sounds so ominous—and it's only a poor little thing trying to get along—Abrazos to you sweeties—and to a few choice others.

Lynn

I'll be here a few weeks still.

The "poor little thing" was cancer of the stomach, lungs, and throat. Riggs called his sister Mattie on June 14, 1954, her birthday, from the hospital, just as cheerful, saying that he had been there "a few days." But the doctor called her, too, and she rushed to New York to stay until the end.

Spud Johnson heard from Riggs that, although he had been feeling rotten for some time, he felt that he was getting better. Johnson wrote late in June that he was going to Europe and and thought he would drive a car from New Mexico to New thought he would drive a car from New Mexico to New York, and he wanted to leave the car at Lynn's place on Shelter Island. He got a telegram in return from Memorial Hospital, saying that he could certainly leave the car with the caretaker at the house.

When he arrived at the hospital on June 29, 1954, Johnson was greeted by Lynn's sister, Mattie Riggs Cundiff, and a young actor, a friend of Riggs, who told him Lynn was dying but did not know it. He had had an operation and was under sedation. Terribly shocked, Johnson went in to see Lynn, who "looked ghastly," he said, hooked up to tubes.[12]

Riggs had asked Johnson about finding a house in Taos and immediately wanted to know what he had found. Going along with this charade, like someone in a dream, Johnson described a charming old house. It was out on the same ridge, he said, where their friends Dorothy Brett and Frieda Lawrence lived, with a wonderful view of the mountains on one side and the desert on another, and a row of trees on the knoll behind. It was also near Bill Goyen, a young writer who had been to see Riggs in New York.

Johnson told the rest of the story in these words:

> He was very pleased and said it sounded just about what he would like and he *staggered* me by saying well, how much was it? Why, I had never got that far at home and so I had no idea. So I simply pulled out of the air $10,000. He said, "That sounds reasonable," and I promised I'd come the next day and I would sort of make a drawing of exactly where it was . . . and of course I had to leave just exhausted, pretending that nothing was the matter and, if possible, not giving him any hint that it was a final goodbye or anything like that. . . .
>
> I went out of the hospital, and it was raining. I luckily had a raincoat and walked all the way from wherever it was to the hotel, crying in the rain. Of course, nobody would have known it because I was dripping rain all over.
>
> And the next morning someone phoned that he had died. . . . I probably was the last to see him of his old friends. . . .
>
> It was a long walk, in the rain.

APPENDIX: THE WORKS OF LYNN RIGGS

Appendix: The Works of Lynn Riggs (in Chronological Order)

Name	Description	Date	Disposition of Manuscript	Play Production
Cuckoo	One-act farce	1923	MS in Lynn Riggs Memorial, Rogers State College Library, Claremore, Oklahoma	University of Oklahoma, summer, 1923
Knives from Syria	One-act play	1925	*One-Act Plays for Stage and Study, Third Series* (New York: Samuel French, Inc., 1927)	Santa Fe Players, May–June, 1925
Big Lake	Two-act play	1925	Samuel French, Inc., 1925	American Laboratory Theatre, New York, April, 1927; Tulsa Little Theater, March, 1928
Sump'n Like Wings	Three-act play	1925-31	*Sump'n Like Wings* and *A Lantern to See By* (Samuel French, Inc., 1925).	Detroit Playhouse, 1931; Brussels, Belgium, 1932
A Lantern to See By	Three-act play	1926, 1930	*Sump'n Like Wings* and *A Lantern to See By* (Samuel French, Inc., 1925)	Detroit Playhouse, September, 1930; Hedgerow Theater, Pennsylvania, March, 1933
The Lonesome West	Three-act play	1927	MS in New York Public Library	Hedgerow Theater, June, 1936; Iowa State University, November 15–17, 1932
Rancor	Three-act play	1927	MSS in New York Public Library and Hedgerow Theater Library	Hedgerow Theater, July, 1928; Santa Fe Players, 1931; Syracuse University, 1931; Denver University, 1932; Valparaiso University and Tulsa University, 1933
Reckless	One-act play, (incorporated in *Roadside*)	1927	*One-Act Plays for Stage and Study, Fourth Series* (Samuel French, Inc., 1928)	None

Title	Description	Date	Publisher	Production/Notes
Roadside (revised as Borned in Texas)	Four-act play	1927–29	Samuel French, Inc., 1930	Roadside: New Haven, September, 1930; New York Longacre, September, 1930; Hedgerow Theater, 1931; Cleveland, Portland, Kalamazoo, Carmel, and Pasadena community theatres, 1932–35; Tulsa community theatre, 1941; Baylor University, November, 1941. Borned in Texas: Stamford, Connecticut, June, 1945; University of Tulsa, 1982.
The Domino Parlor (revised as Hang On to Love)	Three-act play	1928, 1946	Samuel French, Inc., 1948	Springdale, Connecticut, 1928; Long Island, New York; and Newark, New Jersey, 1946
Green Grow the Lilacs	Six-act play	1929	Samuel French, Inc., 1930	Theatre Guild, New York, January, 1931, and continuing throughout the U.S.
Cowboy Songs, Folk Songs, and Ballads from "Green Grow the Lilacs"	Booklet (anthology)	1932	Samuel French, Inc., 1932	
"We Moved to Pomona"	Short story set in Arizona and California		The Laughing Horse (Santa Fe) 20 (Summer, 1938)	
The Iron Dish	Book of poems, many set in Santa Fe	1925–29	New York: Doubleday-Doran Co., 1930	

(continued)

Appendix: (*continued*)

Name	Description	Date	Disposition of Manuscript	Play Production
The Cherokee Night	Seven-scene play	1930	*Russet Mantle* and *The Cherokee Night* (Samuel French, Inc., 1936)	Hedgerow Theater, June, 1932; University of Iowa, 1932; Syracuse University, 1934; Federal Theatre, New York, 1936
The Son of Perdition (from novel by James Gould Cozzens)	Four-act play, set in Cuba	1931	MS in Riggs Memorial, Oklahoma	Hedgerow Theater, February, 1933
More Sky	Four-act play, set in Atlantis	1933	MS in Riggs Memorial, Claremore, Oklahoma	Northwestern University, July, 1934
Russet Mantle	Three-act play, set in New Mexico	1934, 1935	*Russet Mantle* and *The Cherokee Night* (Samuel French, Inc., 1936)	New York, 1936
A World Elsewhere	Two-act play, set in Mexico	1935–39	*Four Plays* (Samuel French, Inc., 1947; briefer version in *The Best One-Act Plays of 1939*, ed. Margaret Mayorga (Samuel French, Inc., 1940)	San Diego, California, April 8–13, 1940; University of Iowa, April, 1948.
The Year of Pilar	Eight-act tragedy, set in New York and Mexico	1938	*Four Plays* (Samuel French, Inc., 1947)	None
A Cow in a Trailer (with Ramon Naya, and with music by Jerome Moross)	Nine-act musical-comedy journey across U.S.A.	1939	Unavailable	Partial radio performance, CBS Radio, April, 1940

Title	Type	Year	Publication	Production
The Hunger I Got	One-act play	1939	Published by Dramatists Play Service, 1939; also in One-Act Plays for Stage and Study, Tenth Series (Samuel French, Inc., 1949)	None
The Cream in the Well	Two-act tragedy	1940	Four Plays (Samuel French, Inc., 1947).	National Theater, Washington, D.C., January 14, 1941; Booth Theater, New York, January 20, 1941
The Dark Encounter	Two-act play, set on Cape Cod	1944	Four Plays (Samuel French, Inc., 1947)	None
Laughter from a Cloud	Three-act comedy, set in New Mexico	1944, 1945	MS in Riggs Memorial, Claremore, Oklahoma	Tanglewood Theater, Falmouth, Massachusetts, August, 1947
Tragic Ground (from novel of Erskine Caldwell)	Play set in Georgia	1944–46	Lost	
The Oedipus Story	Dance drama, set in "a lonely place"		MS in Riggs Memorial, Claremore, Oklahoma	None
All the Way Home (revision of The Verdigris Primitives)	Three-act play	1948	MS in Riggs Memorial, Claremore, Oklahoma	Ridgefield, Connecticut, and New Jersey, August, 1948
Out of Dust	Three-act play, set in Oklahoma	1948	MS in Riggs Memorial, Claremore, Oklahoma	Westport, Connecticut, August, 1949
Someone to Remember	Three-act play for television, set in the Midwest	Early 1954	Unavailable	

(continued)

Appendix: (continued)

Name	Description	Date	Disposition of Manuscript	Play Production
The Boy with Tyford Fever or Some Sweet Day	Two-act play, set in Oklahoma	1950–53	MS in Riggs Memorial, Claremore, Oklahoma; University of Tulsa Library	Philco-Goodyear TV Playhouse, 1953
Song in the A.M.	One-act TV play, based on Some Sweet Day	1953	Unavailable	
Toward the Western Sky (with music by Nathan Kroll)	Six-scene historical play set in the Western Reserve	1951	Cleveland: Press of Western Reserve University, 1951; MS in library of University of New Mexico, Albuquerque	Western Reserve University, 1951
"Eben, the Hound, and the Hare"	Short story, set on Shelter Island, New York	1952	Gentry no. 7 (Summer, 1953)	
The Affair at Easter	Unfinished novel, set in Sapulpa, Oklahoma	1953	MS in possession of Riggs heirs	
This Book, This Hill, These People: Poems by Lynn Riggs	Poems of many moods, some previously published in magazines	1930–48	Lynn Chase Publishing Company, 1734 W. Woodrow St., Tulsa, Okla. 74127, 1982	

MOVIE SCRIPTS (WRITTEN ALONE OR IN COLLABORATION)

Beyond Victory	1930	Pathé Studios
Siren Song	1930	Pathé Studios
Laughing Boy	1930	Metro-Goldwyn Mayer Studio
Stingaree	1933	RKO
Andrew's Harvest	1934	Paramount
Family Man	1934	RKO
Wicked Woman	1934	MGM
Delay in the Sun	1935	Universal
The Plainsman	1935	Paramount
The Garden of Allah	1936	Selznick International

NOTES

Chapter 1. The Golden World of Santa Fe (1923–25)

1. "The Shaped Room," *This Book, This Hill, These People: Poems by Lynn Riggs*, 41. Unless otherwise stated, the poetry of Lynn Riggs is quoted from this book.

2. John Gaw Meem File, Archives, State of New Mexico, Santa Fe. Clippings and photographs describe Sunmount's facilities and history. The sanatorium became Brun's Army Hospital between 1938 and 1940, then an unsuccessful inn, and eventually a Roman Catholic convent.

3. Lynn Riggs to Witter Bynner, 14 October 1923, Bynner Papers, Houghton Library, Harvard University. All quoted letters from Riggs to Bynner are in this collection.

4. "Dr. Frank S. Mera Feted by Friends upon 90th Birthdate," *Santa Fe New Mexican*, 16 March 1969.

5. Lynn Riggs to Walter S. Campbell, 25 November 1923, Campbell Papers, Western History Collections, University of Oklahoma. All quoted letters to Campbell are in this collection.

6. Willard ("Spud") Johnson, personal interview tape and transcript by Dr. Arrell Morgan Gibson, 4 January 1968, Riggs File, Western History Collections, University of Oklahoma.

7. *The Laughing Horse* 1–21, supplements 1–2 (Taos: Laughing Horse Press, 1921–39; reprint, New York: Kraus Reprint Corp., 1967), at University of New Mexico Library, Albuquerque.

8. T. M. Pearce, *Mary Hunter Austin*, 50.

9. Mary H. Austin, *Earth Horizon*, 363.

10. The White residence is now the School for American Re-

8. Leo Morrison to Frances Baker, 27 August 1957, Kaho papers.

9. Betty Kirk Boyer, personal-interview tape, Riggs File, Western History Collections, University of Oklahoma, 4 January 1968.

10. Ibid.

Chapter 4. The Big Time: Broadway, Yaddo, Paris (1925–28)

1. "You'd Think," *This Book, This Hill, These People: Poems by Lynn Riggs*, 16.

2. Letter from William T. Covington II, archivist, Illinois Institute of Technology at Chicago, to author, 10 February 1981. In 1940, Lewis Institute merged as Lewis College of Sciences and Letters with the Illinois Institute of Technology at Chicago.

3. Barrett H. Clark, "Introduction," to Lynn Riggs, *Big Lake.*

4. Charles Aughtry, "Lynn Riggs, Dramatist: A Critical Biography," Ph.D. diss., 24.

5. Riggs to Betty Kirk Boyer, July, 1925, Riggs Files, Western History Collections, University of Oklahoma.

6. Riggs to Witter Bynner, 26 July 1926, Bynner Papers.

7. Land Records, Rogers County Court House, Claremore, Oklahoma.

8. Barrett H. Clark, *An Hour of American Drama*, 153.

9. Riggs to Clark, 2 June 1927, Clark Papers.

10. Descriptions and history of Yaddo are condensed from a small book by Marjorie Peabody Waite, *Yaddo, Yesterday and Today.*

11. Walter S. Campbell, Journal, Campbell Papers, Western History Collections, University of Oklahoma.

12. M. Abbott Van Nostrand, Chairman, Samuel French, Inc., personal interview with author, New York, 16 May 1980. Nostrand said he remembered that Lynn Riggs was "always sending telegrams asking for money."

13. Henry Roth, "Lynn Riggs and the Individual," in B. A. Botkin ed., *Folk-Say, A Regional Miscellany: 1930*, 390.

14. Riggs File, John Simon Guggenheim Memorial Foundation. All Riggs letters to the foundation are in this file unless otherwise stated.

15. Riggs's itinerary is gleaned from newspaper and magazine clippings, programs, and playbills in his four large scrapbooks, courtesy of his niece Bernice Cundiff Hodges.

16. Paul Green, personal interview with author, Chapel Hill, North Carolina, 14 May 1980.

search, Santa Fe. Also located in the compound is the Witter Bynner Foundation for Poetry.

11. "Biographical Introduction," *Selected Poems of Witter Bynner,* ed. James Kraft (New York: Farrar, Straus & Giroux, 1978), xlix.

12. Ibid.

13. *This Book, This Hill, These People: Poems by Lynn Riggs,* 42.

14. Willard ("Spud") Johnson, personal interview by Dr. Arrell Morgan Gibson, 4 January 1968.

15. Ida Rauh Eastman file, Billy Rose Theatre Collection, New York Public Library.

16. Lynn Riggs to Betty Kirk, 6 January 1925, Riggs File, Western History Collections, University of Oklahoma. All letters quoted to Betty Kirk Boyer are from this collection.

17. S. Marion Tucker and Alan S. Downer, eds., *Twenty-Five Modern Plays,* 803.

18. Charles Aughtry, "Lynn Riggs, Dramatist: A Critical Biography," Ph.D. diss., Brown University, 1959, 22.

Chapter 2. Growing Up: Oklahoma Territory Childhood (1899–1920)

1. "Listen, Mind," *This Book, This Hill, These People: Poems by Lynn Riggs,* 52.

2. Genealogical research and consultation with relatives provided data on Lynn Riggs's ancestors. Census records of 1870, Laclede County, Missouri, and of 1900, Indian Territory, list Joseph and William Grant Riggs and their families. Dawes Cherokee Nation Rolls, 1902, Cooweescoowee District, list Rose Ella Riggs, no. 954. The Indian Archives, Oklahoma Historical Society, Oklahoma City, provides marriage records of W. G. Riggs and Rose E. Gillis. The census of 1890 lists the family. Markers in Woodlawn and Buster cemeteries, Claremore, verify dates of birth and death. Joseph Riggs's military records, marriage license, and his widow's pension records are in the National Archives, Washington, D.C.

3. Arrell Morgan Gibson, *The Oklahoma Story,* 182.

4. *Starr's History of the Cherokee Indian,* ed. Jack Gregory and Rennard Strickland, 566.

5. Information on land descriptions and mortgages is from Land Records, Rogers County Court House, Claremore, Oklahoma.

6. Eloise Wilson, "Lynn Riggs, Oklahoma Dramatist," Ph.D. diss., University of Pennsylvania, 1957, 3, 5.

7. Riggs to Marion Starr Mumford, 22 November 1947, in Lynn Riggs Memorial, Rogers State College Library, Claremore, Oklahoma.

8. Lillie Brice Warner, cousin of Lynn Riggs, personal interview with author, Sapulpa, Oklahoma, 16 July 1982.

9. Freeda Martin, telephone interview with author, 8 June 1977.

10. Riggs to Barrett H. Clark, 23 July 1931, Clark Papers, Beinecke Library, Yale University, New Haven, Connecticut. All quoted letters and telegrams from Riggs to Clark are in this collection unless otherwise stated.

11. Bernice Cundiff Hodges, niece of Lynn Riggs, personal interview with author, 14 July 1981.

12. Riggs to Clark, 28 June 1928, Clark Papers.

13. Goldwyn Pictures to Riggs, 10 January 1920, Lynn Riggs Memorial, Rogers State Library, Claremore, Oklahoma.

14. Maggie Culver Fry, "Memories of Lynn Riggs," *Oklahoma Today* 10 (Winter 1959–60): 32. Also, Joseph Benton, "Some Personal Remembrances About Lynn Riggs," *Chronicles of Oklahoma* 34 (Autumn, 1956): 296.

15. Lillie Warner said that Riggs's father did not support him financially in college. Also, his sister Mattie Cundiff told Charles Aughtry that Lynn entered the University of Oklahoma against the wishes of his father ("Lynn Riggs, Dramatist: A Critical Biography," Ph.D. diss., 11).

Chapter 3. Breaking Out: Oklahoma University (1920–23)

1. "Epitaph," *This Book, This Hill, These People: Poems by Lynn Riggs*, 26.

2. Lynn Riggs to Barrett Clark, November 1928, Clark Papers. (For the context of this statement by Riggs, see the extended quotation from this letter in Chapter 5.)

3. Joseph Benton, "Some Personal Remembrances About Lynn Riggs," 300. Benton expressed a similar sentiment in notes that he sent in 1957 to Frances Baker of Quapaw, Oklahoma, for a potential biography of Lynn Riggs. These notes are in the Noel Kaho papers, property of Sallie Kaho.

4. Lynn Riggs to Witter Bynner, 6 December, 1922, Bynner Paper

5. Benton, "Some Personal Remembrances," 298.

6. Riggs to Bynner, 14 February, 1922.

7. Benton notes to Frances Baker, 1957.

17. Clark, *An Hour of American Drama*, 153.
18. Thomas Erhard, *Lynn Riggs, Southwest Playwright*, 10.

Chapter 5. Green Grows the Imagination in France
(1928–1929)

1. Lynn Riggs, "But Momentary—," *This Book, This Hill, These People: Poems by Lynn Riggs*, 13.
2. Lynn Riggs to Barrett H. Clark, 14 August 1928, Clark Papers.
3. Morley Callaghan, *That Summer in Paris*, 113.
4. Barrett H. Clark, "Broadway Opens Shop Again," *The Drama* 20 (October, 1928):11.
5. George Seldes, telephone interview with the author, 17 March 1982.
6. Ibid.
7. Riggs File, John Simon Guggenheim Memorial Foundation, New York.
8. Quoted in *Coe Spectator*, 18 February 1931.
9. Lynn Riggs, "Preface," *Green Grow the Lilacs*, vii.
10. Ibid., viii.
11. Lynn Riggs to Barrett H. Clark, March 10, 1929, Clark Papers.
12. Lynn Riggs to Walter S. Campbell, 13 March 1929, Campbell Papers.
13. Lynn Riggs to Barrett H. Clark, April 7, 1929, Clark Papers.

Chapter 6. Success Without Stability: The Debut of
Green Grow the Lilacs (1929–1931)

1. Lynn Riggs, "Unless Oblation . . . ," *This Book, This Hill, These People: Poems by Lynn Riggs*, 57.
2. Lynn Riggs to Barrett H. Clark, 1 May 1929, Clark Papers.
3. Lynn Riggs to Paul Green, Green Papers.
4. Stanley Vestal, "Lynn Riggs, Poet and Dramatist," *Southwest Review* 15 (Autumn, 1929):64.
5. Ibid., 68.
6. Ibid., 71.
7. Riggs File, John Simon Guggenheim Memorial Foundation.
8. Henry Roth, "Lynn Riggs and the Individual," 386–95.
9. Quoted in Eloise Wilson, "Lynn Riggs, Oklahoma Dramatist," Ph.D. diss., 19.

10. Lynn Riggs to Witter Bynner, 19 October 1930, Bynner Papers.
11. S. Marion Tucker and Alan S. Downer, eds., *Twenty-Five Modern Plays*, 222.
12. Paul Green, personal interview with author, Chapel Hill, North Carolina, 14 May 1980.
13. Clippings quoted are from Riggs's personal scrapbooks, courtesy of Bernice Cundiff Hodges. They provide sources and dates, but no page numbers.
14. Brooks Atkinson, "Introduction," to Lynn Riggs, *Green Grow the Lilacs* (Norman: Limited editions printed by the University of Oklahoma Press, 1954).
15. *Sooner Magazine*, 1931, 209.
16. Burns Mantle, ed., *Best Plays: Yearbook of the Drama in America*, *1931*, 222.
17. Arthur E. Waterman, *Susan Glaspell*, preface.
18. M. Abbott Van Nostrand, chairman, Samuel French, Inc., to author, 8 June 1981.

Chapter 7. Bicoastal Commuting and Paying the Bills
(1931–1934)

1. Lynn Riggs, "Telling Myself This and That," *This Book, This Hill, These People: Poems by Lynn Riggs*, 56.
2. Lynn Riggs to Betty Kirk Boyer, 31 January 1931, Riggs File.
3. Frederick Koch, "Playboy of Oklahoma," *Carolina Play-Book* 4 (June, 1931): 62.
4. *Tulsa World*, 5 May 1931. All quotations of periodicals are from clippings in Riggs's personal scrapbooks, courtesy of Bernice Cundiff Hodges.
5. Lynn Riggs to Paul Green, 8 May 1931, Green Papers. All quoted letters to Green are in this collection.
6. Lynn Riggs to Barrett Clark, 18 June 1931, Clark Papers.
7. Taped interview with Betty Kirk Boyer and Willard ("Spud") Johnson, by Arrell M. Gibson, 4 January 1968, Riggs File, Western History Collections, University of Oklahoma Library.
8. Lynn Riggs to Henry Moe, Riggs File, John Simon Guggenheim Memorial Foundation, New York.
9. Barrett H. Clark, "American Drama in Its Second Decade," *English Journal* 21 (January, 1932): 11.
10. Barrett H. Clark, *Intimate Portraits*, 216.
11. Charles Aughtry, "Lynn Riggs, Dramatist: A Critical Biography," Ph.D. diss., 46.

12. Paul Green, personal interview, Chapel Hill, North Carolina, 14 May 1980.
13. George O'Neil File, Billy Rose Theatre Collection, New York Public Library at Lincoln Center, New York City.
14. Paul Green, personal interview, Chapel Hill, North Carolina, 14 May 1980.
15. Emily Hughes, personal interview, Santa Fe, New Mexico, August, 1979.
16. Bob Thomas, *Joan Crawford: A Biography*, 108.
17. Norman S. McGee to author, 2 January 1982.
18. Lee Mitchell, "A Designer at Work," *Theatre Arts Monthly* 18 (November, 1934): 875.
19. Land Records, Rogers County Court House, Claremore, Oklahoma.

Chapter 8. The Santa Fe House and the Mexican Plays (1935–1940)

1. Lynn Riggs, "The Stair Ascending," *This Book, This Hill, These People: Poems by Lynn Riggs*, 23.
2. Lynn Riggs to Barrett H. Clark, 12 February 1935, Clark Papers.
3. Arrell Morgan Gibson, *The Santa Fe and Taos Colonies: Age of the Muses, 1900–1942*, 195.
4. Lynn Riggs to Paul Green, 25 October 1935, Green Papers.
5. Spud Johnson, taped interview by Arrell M. Gibson, 4 January 1968.
6. Joseph Benton, "Some Personal Remembrances About Lynn Riggs," 299.
7. Robert Benchley, *The New Yorker*, 25 January 1936. All quotations from magazines and newspapers are from Riggs's personal scrapbooks.
8. Lynn Riggs to Betty Kirk Boyer, 1 June 1936, Riggs File, Western History Collections.
9. Betty Kirk Boyer, taped interview by Arrell M. Gibson, 4 January 1968, Western History Collections, University of Oklahoma. All quoted comments by Betty Kirk Boyer are from this interview unless otherwise stated.
10. Santa Fe *New Mexican*, 1 February 1936, from Riggs's personal scrapbook, courtesy of Bernice C. Hodges.
11. Lynn Riggs to Spud Johnson, 26 June 1936, Riggs File, Western History Collections, University of Oklahoma.
12. "High, Wide and Handsome," *The Nation*, 16 December 1931, 674.

13. Lynn Riggs to Miriam Howell, 17 March 1937, copy to Barrett H. Clark, Clark Papers.

14. See n. 9, above.

15. Lynn Riggs to Witter Bynner, 12 June 1937, Bynner Papers.

16. Charles Aughtry, "Lynn Riggs, Dramatist: A Critical Biography," Ph.D. diss., 61.

17. Joseph Benton to Noel Kaho, 8 July 1954, among Kaho's personal papers in the possession of Sallie Kaho.

18. John Gassner, "Our Lost Playwrights," *Theatre Arts* 38 (August, 1954): 24. Naya's play *Mexican Mural* eventually was produced in New York. See the review by John Gassner in *Current History* 2 (August, 1942): 472.

19. Paul Green, personal interview with author, Chapel Hill, N.C., 14 May 1980.

Chapter 9. New York Years: Shelter Island Home (1941–50)

1. Lynn Riggs, "The True Seducers," *This Book, This Hill, These People: Poems by Lynn Riggs,* 12.

2. Joseph Wood Krutch, "Tragedy Is Not Easy," *The Nation,* 1 February 1941, 137.

3. Lynn Riggs to Paul Green, 7 February 1941, Green Papers.

4. "Drama Mailbag," *The New York Times,* 2 February and 9 March 1941. All quotations from newspapers and playbills are from Riggs's personal scrapbooks.

5. Spud Johnson, taped interview by Arrell M. Gibson, 4 January 1968, Riggs File, Western History Collections, University of Oklahoma.

6. *Waco Sunday Tribune-Herald,* 27 July 1941; Santa Fe *New Mexican,* 24 July 1941.

7. Paul Baker, personal interviewer with author, Dallas Theatre Center, 15 October 1979.

8. Virgil Beavers and Gene McKinney, telephone interviews with author, 15 October 1979.

9. Jacque Hardré, personal interview with author, Chapel Hill, N.C., 15 May 1980.

10. This bar panel and a section of the publication *Old American Songs (Newly Arranged)* are in the Lynn Riggs Memorial, Rogers State College Library, Claremore, Oklahoma.

11. Lynn Riggs to Henry Moe, Riggs File, John Simon Guggenheim Memorial Foundation.

12. Edrye Riggs, telephone interview, 18 August 1980.

13. Lynn Riggs to Betty Kirk Boyer, 20 December 1943, Riggs File, Western History Collections.
14. Eloise Wilson, "Lynn Riggs: Oklahoma Dramatist," Ph.D. diss., 29.
15. Riggs kept a record in his scrapbooks of the plays he had written and their dates.
16. Lynn Riggs to Marion Starr Mumford, 22 November 1941, in Lynn Riggs Memorial.
17. Lynn Riggs to Spud Johnson, 20 May, 1947, Riggs File, Western History Collections, University of Oklahoma.
18. Betty Kirk Boyer, taped interview by Arrell M. Gibson, 3, 4 January 1968.
19. Nathan Kroll, personal interview with author, New York City, 16 May 1980.
20. Eloise Wilson, "Lynn Riggs: Oklahoma Dramatist," Ph.D. diss., 31.
21. Lynn Riggs to Witter Bynner, 11 April 1948, Bynner Papers.
22. Lynn Riggs to W. S. Campbell, 17 April 1948, Campbell Papers, Western History Collections.
23. The program and clippings for this event are in Riggs's personal scrapbooks.
24. Eloise Wilson, "Lynn Riggs: Oklahoma Dramatist," Ph.D. diss., 34.
25. Charles Aughtry, "Lynn Riggs, Dramatist: A Critical Biography," Ph.D. diss., 89.

Chapter 10. Reflected Glory: *Green Grow the Lilacs* Returns as *Oklahoma!*

1. Lynn Riggs, "It Will Be Morning," *This Book, This Hill, These People: Poems by Lynn Riggs*, 47.
2. Theresa Helburn, *A Wayward Quest*, 28.
3. Ibid., 284.
4. Album of Decca record, "Selections from Theatre Guild Musical Play *Oklahoma!* featuring members of the original New York production, 1943.
5. Oscar Hammerstein, *New York Times*, clipping in one of Riggs's personal scrapbooks.
6. *Green Grow the Lilacs* (New York: Samuel French, Inc., 1929), 3.
7. Decca record album.
8. Helburn, *A Wayward Quest*, 290.
9. Riggs, *Green Grow the Lilacs*, 157.

10. Ibid., 146.

11. Ibid.

12. *Dayton Herald*, 19 April 1943.

13. Charles Aughtry, "Lynn Riggs, Dramatist: A Critical Biography," Ph.D. diss., 74.

14. Richard Watts, Jr., *New York Herald-Tribune*, 8 August 1943.

15. Correspondence, news releases and clippings regarding the Claremore celebration are in the papers of Dr. Noel Kaho, used courtesy of his daughter, Sallie Kaho.

Chapter 11. Facing Toward the Western Sky (1951–1954)

1. Lynn Riggs, "The Shaped Room," *This Book, This Hill, These People: Poems by Lynn Riggs*, 41.

2. Lynn Riggs to Witter Bynner, 22 February 1950, Bynner Papers.

3. Paul Green, personal interview with author, Chapel Hill, North Carolina, 14 May 1980.

4. Lynn Riggs poem, "All Hallow's Eve," *This Book, This Hill, These People*, 35.

5. Nathan Kroll, personal interview with author, New York City, 16 May 1980.

6. Eloise Wilson, "Lynn Riggs: Oklahoma Dramatist," Ph.D. diss., 37.

7. Lynn Riggs to Jacque Hardré, 4 July 1952 letters in personal papers of Mr. Hardré. Further comments are from Jacques Hardré's personal interview with author, Chapel Hill, N.C., 15 May 1980.

8. Lynn Riggs to Paul Green, 27 August 1952, Green Papers.

9. Paul Green to Lynn Riggs, 4 September 1952, Green Papers. This manuscript, "Hamlet Not the Only," or "Of Oak and Innocence," makes up the major part of *This Book, This Hill, These People: Poems by Lynn Riggs*, published in 1982 by the author, a memorial to Lynn Riggs for the state of Oklahoma's Diamond Jubilee.

10. Lynn Riggs to Spud Johnson, 17 March 1953, Riggs File, Western History Collections, University of Oklahoma.

11. Lynn Riggs, "Eben, the Hound, and the Hare," *Gentry*, Summer, 1953, 92, 93.

12. Spud Johnson, taped interview by Arrell M. Gibson, Riggs File, Western History Collections, University of Oklahoma. Library, Norman, Oklahoma, 4 January 1968.

BIBLIOGRAPHY

A. PRIMARY SOURCES

1. Published Plays by Lynn Riggs

Big Lake. New York: Samuel French, Inc., 1925.

Sump'n Like Wings. New York: Samuel French, Inc., 1925.

A Lantern to See By. New York: Samuel French, Inc., 1925.

Knives from Syria. In *One-Act Plays for Stage and Study, Third Series.* New York: Samuel French, Inc., 1928.

Reckless. In *One-Act Plays for Stage and Study, Fourth Series.* New York: Samuel French, Inc., 1928.

Green Grow the Lilacs. New York: Samuel French, Inc., 1930.

Roadside. New York: Samuel French, Inc., 1930.

Russet Mantle and *The Cherokee Night.* New York: Samuel French, Inc., 1936.

The Hunger I Got. New York: Dramatists Play Service, 1939; and in *One-Act Plays for Stage and Study, Tenth Series.* (New York: Samuel French, Inc., 1949).

A World Elsewhere. In *The Best One-Act Plays of 1939,* ed. Margaret Mayorga. New York: Samuel French, Inc., 1940.

A World Elsewhere. In Lynn Riggs, *Four Plays.* New York: Samuel French, Inc., 1947.

The Year of Pilar. In Lynn Riggs, *Four Plays.* New York: Samuel French, Inc., 1947.

The Cream in the Well. In Lynn Riggs, *Four Plays.* New York: Samuel French, Inc., 1947.

The Dark Encounter. In Lynn Riggs, *Four Plays.* New York: Samuel French, Inc., 1947.

219

The Domino Parlor. Revised as *Hang On to Love.* New York: Samuel
French, Inc., 1948.
Toward the Western Sky. Cleveland: Press of Western Reserve University, 1951.

2. Plays by Lynn Riggs Produced But Not Published

Cuckoo. 1923. Ms. in Lynn Riggs Memorial, Rogers State College Library, Claremore, Oklahoma.
The Lonesome West. 1927. Ms. in New York Public Library
Rancor. 1927. Mss. in New York Public Library and Hedgerow Theater Library.
The Son of Perdition. 1931. Ms. in Lynn Riggs Memorial, Rogers State College, Claremore, Oklahoma.
More Sky. 1933. Ms. in Lynn Riggs Memorial, Claremore.
Laughter from a Cloud. 1944. Ms. in Lynn Riggs Memorial, Claremore.
All the Way Home. Formerly *The Verdigris Primitives.* 1948. Ms. in Lynn Riggs Memorial, Claremore.
Out of Dust. 1948. Ms. in Lynn Riggs Memorial, Claremore.
Some Sweet Day. 1953. Originally *The Boy with Tyford Fever.* Typescripts in Lynn Riggs Memorial and University of Tulsa Library.

3. Other Works by Lynn Riggs

Cowboy Songs, Folk Songs and Ballads from "Green Grow the Lilacs." Compiled by Lynn Riggs. New York: Samuel French, Inc., 1932.
"Eben, the Hound, and the Hare." Short story. *Gentry,* no. 7 (Summer, 1953).
The Iron Dish. Poetry. New York: Doubleday-Doran, 1930.
This Book, This Hill, These People: Poems by Lynn Riggs. Edited by Phyllis Braunlich. Lynn Chase Publishing Co., 1734 W. Woodrow St., Tulsa, Okla. 74127, 1982. Based on a 1952 manuscript, "Hamlet Not the Only."
"We Moved to Pomona." Short story. *The Laughing Horse* 20 (Summer, 1938).

4. Articles by Lynn Riggs

"A Credo for the Tributary Theatre," *Theatre Arts* 25 (February, 1941):16.
"High, Wide and Handsome." *The Nation,* 16 December 1931, p. 674.
"We Speak for Ourselves." *Theatre Arts* 27 (December, 1943):752–57.
"When People Say 'Folk Drama.'" *The Carolina Play-Book* 4 (June, 1931):39–41.

5. Scrapbooks of Lynn Riggs

Four oversize books of his collected clippings from newspapers,
magazine articles, playbills, letters, telegrams, military-service
documents, and his personal record of plays that he wrote. Most
items give dates but not page numbers. These scrapbooks were
made available to the author by Mrs. Bernice Cundiff Hodges,
niece of Lynn Riggs, Muskogee, Oklahoma.

6. Letters by Lynn Riggs in Libraries and Private Collections

Letters to Joseph Benton. Western History Collections, University of
Oklahoma, Norman.
Letters to Betty Kirk Boyer. Riggs File. Western History Collections,
University of Oklahoma, Norman.
Letters to Witter Bynner. Bynner Papers. Houghton Library, Har-
vard University, Cambridge, Massachusetts.
Letters to Walter S. Campbell. Campbell Papers, Western History
Collections, University of Oklahoma, Norman.
Letters to Barrett H. Clark. Clark Papers. Beinecke Library, Yale Uni-
versity, New Haven, Connecticut.
Letters to Paul Eliot Green. Green Papers. University of North Caro-
lina Library, Chapel Hill, North Carolina.
Letters to Guggenheim Foundation and Henry Allen Moe, secretary.
Riggs File. John Simon Guggenheim Memorial Foundation, 90
Park Avenue, New York City.
Letters to Willard ("Spud") Johnson. Riggs File. Western History
Collections, University of Oklahoma, Norman.
Letters to Jacques Hardré. Personal papers. Chapel Hill, North
Carolina.
Letters to Alice Corbin Henderson. Personal papers formerly in the
possession of her daughter, Alice Rossin, Tesuque, New Mexico,
now at University of Texas, Austin.
Letters to Dr. Noel Kaho. Personal papers in the possession of his
daughter Sallie Kaho.
Miscellaneous letters. Lynn Riggs Memorial, Rogers State College
Library, Claremore, Oklahoma.

7. Interviews

Baker, Paul. Personal interview, Dallas Theatre Center, Dallas, Texas,
15 October 1979.
Beavers, Virgil. Telephone interview, Dallas, Texas, 15 October 1979.
Boyer, Betty Kirk. Interviews taped by Dr. Arrell M. Gibson, 3,

4 January 1968. Riggs File, Western History Collections, University of Oklahoma.

Cundiff, Leo (nephew of Lynn Riggs). Personal and telephone interviews, Tulsa, Oklahoma, on numerous occasions since 1977.

Green, Paul Eliot. Personal interview, Chapel Hill, N.C., 14 May 1980.

Hardré, Jacques. Personal interview, Chapel Hill, N.C., 15 May 1980.

Hodges, Bernice Cundiff (niece of Lynn Riggs). Personal and telephone interviews, Muskogee, Okla., on numerous occasions since 1977.

Holm, Celeste. Telephone interview, New York City, 9 July 1982.

Horgan, Paul. Telephone interview, Middletown, Conn., 18 July 1981.

Hughes, Emily (Mrs. James). Personal interviews, Santa Fe, August, 1979 and May, 1981.

Johnson, Willard ("Spud"). Interviews taped by Dr. Arrell M. Gibson, 3, 4 January 1968. Riggs File, Western History Collections, University of Oklahoma.

Kroll, Nathan. Personal interview, New York City, 16 May 1980.

McGee, Norman. Telephone interview, Sedona, Ariz., 18 July 1981.

Martin, Freeda. Telephone interview, Tulsa, Okla., 8 June 1977.

McKinney, Gene. Telephone interview, Waco, Texas, 15 October 1979.

Riggs, Edrye (Mrs. Joe). Telephone interview, Ironwood, Mich., 18 August 1980.

Ritchie, Ward. Telephone interview, Laguna Beach, Calif., 20 May 1981.

Seldes, George. Telephone interview, Windsor, Vt., 17 March 1982.

Van Nostrand, M. Abbott. Personal interview, Samuel French, Inc., New York City, 16 May 1980.

Warner, Lillie Brice. Personal interviews, 16 and 25 July 1982.

B. Secondary Sources

1. Books and Dissertations

Aughtry, Charles. "Lynn Riggs, Dramatist: A Critical Biography." Ph.D. diss., Brown University, 1959.

Austin, Mary. *Earth Horizon*. Boston: Houghton-Mifflin, 1932.

Callaghan, Morley. *That Summer in Paris*. New York: Coward, McCann, 1963.

Chapman, John, ed. *The Best Plays of 1950–1951* New York: Dodd, Mead, 1951.

Clark, Barrett H. *An Hour of American Drama*. Philadelphia: J. B. Lippincott, 1930.

———. *Intimate Portraits*. Bristol, Conn.: Hildreth Press, 1951.

——— and George Freedley, eds. *A History of American Drama*. New York: D. Appleton-Century, 1947.

Clurman, Harold. *The Fervent Years*. New York: A. A. Knopf, 1945.

Downer, Alan S. *Fifty Years of American Drama, 1900–1950*. Chicago: Regnery, 1951.

Erhard, Thomas. *Lynn Riggs, Southwest Playwright*. Southwest Writers Series, no. 29. 44 pp. Austin, Texas: Steck-Vaughn, 1970.

Gibson, Arrell Morgan. *The Oklahoma Story*. Norman: University of Oklahoma Press, 1978.

———. *The Santa Fe and Taos Colonies: Age of the Muses, 1900–1942*. Norman: University of Oklahoma Press, 1983.

Green, Paul. *Dramatic Heritage*. New York: Samuel French, 1953.

Helburn, Theresa. *A Wayward Quest*. Boston: Little, Brown, 1960.

Kraft, James, ed. *Selected Poems of Witter Bynner*. New York: Farrar, Straus & Giroux, 1978.

Mantle, Burns, ed. *Best Plays: Yearbook of the Drama in America, 1931*. New York: Dodd, Mead, 1931.

Marable, Mary Hays, and Elaine Boylan. *A Handbook of Oklahoma Writers*. Norman: University of Oklahoma Press, 1939.

Pearce, T. M., *Mary Hunter Austin*. New York: Twayne Publishers, Inc., 1965.

Plays, Players, and Playwrights: An Illustrated History of the Theatre. New York: Hart Publishing, 1971.

Seeger, Alan. *Poems*. Introduction by William Archer. New York: Scribner's, 1916.

Sievers, W. David. *Freud on Broadway: A History of Psychoanalysis and the American Drama*. New York: Hermitage House, 1955.

The Sooner Yearbook. Norman: University of Oklahoma, 1920–24.

Starr's History of the Cherokee Indian. Jack Gregory and Rennard Strickland, eds., 1922. Reprint, Fayetteville, Ark.: Indian Heritage Association, University of Arkansas, 1967.

Thomas, Bob. *Joan Crawford: A Biography*. New York: Bantam Books, 1978.

Tucker, S. Marion, and Alan S. Downer, eds. *Twenty-Five Modern Plays*. New York: Harper & Row, 1953.

Waite, Marjorie Peabody. *Yaddo, Yesterday and Today*. Albany, N.Y.: Argus Press, 1933.

Waterman, Arthur E. *Susan Glaspell*. Modern Authors Series. New York: Twayne, 1966.

Wilson, Eloise. "Lynn Riggs: Oklahoma Dramatist." Ph.D. diss., University of Pennsylvania, 1957.

2. Articles

Benton, Joseph. "Some Personal Remembrances About Lynn Riggs." *Chronicles of Oklahoma* 34 (Autumn, 1956): 296–301.
Braunlich, Phyllis Cole. "The Cherokee Night of R. Lynn Riggs." *Midwest Quarterly* 30 (Autumn, 1988).
Caldwell, Richard. "Southern Personalities." *Holland's,* January, 1937, p. 12.
Carb, David. "The Hedgerow Players: A Little Theater Bulwark." *The Literary Digest,* April 23, 1934, p. 43.
Clark, Barrett H. "American Drama in Its Second Decade." *English Journal* 21 (January, 1932): 1–11.
———. "Broadway Opens Shop Again." *The Drama* 20 (October, 1928): 9–11.
———. "The Critics and Roadside." *The Drama* 21 (November, 1930): 17.
Clurman, Harold. "Theatre." *New Republic,* 4 September 1950, p. 23.
Fry, Maggie Culver. "Memories of Lynn Riggs." *Oklahoma Today* 10, no. 1 (Winter, 1959–60).
Gassner, John. "Our Lost Playwrights." *Theatre Arts* 38 (August, 1954): 19–21.
Gregory, Horace. "Lynn Riggs as Poet." *The Nation,* 17 January 1931, 22.
Harris, Harry. "Theatre in a Mill." *Theatre Arts,* October, 1941, pp. 766–70.
Isaacs, Edith J. R. "Plays for Puritans and Others." *Theatre Arts* 20 (March, 1936): 176–78.
Johnson, Willard, ed. *The Laughing Horse* (Taos: Laughing Horse Press, 1921–39). Reprint, New York: Kraus Reprint Corp., 1967.
Koch, Frederick. "Playboy of Oklahoma." *The Carolina Play-Book* 4 (June, 1931): 62.
Krutch, Joseph Wood. "Tragedy Is Not Easy." *The Nation,* 1 February 1941, p. 137.
Milburn, Vivien. "In Bold Relief." *The Bandwagon,* 1932.
Mitchell, Lee. "A Designer at Work." *Theatre Arts* 18 (November, 1934): 874–77.
Roth, Henry. "Lynn Riggs and the Individual." Pp. 386–95 in B. A. Botkin, ed. *Folk-Say: A Regional Miscellany, 1930* Norman: University of Oklahoma Press, 1930.

Sper, Felix. "The Stage and Screen." *Commonweal*, 31 January 1941,
    p. 375.
University of Oklahoma Magazine, December, 1921; February, 1922;
    October, 1922; March, 1923; February, 1926.
Vestal, Stanley (Walter S. Campbell). "Lynn Riggs, Poet and Drama-
    tist." *Southwest Review* 15 (Autumn, 1929): 64–71.
Zabel, Morton D. "Lynn Riggs's Poems." *New Republic*, 19 November
    1930, p. 25.

INDEX